Aural Matters

*A Student's Guide to Aural Perception
at Advanced Level*

David Bowman
and
Paul Terry

With a chapter on World Music
by Dr. Mark Lockett

ED 12430

SCHOTT
EDUCATIONAL
PUBLICATIONS

Mainz • London • Madrid • New York • Paris • Tokyo • Toronto

For Jill and John

The authors and publisher would like to thank Peter Nickol and Kev Smith
for their assistance in the compilation of the anthology of recorded examples
that accompanies this book, and Dave Richardson for his advice on folk music.

British Library Cataloguing-in-Publication Data.
A catalogue record for this book is available from the British Library.

ISBN 0 946535 22 1

ED 12430
© 1993 Schott & Co. Ltd, London

Typeset by Musonix Typesetting
Printed in England

Contents

The recordings

The two compact discs that accompany this book contain nearly two and a half hours of music for use in the tests and to illustrate the text. Some CD players can access only a limited number of tracks directly, but on all players it is possible to play the later tracks by pressing the track advance button the requisite number of times.

The symbols ⊚ and ⊚ refer to the first and second CD respectively.

The answers

Model answers are given to each of the questions from the 112 tests included in this book. The authors should like to point out, however, that these are intended primarily to assist students working with *Aural Matters* on their own and do not, particularly for the tests in Part II, represent the only answers that would be acceptable in a public examination. Responses that are accurate and unambiguous, or which make reference to different (but valid) points in answer to the question posed, always receive credit in the mark-schemes for such examinations.

Also available

To supplement the listening tests and background information the reader is referred to *Sound Matters* (Schott & Co. Ltd, 1989), an anthology of 72 extracts of printed and recorded music, available with Teacher's Manual and Pupils' Questions:

ED 12351 Score
ED 12353 Two Cassettes
ED 12352 Teacher's Manual (with pupils' questions)

Prelude

This book, with its two compact discs, is intended for students rather than teachers. It aims to demonstrate fundamental techniques of aural perception which can be applied, not only in the examination room, but also in the reader's general approach to a variety of styles ranging from Palestrina to jazz fusion and from British folk music to Indonesian gamelan music. The paramount importance of aural perception in musical education has been recognized in every type of syllabus, from those designed for primary-school children through to those used in universities and colleges of music. The principal aims of all of them are to enable students to hear the detail below the surface of music and to broaden their knowledge of musical styles. Ultimately they aim to increase delight in the never-ending variety of musical sounds and to provide the basis for a deeper understanding of the significance of those sounds. These are also the ultimate aims of this book.

Although *Aural Matters* has been designed as a work-book for Advanced level candidates, it begins where its sister volume *Sound Matters* ended—at GCSE level. More able candidates for this latter examination will find that much of the teaching and many of the tests in this book will be useful in the last terms of a GCSE course. Used in this way *Aural Matters* will bridge the much feared gap between GCSE and Advanced level. At the other end of the scale, there can be little doubt that many undergraduates find aural perception one of the most difficult components in degree and diploma courses. This book could well provide the firm foundations which they require. Just as *Aural Matters* could bridge the gap between GCSE and Advanced Level, so too could it bridge the gap between school and higher education.

A few words of warning. Although the tests in this book reflect Advanced level syllabuses in aural perception, you would be well advised to check the syllabus of the examining body whose examinations you intend to sit since these are constantly under review. You should also know that tests in operational examinations are subjected to rigorous scrutiny and moderation in order to ensure that they cover the extent and depth of the skills required in the time allotted for the paper. Since *Aural Matters* is meant to be a progressive self-help textbook, the earlier tests will be much easier than those you will encounter in the examination room, while some of the later ones include questions that may require more time to answer, along with extra playings of the recordings. You will need to supplement the tests in this book with additional material, particularly for the dictation and discrimination exercises in Part I. There is, fortunately, already a copious supply of these latter tests in the past papers that are available from the various examining bodies. Towards the end of your course you will need experience in working tests in the exact format and in the precise time allowed in the examination you intend to sit. If you have worked conscientiously through *Aural Matters* these tests should provide few problems.

Finally, you should recognize that all activities in music are interconnected. When you compose you should try to hear the sounds you are writing before testing them out on an instrument. When you analyse someone else's composition your analysis should be based upon what you can hear and not upon a fanciful idea derived from the written notation alone. When you play an instrument you should listen to yourself critically as well as noting how your performance relates to others when playing in ensemble. Singing is perhaps the most useful ally of aural perception, since it most accurately represents the sounds which you have imagined with your inner ear. So it is with song that we will begin.

Melody Dictation

The ability to write the sounds you hear in accurate musical notation is one of the most useful of musical skills because notation is the principal means by which music is presented for interpretation by others. It is, in fact, the link between composing and performing. Skill in writing from aural dictation will also help you to understand better the relationship between the printed symbols of music and the actual sounds they represent. This, in turn, can help the accuracy of your performing (especially when sight-reading and sight-singing) and improve your ability to recognize precise detail when listening to music.

A few people can manage pitch dictation with seemingly little effort—probably because, in earlier years, they learnt to associate the symbols of music directly with the individual sounds they represent rather than with, say, a certain fingering. This can become such an automatic process that it possible to hear a note and instantly name it as an A or a C, or whatever. Those who can do this are said to have 'absolute pitch'. Although this may seem an extraordinary gift, it is little different to describing colours as 'red', 'orange' and so forth, and involves precisely the same activity of giving a label to a frequency of vibrations.

Whatever the starting point, it is always possible to improve your level of aural perception and, especially if you feel you are starting from a rather basic position, you can have the fun and satisfaction of making very considerable progress over an extended period. Like all things worthwhile, though, this will only happen with regular practice and continual appreciation of the need to be aware of what you hear. The routines on page 6 need take little more than a minute or so of your time, but they do need to be practised frequently (preferably at least twice a day) if you are to benefit. You will almost certainly not be aware of any day-to-day improvement, but we are happy to challenge you now to make a note of what you can and cannot do in aural tests, and then to compare this with your own assessment of your abilities in a year's time.

Self-Help Ideas

Aural dictation is the opposite of sight-singing. When singing, you see the printed symbols and have to turn them into sounds. In aural tests, you hear the sounds and have to turn them into symbols. Singing and aural work are thus inextricably linked. One of the most enjoyable ways of practising sight-singing is to join a choir, especially one that rehearses a wide variety of music. It is particularly useful if you can manage one of the lower parts, as these will need greater note-reading ability, being less easy to pick up 'by ear' than the often more predictable top line. However, joining a choir will only improve your aural ability if you concentrate on reading your part from the score—just tagging along with the others will not produce the desired improvement!

Just as useful as choral singing is practising individual vocal exercises in private. For aural purposes, vocal quality is not important: don't worry if you think the tone sounds horrible—you can always whistle or hum if you wish—but do concentrate on accurate pitch and rhythm. The following exercises can be practised while waiting for the bus, or in the bath (the acoustics of bathrooms always seem to make singing easier) or anywhere you have a minute or two on your own. They are particularly useful as warm-up exercises for sharpening-up the ear before an aural lesson or test. It is important that you understand the purpose of each exercise—don't go into auto-pilot mode and rattle through them as if you were practising scales. Make a conscious note of what you are singing (the difference between tones and semitones, for example). In the early stages, it is important to have a reference point to check accuracy: a piano or other instrument for pitch, and a metronome or loudly ticking clock for rhythm.

Use your voice and ear first and then check your results against this chosen source of reference. Frequent short bursts of practice should enable you to dispense with such aids after a time, especially in the easier exercises.

The secret of success in dictation tests is the accurate recognition of intervals. Some people use the starting notes of well-known songs to remind them of each interval. We don't recommend this: it is all too easy to get the titles confused, and the same interval can actually sound quite different in some new context— F up to A in the key of F, for example, may well not sound to you as being quite the same major third as F up to A in the key of D minor.

A more reliable method is to develop the ability to sing a scale accurately and without accompaniment, using either note numbers or, if you prefer, 'doh–ray–me', etc. The exercises below begin with the basics: we suggest that you start at whichever level suits you best. You can sing, hum or whistle—and remember that it's OK to make mistakes. If any kind of singing worries you, try the following tips:

- ❏ Singing is easier if you stand up.

- ❏ Try not to let the muscles around your lips and throat get tight: make a conscious effort to keep your whole body relaxed.

- ❏ Let your jaw drop down in a loose, gormless expression and keep your teeth well apart.

- ❏ Sing to the sound 'ah' or 'ee' (the brighter sound of the latter will help any tendency to sing flat). If you prefer humming, use the sound '-ng' (like the end of the word 'running') to help your teeth stay apart.

- ❏ Take a much bigger breath than you think you will need and concentrate on filling the lowest part of your lungs—but don't tense your shoulders.

- ❏ Make sure nobody is around and then sing or hum as loudly as you dare: if you feel your nose and the roof of your mouth vibrating, you will know you are doing really well.

Pitch Warm-Up Schedule

Devise your own training schedule for the exercises below and later in this chapter, but try to observe the following points:

- ❏ Practise for no more than two or three minutes.

- ❏ Practise at least twice every day.

- ❏ Practise very slowly.

- ❏ Mentally register the relative pitch of each note as you sing, using note numbers or sol-fa syllables.

- ❏ Check your accuracy against an instrument frequently in the early stages.

Choose any comfortably low starting note. Sing up to the third note of a major scale, pause, and sing back down again. Once you feel confident, miss out the middle note on the descent, jumping a third to the tonic. Finally, miss out the middle note on the ascent as well, so that you are now singing rising and falling major thirds:

Repeat the entire exercise, starting on various different key notes. Be careful that you keep to the same pattern of major thirds—don't let the top note slip down to a minor third.

When you are satisfied that you can sing and recognize this pattern, extend the exercise to cover the first *four* notes of the major scale. The distance between the third and fourth notes is a semitone: keep these two notes close in pitch, and repeat the semitone, noticing how different it is to the intervals of a tone in the first part of the scale:

The interval of a semitone between the third and fourth notes of the scale means that there are always two different sizes of third in this group of notes. The interval from the first to the third of the scale is a major third (two tones) while the interval from the second to the fourth is a minor third (one-and-a-half tones). Try singing these first four notes in different patterns, such as the following, making sure that you are aware of the very different flavour of these two types of third (the descending minor third is always recognizable as the distinctive sound that young children make when pitching cries like 'coo-ee' and 'mummy').

Continue making up your own permutations of these four notes: the important thing is to know where you are in the scale, whether using sol-fa, note numbers or letter names, and consciously to return to the tonic in order to check that you have not lost your position. Once you feel secure, try the following routine, which adds a second **tetrachord** (four-note scale segment) to the first, thus completing the full major scale (T=tone, S=semitone):

The two tetrachords have identically spaced intervals: tone–tone–semitone. Clearly, if you hear a semitone in a diatonic major melody, the two notes must be either the third and fourth of the scale, or the leading note and tonic.

Practise major scales in a variety of keys descending and ascending—vocally, the descending version is a better exercise, since it will stop you pushing your 'chest voice' up too high. As you sing, make a conscious effort to notice the unique sound of each degree of the scale in relation to its neighbours. Most importantly, to absorb the different feel of the *subdominant* (the note on which the first tetrachord comes to rest when singing up the scale) and the *dominant* (on which the second then starts).

Finally, try different permutations of these notes. Again, concentrate on knowing precisely where you are in the scale at all times. We suggest that you start by exploring how the notes of the tonic triad are formed from notes 1, 3 and 5 of the major scale and on the difference between the dominant and the subdominant. The second stave below suggests some ways of then using familiar fragments to extend the exercise to include the the sixth degree of the scale:

[7]

Most tonal melodies consist largely of simple scale-based patterns and triadic shapes like these, so it is important that this type of exercise is practised until you feel fully confident in naming the notes of the major scale and would no more mistake the fifth degree of the scale for the fourth than you would identify the colour of grass as purple.

Working the Tests

Throughout this book all parts played by transposing instruments (such as the clarinet, horn and trumpet) are always written at their sounding pitch, so you need not worry about transposition.

In an examination it is likely that you will be given two melodies, either of which may be played with or without accompaniment. The first may be diatonic (using only the notes of its key), may be played three times, and will probably have at least half of the notes given. The second may contain accidentals, may be played four times, and is likely to have little (if any) of the music printed. In this chapter we have graded the melodies by difficulty, gradually moving from the first type to the second. Listen to each melody as many times as you need, but aim for a maximum of three to four playings as soon as you can.

In each test you will hear the key chord and key note played on the piano before the test begins, along with an indication of the speed of the pulse.

A simple musical 'shorthand' will help writing at speed. Try using just a dot on the correct line or space of the stave for pitch—keep to a single movement of the pencil and don't waste time filling in the note heads. Also indicate rhythms with single strokes: a vertical line for a crotchet, a hooked line (⌠) for a quaver and no stroke at all for a minim. Allow 30 seconds between each playing of the test, during which time you can turn confirmed shorthand into proper notation. Try to memorize each melody, or at least the end of it, so that you can continue to hear it 'in your head' during these gaps.

When working the test, keep the key note in the back of your mind as a reference point (although humming it throughout is not recommended, since the inevitable clashes will make it difficult to focus on other pitches). It is also a good idea to keep a steady pulse going, for example, by wriggling your toes inside your shoe—again, an audible foot-tapping is likely to be too distracting. If you find rhythm particularly difficult, make sure that this pulse is as regular as a ticking clock: it is all too easy to start tapping along with the varying note-lengths of the melody unless you are careful about this.

🔘 Tracks 1–2

============================= *Test 1* =============================

Complete these melodies. They move mainly by step but include an occasional leap of a major third. The rhythms use only crotchets, quavers and minims.

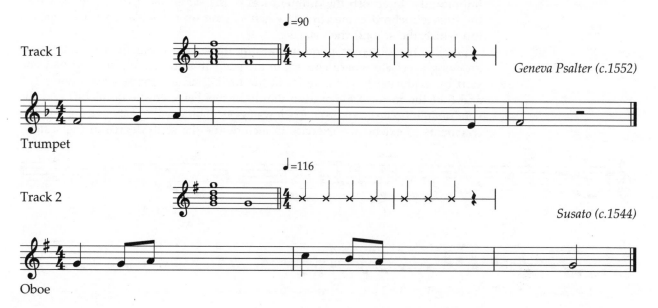

Track 1

Geneva Psalter (c.1552)

Trumpet

Track 2

Susato (c.1544)

Oboe

With all of the tests in this book, it is likely that you will need more practice material than we have room to provide here. Use every opportunity to exercise your aural skills, not only in formal tests, but also when listening to music of every kind. Try to register what is happening in, say, a melody or a bass part of a favourite piece of music for which you don't have a score. Concentrate on just a tiny section; memorize it; conceptualize it (that is, work out precisely what the music is doing) and then write it down or pick out the notes on your instrument.

Anacrusic Starts

Each of the melodies in the next test begins with an **anacrusis** (an upbeat). It is the convention with anacrusic melodies to trim the length of their final notes (or rests) so that the incomplete first and last bars together total a full bar. Look carefully at the printed examples for Tracks 4 and 5 below and ensure you follow suit for the melody on Track 3.

Tracks 3–5

Complete the following melodies, the notes of which move mainly by step but which also include occasional leaps of a major third and perfect fourth. The rhythms use entirely crotchets, quavers and minims.

Compound Time

The melodies in the next test are both in ⁶⁄₈ time. In a slow ⁶⁄₈ metre you should count a quaver pulse (six quavers per bar in the first example). If the music is too fast to count quavers the pulse will be in *dotted*-crotchet beats—so all 'one beat' notes will need a dot. Shorter notes will need beaming in units of a dotted crotchet (three quavers, six semiquavers, and so forth) whether counting in quavers or dotted crotchets. Look carefully at the metronome mark and at the notes representing the metronome pulse and you will be able to work out in advance which method to adopt. Notice that the metronome speed for the second melody in this test is slower than for the first, but the music will sound *faster* because the pulse is expressed as a dotted-crotchet beat. Be careful to calculate the effect the anacrusis will have on the final note of this melody.

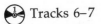
Test 3

Complete the following melodies, the notes of which move mainly by step but which also include occasional leaps of a major third and perfect fourth.

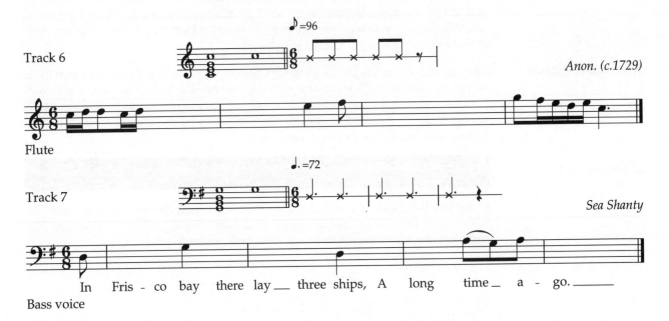

Track 6

Flute

Anon. (c.1729)

Track 7

Sea Shanty

In Fris - co bay there lay — three ships, A long time — a - go. ———

Bass voice

Dotted Rhythms

Dotted rhythms occur in music of almost all types, but it easy to confuse the two most common patterns, the dotted crotchet–quaver pair, and the dotted quaver–semiquaver pair. There is a simple way to tell the difference, though. Since a dot makes a note longer, the dotted crotchet will always last for more than a beat—in other words, you will hear *two* pulses during the length of the note. This is shown by the pairs of beats marked with arrows in the example below. The dotted quaver–semiquaver pair, on the other hand, is completely over within the space of a single beat.

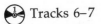 Track 8

Listen to the melody on Track 8 and follow the score below. The metronome continues while the clarinet is playing—play the track several times until you are sure that you can hear two beats during the length of a dotted crotchet, and that you can differentiate the two main types of dotted rhythm.

Chopin

Track 8   Oboe

♩=96

There is an important point to keep in mind when using dotted rhythms in simple time. The dotted note usually comes *on* the beat and is *followed* by a rhythm that equates to the length represented by the dot. A dotted quaver, for example, will normally be followed by a semiquaver or by two demisemiquavers. A common mistake is to write the shorter note first, on the beat (and then to make the other notes fit around it), when it should actually have been deducted from the length of the previous note:

The pattern of a semiquaver followed by a dotted quaver occurs in some types of music (the pattern is known as a **Scotch snap** or **Lombardic rhythm**) but it is very much rarer than the common dotted quaver–semiquaver group.

In ⁶⁄₈ time the dotted crotchet occupies a complete pulse, so no further notes are required to complete the beat, but shorter note values follow the same principle as those in simple time.

The starting notes are not given in the first two melodies below. They should not prove difficult to locate as you will hear the key note before each is played, and both melodies arrive on their tonics very soon after they start. Remember that most tonal melodies start on one of the notes of the tonic triad (those with an anacrusic start sometimes begin on the leading note)—although this is not an invariable rule, as the third melody below shows.

Try to get used to 'pattern spotting' when listening. Scale patterns are the most common, closely followed by triadic patterns. A clear example is given in the middle of the printed music for Track 10, where the bassoon ascends the tonic triad, with a wiggle on a passing B at the end of the bar. Listen out for a similarly triadic pattern in bar 3 of the melody on Track 11.

Tracks 9–11

Minor Keys

By now you should be extending your vocal practice routine to include the larger intervals of the sixth (major and minor), minor seventh (the major seventh is rare in melodic writing) and octave. Once you feel secure in singing and recognizing these, move on to the minor scale. Start, as you did in major keys, by singing up to the third of the scale and back, making sure that you are clear about the difference between major and minor thirds. Then extend the exercise down to include the leading note, just below the tonic, and up to include the first five degrees of the scale, outlining a tonic minor triad:

The upper part of the minor scale is more problematic. In melody writing you are much more likely to encounter the melodic minor scale than the harmonic minor. You must therefore be prepared for both raised and lowered forms of the sixth and seventh degrees. Once again, make sure that you can sing and recognize both forms, using patterns like this:

Don't assume that the descending form will always be used in falling phrases, or vice versa—listen carefully to the end of the melody on Track 12. One of the most common problems in minor keys, though, is simply forgetting to write in the accidental for the raised leading note when necessary. It is therefore a good idea to write the name of the raised leading note at the start of the exercise before you listen (like the encircled reminders above the staves in Test 5).

We have given very little help for the melody on Track 13, but you should be able to recognize the shape of its opening pattern of pitches—there is plenty of stepwise movement after the opening. The melody on Track 14, on the other hand, has some tricky leaps: try to spot signposts such as the dominant, and the leading note–tonic pattern, and this will help locate the surrounding pitches.

Tracks 12–14

=== *Test 5* ===

Complete the following minor key melodies.

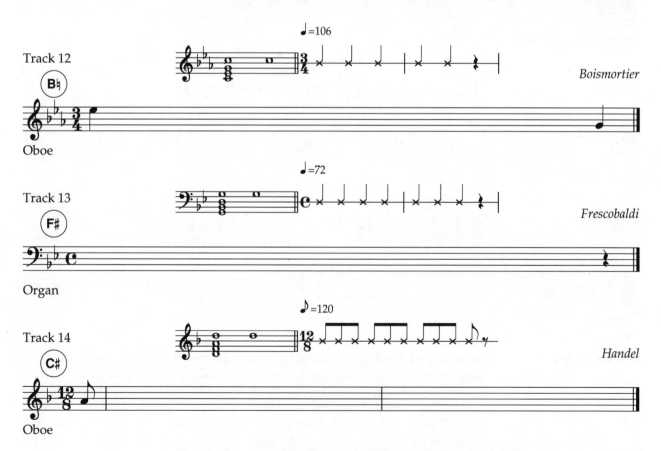

The final test in this chapter includes melodies that contain some features of rhythm and pitch that we have not yet touched upon, and that may occasionally be encountered in examinations. Tied notes are similar to dotted notes. While a dot can be used to extend a note by half of its length, a tie usually has to be used if the note is to be prolonged across a bar-line or if the note needs to be lengthened by some amount other than half of its value. As with dotted notes, you should feel the pulse continuing regularly beneath the tied note, and the melody swiftly moving off (usually on the half beat) after the tie. Here are two of the most common patterns:

The melody on Track 17 has a triplet printed in the second bar: keep to a steady pulse and you should be able to recognize such totally even threefold divisions of the beat elsewhere. Finally, we have included a melody in this test that uses a simple chromatic passing-note of the type that may occasionally be encountered in melody dictation tests.

Track 15–18

Test 6

Complete the following melodies.

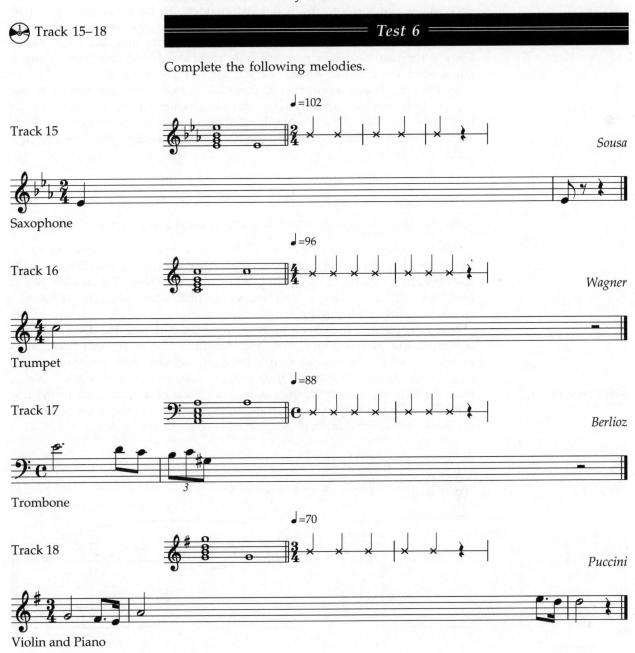

[13]

Two-Part Dictation

Writing two simultaneous melodies demands the fullest concentration, so we recommend that you don't start the tests in this chapter until you start to feel confident about your melody-writing skills. Make sure that you persevere with the vocal exercises suggested in the last chapter as these should benefit your response to all of the tests in Part I of this book. Also remember that melodies in tonal music are based largely on simple scale and triad patterns—this knowledge should again prove useful.

These tests each consist of a short passage of two-part music, up to about eight bars in length. Short sections of the music in either or both of the parts are printed as a guide and you will be given the key chord and the pulse before each playing of the test. As in the last chapter, we have provided you with much of the printed music in the first few tests and, again, we suggest that you listen to the CD as many times as you need in order to complete your answer. Only when you are achieving reasonable accuracy should you start aiming to cut down the number of repetitions to a total of five playings.

Writing down two simultaneous melodies is not the whole answer to this type of test, because harmony arises out of the counterpoint generated by the two parts, and this gives you another reference point for checking your work. At the very least, aim to recognize the distinctive sounds of the three principal types of interval:

- ❐ Smooth-sounding (concords): thirds and sixths.

- ❐ Hollow-sounding (perfect intervals): fourths, fifths and octaves.

- ❐ Harsh-sounding (discords): seconds, sevenths and tritones.

When working the tests, you may prefer to concentrate on just one of the two parts at each playing, but do also spend some time listening 'vertically' to the intervals made by the parts in combination. This should then alert you to problems such as writing a 'hollow' perfect fifth when you actually heard a smooth-sounding, concordant sixth.

Many people find it difficult to listen to a bass part with the distraction of a melody being played above. You may therefore like to try this preliminary exercise, in which the bassoon part is the main melody—quite possibly one that you already know. Over this a flute plays the simple, printed descant. Notice how the bassoon melody is, once again, made up of a tonic triad in the first phrase and largely stepwise movement in the second. Complete the notation of the bassoon part (the rhythm uses entirely crotchets and quavers):

 Track 19

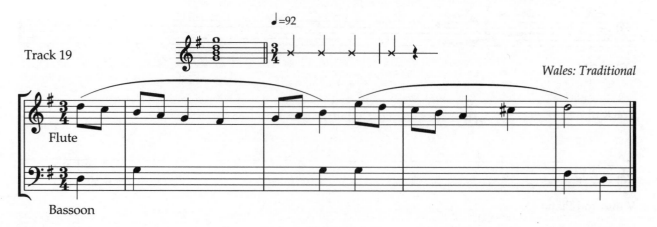

Track 19

Wales: Traditional

Flute

Bassoon

If you listened 'vertically', as well as 'horizontally', to *The Ash Grove*, you probably noticed a high proportion of 'smooth' intervals—thirds and sixths—on the main beats, with passing-notes in both parts causing almost unnoticeably mild dissonances between these beats. This should cause you to ask questions such as 'what was the sound of the interval below the C sharp?'—if it was smooth, did the bassoon play A or E? No other note would be possible. Try to apply this type of harmonic thought throughout these tests: not only will it improve your accuracy, but it will help you develop the skills needed for later sections of this book.

Track 4

==================================== *Test 7* ====================================

In the last chapter, you completed a melody by Mozart, played on the piano. Here is that melody, with the start of the bass part that accompanies it. You can see that this is purely functional in the first two bars: that is, it merely outlines tonic and dominant harmonies. Make sure you can hear this, and then complete the rest of the bass part, which takes on a more melodic character. Again, only crotchets and quavers are needed for the rhythm.

Track 4

Mozart

The extract on Track 4 is taken from a set of variations Mozart wrote at the age of ten; the next is taken from a set of violin duets (here played on flute and oboe to help distinguish the parts) written by his father some years later.

Follow the incomplete score below as you listen to Track 20. The oboe part starts in almost the same way as the flute, one bar later and an interval of a fourth lower. This is an example of **imitation**—a contrapuntal device in which the same or a similar motif is presented successively by different parts. It is like the start of a round or a canon, but here the imitation is not exact (the first interval is changed) and the device stops after only a few notes—in a canon, the imitation is exact and continues throughout the entire piece. Two-part music is often imitative in places, and there are further examples in this extract, but you should not expect simply to replicate the upper part for note after note: any imitation is likely to be short-lived and not exact in an examination.

Track 20

==================================== *Test 8* ====================================

Complete the missing beats in both parts of the following: notice that the time signature indicates a duple pulse, in minims.

Track 20

Leopold Mozart

The melodies in the next test each include imitation at some point. Notice the duple pulse (two *minims* per bar) of the first melody and both the ascending and descending forms of the melodic minor scale in the printed passage—don't forget to check whether you need C sharps or C naturals in the parts that you have to add. The rhythm of this melody still uses only crotchets and quavers, but you must be prepared for some dotted rhythms in the other two extracts.

 Tracks 21–23

Test 9

Complete the missing portions in the following passages.

The two-part passages on the next page provide rather less in the way of printed reference points. Do not panic! Use your own reference points, in the form of your knowledge and awareness of the sound of such critical signposts as the tonic, dominant and leading note of a key.

Be prepared for the occasional rhythmic difficulty, such as tied notes, in these passages and listen out for any chromatic notes or notes foreign to the key which cause a modulation to occur. These will need appropriate accidentals, possibly including an accidental to cancel a previous chromaticism. As in melody dictation, these are likely to be simple chromatic passing-notes or accidentals that cause a modulation to a closely related key.

Complete the missing portions of the following passages.

Keys, Chords and Cadences

Keys, chords and cadences are three components of music that are closely related. Cadences are defined by the chords of which they are comprised, and chords and cadences together have an important rôle in defining key.

In each of these tests you will be given a 'skeleton score' of the music you hear. This is a reduction of the parts onto two staves (like piano music) with some sections showing just part of the texture, or perhaps a rhythm to help you keep your place, and also with some bars that are completely blank.

Before embarking on these tests ensure that you are well used to listening to a bass part independently of the main melodic line above, since recognition of chords depends on the identification of their bass notes. The two-part exercises in the last chapter will be a useful starting point for this. Also make sure that you are totally familiar with the construction of common chords (major and minor triads and their inversions) in a variety of keys. The notes in this chapter are intended as a brief reminder and not a complete guide to harmonic theory. You can hear many of the points below illustrated in the music for Test 12.

Triads

In C major, the triads formed on each note of the scale are:

In any major key the primary triads (chords I, IV and V) are always major and chords II, III and VI are always minor, providing there are no chromatic alterations. The lowest note of each of the triads shown above is called the root. When the root is in the bass, with the other notes arranged above it at intervals of a third and a fifth (or their compound equivalents, such as a tenth and a twelfth), the triad is in **root position**. The root of the triad provides its description, whether using letter-names or Roman numerals.

The major or minor quality of common chords (major and minor triads in root position) is determined by the interval between the root and the third (middle note). If the third is major, the triad is major; if the third is minor, the triad is minor. The outer notes of root position triads in a major key always form a perfect fifth, except in the unique case of chord VII, where they are a diminished fifth apart, making the chord a diminished triad.

It is, of course, important to get used to recognizing that minor chords occur in major keys and that major chords occur in minor keys.

Cadences

A cadence is a formula that signifies the end of a musical phrase, like punctuation in written language. For our purposes a cadence may be regarded as a harmonic formula, usually consisting of a pair of chords, that also often has the important function of defining the key of the music. Many possible combinations of chords can be used to form a cadence. The following four patterns have names and, of these, the first two are the most common:

❐ Perfect   V–I

❐ Imperfect   Ending on chord V

❐ Plagal   IV–I (listen for the characteristic 'fah–doh' pattern)

❐ Interrupted   V–any chord except I

Working the Tests

As with the other dictation tests, listen to the recordings as many times as you need in the early stages, but aim ultimately for a maximum of five playings. The music on Track 27 is a hymn tune by Henry Gauntlett, composer of 'Once in Royal David's City'. Most music does not, of course, change chord on almost every beat as chorales and other hymn tunes generally do, but this piece provides some clear examples of the simple use of chords and cadences and should therefore be useful as a source for aural reference.

In the questions, small numbers refer to beats of the bar (e.g., 8^2 means bar 8, beat 2). When you are asked to identify a chord, you may use letter names or Roman numerals. If you prefer letter names you will need to remember to add a lower-case 'm' for the minor triads and 'dim' for the diminished triad. If you prefer Roman numerals you will need to state the key if the music has modulated away from the tonic (e.g., D major: IV).

 Track 27

Test 12

Listen to the music on Track 27 as you follow the skeleton score below.

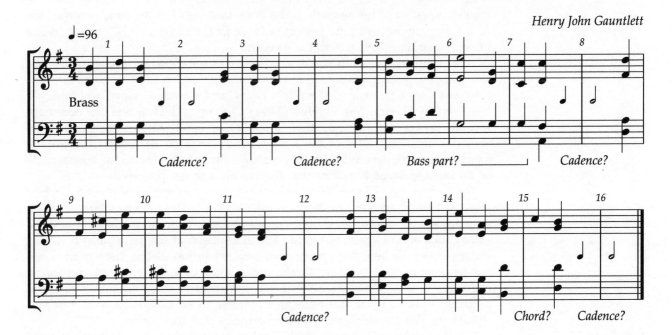

Henry John Gauntlett

(a) Identify the cadences at bars:

  (i) 1^3–2^2,

  (ii) 3^3–4^2,

  (iii) 7^3–8^2,

  (iv) 15^3–16^2.

(b) Describe the bass part under the incomplete chords shown in bars 5^2–7^1.

(c) Is the chord on the first beat of bar 15 a major triad or a minor triad? Listen carefully to the bass note of this chord and then identify it precisely.

d) The music at the start of the second line has modulated to D major, the dominant key. Identify the cadence at 11^3–12^2 in terms of this new key.

Inverted Chords

When the root of a chord is not its lowest note, the chord is inverted. If the third of the chord is in the bass (the note B in a G major triad) then the chord is in **first inversion** (notated Ib, or G/B). Listen carefully to this chord in bar 1^1 and compare it with the root position triad of G on the beat before.

If the fifth is in the bass (D in a G major triad) then the chord is in **second inversion** (Ic, or G/D). Chord Ic often occurs before a cadence, where it is known as a **cadential second inversion**. Listen to the example at bar 15^2 and make a mental note of this common pattern.

You will see from this that the relationship of the bass note with the rest of the chord is of vital importance in determining inversions. Conversely, it does not matter how the other notes of the triad are arranged above the bass. When you are asked to identify a chord, don't forget to add a letter to show the inversion, unless the chord is in root position. If you use Roman numerals, the letter 'b' indicates a first inversion and the letter 'c' a second inversion. If you prefer letter names for chords, add the actual bass note after a diagonal slash (G/D, for example) unless the chord is in root position.

Sevenths and Suspensions

Triads in root position are, of course, formed from alternate notes of the scale. If the next note in series is added to those already there (G–B–D–F, for example) a seventh chord is created—so called because the new note forms an interval of a seventh from the root. The most common is the seventh on V: in other words, the dominant seventh, notated V^7. In the key of C major the dominant seventh is G^7. Sevenths have three inversions, since there are three possible alternatives to the root as a bass note, the third inversion being V^7d.

Listen once again to the hymn tune on Track 27 and see if you can hear the thickening effect of the seventh in the dominant chord of the final cadence (bar 15^3). Compare this with the perfect cadence in D in bars 11^3–12^1, which uses a plain V–I progression, without a seventh.

Technically, the seventh is a discord and was traditionally 'prepared' by first sounding the discordant note in a concordant context on the previous beat. This note was then left suspended while a new chord sounded below, and finally it 'resolved' by moving (usually down) back to a concord. However, the dominant seventh became so common that it was often used without such treatment. Sevenths on other notes of the scale (and discords of all sorts) were usually handled with caution until the 19th century, either being treated as suspensions or as **appoggiaturas** (discords that resolve but are not prepared).

The hymn tune of Track 27 includes a number of examples of seventh chords: those at bars 5^1 and 13^1 are both chord VI^7 (Em^7). The pattern of preparation, suspension and resolution should be clear by studying the treble part, and the same chord occurs again, but in the key of D major, at bar 10^1. Chord II^7 (Am^7) occurs at bar 7^1: here the preparation and resolution of the discordant G are not so obvious—but they are there, in the tenor part. Listen to the recording one more time and make sure that you can identify these sevenths: they will probably strike you as too mild and familiar to be called discords, but you should register the thickening of the harmony that they cause.

Track 28

The recording on the next track is taken from a piano trio (a work written for violin, cello and piano) by Haydn. Notice the very slow speed indicated by the metronome mark, which shows a quaver pulse. Unlike the hymn tune on the previous track, this extract includes much decoration of its basically simple harmonic scheme. A clear example of a suspension occurs at bar 16^1: the B flat in the violin noticeably clashes with the F major chord played by the other two parts. The note is prepared before the bar-line, sounds on the beat, and is resolved by moving down to the harmony note A.

Many of the shorter notes (semiquavers and demisemiquavers) are passing-notes, that move by step between the harmony notes. In bar 8 the violin leaps to a high G, producing a momentary clash *on* the beat—this is an appoggiatura. Passing-notes, appoggiaturas and suspensions are sometimes called **unessential notes** because they make no fundamental difference to the underlying harmony (although you might rightly say they are 'essential' for maintaining interest in the melody!).

You are asked to identify the cadence in bar 13. You can see from the skeleton score that this reverses the normal harmonic rhythm of a cadence, in which the first chord is more usually on a weak beat and the second on a strong beat. When the principal stress falls on a stronger beat, as here, the cadence is described as a **feminine** cadence. This is not the answer to the question—you will still need to identify it as one of the four main types of cadence!

Study the following skeleton score before listening to the music and answering the questions below.

(a) Identify the chord heard at bar 1^2.

(b) Compare the harmony of bars 3–4 with that of bars 1–2.

(c) Describe the chords heard over the bass notes in bar 9.

(d) Identify the chord heard in bar 10^2 in terms of F major.

(e) Name the cadence in bar 13.

(f) Identify the chord heard in bar 17^1.

(g) The piano plays a tonic chord of F in the final bar.

   (i)   Which note(s) of this chord does the cello play?

   (ii) How does the violin part relate to this chord?

Keys

A key is defined by the set of notes (i.e., the scale) it uses and by a cadence: usually both of these things are necessary for a key to become established. So, if an F sharp occurs in the key of C major *and* there is a cadence in the key of G major, the music can be said to have modulated to G major. If the new key lasts only for a beat or two, it is usually called a **transitory modulation** (or passing modulation). If there is no cadence, and/or the F sharp is cancelled almost immediately, no modulation will have taken place—the passage is simply chromatic in the tonic (or current) key.

[21]

In many cases a modulation will be defined by a perfect cadence using the progression V^7–I in the new key since the dominant seventh has a particular rôle as a key-defining chord. In both major and minor keys it includes the subdominant, dominant and leading note. These are the three notes most likely to be altered if the music changes key: if they are all present in unaltered form, as they are in the dominant seventh, there can be little doubt about the key. Consider the dominant seventh of C: the notes G–B–D–F. It contains B natural, so the music is unlikely to be in a flat key (all flat key signatures contain a B flat). It contains F natural, so the music is unlikely to be in a sharp key (they all contain at least F sharp). That leaves A minor or C. A minor is unlikely as the chord contains G natural (A minor uses G sharp to define the key). Thus, the music must be in C. Whether this is C major or C minor will not become clear until you hear the tonic chord that so often follows a dominant seventh.

Both of the previous recordings in this chapter used a perfect cadence in the dominant in order to modulate to the dominant key, the most common of all modulations. Listen again to Track 28 and notice the dominant seventh of C that clinches the modulation at the end of bar 8. The actual modulatory chord is printed in the music at the end of bar 6: this is chord VIIc (B dim/F), effectively the top three notes of V^7. The return to the tonic is made by a straightforward V^7 of F in bar 10. Similarly, the hymn on Track 27 reached the dominant key of D by means of the last inversion of V^7 at the end of bar 9, resolving (after a double suspension) onto chord Ib on the second beat of bar 10. The return to the tonic was made by the progression V^7b–I in G, on beats 2 and 3 of bar 13.

As you listen to these key changes, concern yourself more with the aural effect of modulations to the dominant and back, rather than with the minutiæ of the precise chords used. Be aware of the tonal centre lifting to a new plain as the tonal centre moves up a fifth, and returning to base as the original tonality is restored. You will find this easier if you step back and almost subconsciously listen for the overall effect of such tonal changes, rather than resolutely trying to hum a tonic note through the modulations.

In these tests you will undoubtedly encounter modulations to closely related keys. In a major key these are the dominant, subdominant and relative minor, all of which are only one sharp or flat removed from the tonic and therefore easy to reach by a change of only one note. A little less closely related are the relative minors of the subdominant and dominant, the dominant of the dominant (D major in the key of C) and the minor key based on the tonic note (the tonic minor: C minor in relation to C major). You may also encounter more distant, tertiary modulations to a third generation of keys: those based on the natural or flattened mediant and submediant (In the key of C: E, E flat, A, A flat). Such complicated options can be rationalized by making a plan of the main related keys. This one is based on G major, the key of the music in the next test:

		IV	I	V
Tonic: G major	*Major keys*	C	G	D
	Relative minor keys	a	e	b

Listen for the brightening effect of modulations in the dominant direction. These always either add one or more sharps to the key, or remove flats currently in effect. Conversely, modulations in the subdominant direction either add flats or remove sharps and have a duller, settling-back effect. Hearing a modulation caused by a sharpened note should make you think first of the dominant direction. In many cases the sharpened note will actually be the leading note of the new key: a C sharp in the key of G could herald a modulation to D, an A sharp could announce a change to B minor, and a D sharp could suggest E minor. However, always listen for the confirming evidence of a cadence, since all of these notes occur in more than one key and the altered note may, in any case, be merely a chromatic note in the tonic, causing no modulation at all.

Before trying the next test, listen to the recording and make sure that you recognize that the chords in bars 2^4 and 4^4 each repeat the previous chord, but in a different spacing, with the bass moving by an interval of an octave. This will show that you are actually listening to the chords themselves.

Melody: Johann Crüger
Harmonization: Mendelssohn

(a) Identify the two chords at 1^1–1^2.

(b) Mention **three** ways in which the V–I progression is decorated at 4^1–4^3.

(c) State the letter name and function of the note played in the bass at 5^1.

(d) Name the cadence in bars 5^4–6^1.

(e) Describe, as fully as you can, the harmonic function of the three notes in the horn part of bar 7 indicated by small notes.

(f) Name the key the music has reached at:

   (i)   bar 10^1,

   (ii)   bar 12^1,

   (iii) bar 14^1.

(g) How does the chord at bar 12^4 relate to the chord at bar 12^1?

(h) Identify the chord heard at bar 15^3.

[23]

There is a suspension at bar 3^3 of the music below. The chord looks like a triad of D major but the second violin plays a G, held over from the previous beat, instead of an F sharp—the resolution onto F sharp occurs in the pure chord of D at the end of the bar. A suspension like this is most accurately described by identifying the suspended note within the harmony. In figures, this is a 4–3 suspension: the dissonant G and its resolution onto a consonant F sharp form, respectively, intervals of a (compound) fourth and third above the bass D. If you prefer to use letter names, describe the chord as it would be without the suspension (i.e., D) and then identify the suspended note in the form of either 'D sus G' or 'D sus 4'.

Track 30 ══════════════ *Test 15* ══════════════

(a) Identify the key of the music in bars 5^1–8^2.

(b) Identify, as precisely as you can, the chords at 1^1, 3^1 and 11^3.

(c) Name the cadences at 5^4–6^1 and 7^3–8^2.

(d) Through which keys does the music pass in bars 9^3–10^1 and 13^1–14^1?

[24]

Minor Keys

Triads on the notes of minor scales follow a less standardized pattern than those in major keys because of the variable inflexion of the sixth and seventh degrees of the scale. The following shows some of the more common possibilities:

In general, 'raised' forms of the sixth and seventh tend to be used at cadences to define the key. Chord V, in particular, is almost always major at cadences. The 'lowered' forms of these notes tend to create harmonic ambiguity, allowing the music easily to slip into related keys. The extract below was first published in 1617, when the tonal system of major and minor keys was still being established. Notice how the minor version of chord V appears in bar 1^3, but its major counterpart is used as the first chord of the cadence in bar 3^3.

Two variations on the standard cadence patterns often occur in minor keys. One is the substitution of a major third in the tonic chord of perfect and plagal cadences. This third is known as a *tierce de Picardie* and turns the tonic triad from minor to major. A clear example can be seen in bar 4 below. When you listen to this, make sure that you can tell the difference between the *tierce de Picardie* and the imperfect cadence in bars 7^3–8^3. This also ends on a major triad, so it is easy to confuse the two. The *tierce de Picardie* is not a cadence, but a modification of a cadence, and it can only occur on a tonic triad.

The other special type of cadence unique to minor keys is the **Phrygian cadence**. This is no more than an imperfect cadence that uses the particular chord pattern of IVb–V. The term survived from the days of the modes, but there is no implication that the cadence is now modal. The extract below also includes a Phrygian cadence—the imperfect cadence in bars 7^3–8^3. Ending slow movements in minor keys with a Phrygian cadence was a favourite device of Baroque composers.

Track 31

Test 16

(a) Identify, as precisely as you can, the chords at 2^1, 5^1 and 6^3.

(b) Fully describe the cadence in bars 11^3–12^3, explaining how the first chord of the cadence has been decorated.

Diminished Sevenths

The diminished seventh is a chord made up of a succession of minor thirds, such as the combination of F sharp–A–C–E flat in bar 8 of the song by Chopin, below. This symmetry results in the chord always having the same internal relationship of intervals, whichever note is in the bass. The chord of the diminished seventh is always chromatic in major keys, but it can be diatonic (i.e., employing only the notes of the current scale) in minor keys when it is used as a seventh on the leading note (e.g., G sharp–B–D–F in the key of A minor). Its quality of mystery, or even horror when played loudly, usually makes it quite distinctive.

Neapolitan Sixths

The Neapolitan sixth is always a chromatic chord, and is the triad on the flattened second degree of the scale. It is normally used in first inversion, giving it the name 'sixth' since, like all first inversions, the root appears a sixth above the bass. The adjective 'Neapolitan' reflects its popularity amongst composers working in Naples in the early 18th century. The chord is so highly chromatic in a major key—it is a chord of D flat major in the key of C, for example—that its use is rare and always startling. It is found much more often in minor keys, most typically as in the example at bar 10 below, where the chord is essentially an F major triad in the key of E minor (the B at the start of the bar is an appoggiatura in the vocal part).

 Track 32

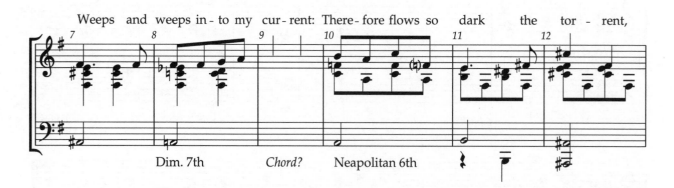

(a) Name the chord played by the piano in bar 2.

(b) How does the harmony of bars 4–6 relate to the harmony of bars 1–3?

(c) Describe the relationship between the singer's note and the printed bass part at:

   (i)   bar 13^1,

   (ii) bar 15^1.

(d) Identify the chords played by the piano at:

   (i)   bar 14^1,

   (ii) bar 16.

(e) This extract starts in the key of G major. In which key does it end?

Secondary Dominants

We normally think of the dominant as the chord a perfect fifth above the current tonic. However, it is possible, with the help of some chromaticism, to create a 'dominant' chord a fifth above any major or minor triad. Look at the chord in bar 5^2 of the music by Tchaikovsky below. It is a chord of A major, with a seventh on the third beat of the bar—just what you would expect for a modulation to the key of D. But when the *chord* of D arrives at the start of bar 6 it contains a C natural. This is hardly a modulation, not even a transitory one! The chord of A is, in this context, a secondary dominant—it is the dominant of the dominant, the most common of all secondary dominants.

Tchaikovsky ends the first line of music with a Phrygian cadence on a chord of B major—a simple modulation from the home key of G to its relative minor, E minor. In the second line he takes the 'long route' back to G by using a series of interconnected secondary dominants, each a fifth apart (B–E–A–D–G):

B ——————→ E ——→ A ——————→ D ——→ G

Track 33

This type of progression is known as a **cycle of fifths**, or even 'circle of fifths' since, if you extend the principle far enough, you would eventually return to the starting chord. When you listen to this track, notice how none of these secondary dominants has time to establish a key—the tonality is quite fluid, even in bar 8 where, without hearing what happens next, it remains unclear whether the final chord is the dominant of G or the tonic of D.

Romantic Harmony

The Lied (German art song) recorded on Track 34 and shown in skeleton score below, was written by Weber in 1809. It illustrates some of the ways in which harmonic vocabulary was extended by composers of the 19th century.

The bass of the piano accompaniment remains on the note E until the second beat of bar 4, although the harmony above this note continues to change. This device is known as a **pedal point**, or just a 'pedal'. The note may be continuous or, as here, re-sounded. If it occurs in an upper part rather than the bass, it is called an 'inverted pedal'. Pedal points most commonly occur on either the tonic or the dominant. The defining characteristic of a pedal is that the harmony should always be changing against it—the simple repetition of the same chord, or the juxtaposition of two chords that simply happen to share a common note, as in bar 18, does not create a pedal.

The chord in bar 7 is one that we have not yet encountered although, in isolation, it may sound familiar. It is a chord of the **augmented sixth**, named after the interval from its root to the augmented sixth above (here, C natural–A sharp). If you think of the A sharp enharmonically respelt as B flat, this might seem to be a dominant seventh of F: the notes C–E–G–B flat. Yet the key of F seems to have nothing to do with this music, which is firmly centred around the sharp keys. The function of the augmented sixth chord is quite different from the dominant seventh. The outside notes are both chromatic in a major key, and both lean onto the dominant note. Here, the key is E and therefore the dominant is B. The C natural leans down onto B and the A sharp leans up onto B. The inside notes of the chord are variable and give rise to such fanciful names as the German, French and Italian sixths. However, it is the root and the augmented sixth above it which are important: the two notes which lean onto, and thereby strengthen, the dominant.

In bar 9 the music changes into a key which is rather distant from the tonic of E major. This is a **tertiary modulation**—a change to a key which is a third or a sixth away from the main tonic. To identify this modulation, listen carefully to the note 'B' established in bar 8. How does this B relate to the new key? Is it the third, fourth, fifth or sixth degree of the key which we are entering?

The singer has an A sharp at the end of bar 16. This is a **chromatic passing-note** since the music is not modulating to B (notice the A naturals and tonic harmony of E in the next bar). The piano also has a chromatic passing-note in this part of the bar, an F double sharp, a third below the singer. These chromatic double passing-notes are one of the fingerprints of early Romantic harmony.

The Ic–V–I progression at the end of the extract is varied by the C sharp above chord V^7 in bar 18^3. Seventh chords consist of alternate notes—intervals of a third stacked above one another (here, B–D sharp–F sharp–A). The C sharp adds one more third above these, forming a **dominant major ninth** (V^9), another Romantic fingerprint. As often happens with this chord, the dissonant ninth resolves by dropping onto the dominant at the end of the bar, so the harmony could equally well be described as a dominant seventh with a long appoggiatura.

 Track 34

Test 18

[28]

(a) Identify how freqently the harmony changes in bars 1–3 and then name each of the chords heard above the tonic pedal in these bars.

(b) Name the three notes heard in the bass in bars 5^1–6^2.

(c) (i) To which key does the music modulate at bar 9?

    (ii) What harmonic device is used to underline this new key?

(d) Identify the two chords heard in bar $15^{1\text{-}2}$.

The remaining tests in this chapter offer further examples of some of the harmonic techniques we have outlined. Remember to concentrate your listening on the bass as you work through these. Juggling the many combinations of notes that make up the varied palette of chords available in different keys is not easy at the speed required in these tests. Making out your own chord and key plans at the start of each extract will help, but ultimately a thorough knowledge of scales and arpeggios will be of great assistance in identification.

Andante espressivo

Debussy

(a) Identify the chords at bar 1^4 and bar 4^4.

(b) Compare the harmony of bar 5 with the harmonization of the same melodic motif in bar 9.

(c) Name the key of the music in bars $11-12^3$ and the key of the music in the section beginning at bar 13.

(d) How do the quavers in the 'cello and piano decorate the harmony in bar 16^{1-2}?

(e) Name the key and the cadence in bars 19–20.

(f) The violin outlines a chord of E minor in the second half of bar 22. What note is played in the bass by the piano at 22^3 to modify this triad?

(g) Identify the chord at bar 23^3.

(h) Explain the decoration of the tonic harmony in the last bar of the extract.

(a) Briefly explain how the bass part harmonizes the melody in bars 5^1–7^1.

(b) Name the key to which the music modulates at bars 9–10.

(c) Identify the chord heard in bar 13.

(d) What does the first violin play in bars 20–23?

(e) Identify the chord heard throughout bars 36–38.

(f) Identify the chord heard in bar 43^{1-2}.

Allegro ♩=88   *Mozart*

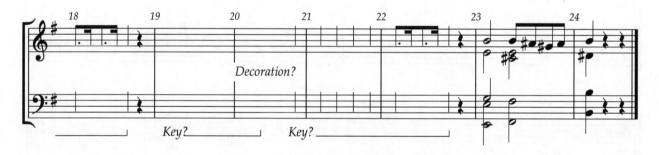

(a) Identify the chord heard in bar 2 and the chord heard in bar 4.

(b) What is the harmonic rôle of the violin part in bars 8–10?

(c) Identify the chord heard in bar $15^{1\text{-}2}$.

(d) A perfect cadence occurs in bars 19–20^2. Explain precisely how the tonic chord is decorated in this cadence (bar $20^{1\text{-}2}$).

(e) The extract end with a series of transitory modulations. Identify the keys passed through in each of the following phrases:

    (i)   bars 16^4–18^3,

    (ii)   bars 19^1–20^2,

    (iii) bars 20^4–22^3.

Intonation

Good intonation refers to the accurate pitch of individual notes sung or played by a musician and is a vital factor in achieving a satisfying musical performance. Unfortunately, it is not always easy to find the opportunity to practise this skill. Pianists, of course, have no direct control over the tuning of their instrument, while players of orchestral instruments often practise alone without the use of a fixed-pitch instrument to act as a reference point. Intonation becomes a critical factor in ensemble music, but in orchestras, bands, choirs and other large groups there may sometimes be so many pitch discrepancies that it is difficult for the individual to concentrate on, and solve, the various problems that arise.

Self-Help Ideas

There are two activities which offer excellent self-help opportunities to refine aural skill in intonation. One is in small ensemble work, with just two or three players, and especially in the performance of solos with piano accompaniment. Pianists, in particular, can benefit greatly from this type of duo work and may encounter some marvellous new repertoire. If you are a pianist, however, you will need to develop confidence in sharing in the discussion and criticism of points of intonation with your soloist. It is important that the music chosen should not, for either participant, pose technical hurdles that impede working on fine detail. Indeed, it is good practice in any ensemble work to ensure that all basic note-learning is mastered before working on the refinement of ensemble.

A second, and similarly very enjoyable, way to practise skills in intonation is once again provided by the human voice. Even if you are not a specialist singer, practising simple *solo* songs with a pianist and singing in a vocal group with only one or two voices per part provide excellent opportunities for working on accurate intonation. The vocal exercises in the first chapter can also be extended to include more detailed practice of intonation. To do this, we suggest you work at a keyboard—even non-pianists should be able to manage this. Give yourself a single pitch in a comfortable part of your range and hold the note down, with the sustaining pedal depressed. As you play, sing this pitch to a very long note. Take care that you centre the pitch very carefully at the start, and then very slightly raise the pitch of your singing, allowing the note to go out of focus before returning to the centre of the note. Do this a number of times, always very slowly, and check that you don't raise the pitch as far as the next semitone above. Savour the effect of this sharpening. You should hear the sung note at first sounding just a little brighter, but then becoming quite unstable—it may well be difficult to hold the pitch steady and you may find yourself being pulled up to the semitone above or back to the original note. If, after several attempts, you are not convinced that you can hear this effect, we suggest you try with a different reference point, since the rapidly decaying tone of a piano is not ideal for the slow speed of this exercise. Other possibilities include an electric keyboard, using a pure, flute-like sound that can sustain indefinitely, or perhaps working in pairs with an instrumentalist or a singer who can hold the steady pitch while you slowly sharpen it.

Once you can hear the gradual brightening and then de-focusing of a sharp pitch, try lowering the pitch of the sustained note. This time, you should at first hear the pitch starting to sound dull, and then again going noticeably out of tune. Check that you haven't flattened it as far as the semitone below.

Finally, try singing a very slow ascending scale. Start each note in tune, checking its pitch against the keyboard, and then very slightly sharpen it before dropping back to the correct pitch. Repeat the exercise, but flatten each note in turn. Then try Test 22 below.

Working the Tests

In each of the tests you will be given the score of a short passage of music for a solo orchestral instrument with piano accompaniment. The recording will contain up to five errors of intonation in the solo part and you have to locate these by encircling the notes concerned, and stating whether they are played sharp or flat. As with all of the tests in this book, you should repeat the passage as many times as you need at first, but with these aim ultimately for no more than four playings. In each of the tests we have graded the errors so that there will always be some that should stand out fairly clearly.

You should be aware that intonation, like most musical parameters, is not a matter that is fixed with scientific precision. Listen carefully to a good violinist and you will hear, for example, that the note 'B' when it is the key note of B major may well not sound at precisely the same pitch as 'B' when it is the leading note of C major. However, in these tests we are not dealing with such natural subtleties of performance but with notes that should, as you work on this skill, strike you as clearly out of tune with the accompaniment.

Track 38

======================================= *Test 22* =======================================

The passage below will be played with four errors of intonation in the oboe part. Locate these errors and describe each as either sharp or flat.

Pachelbel (adapted)

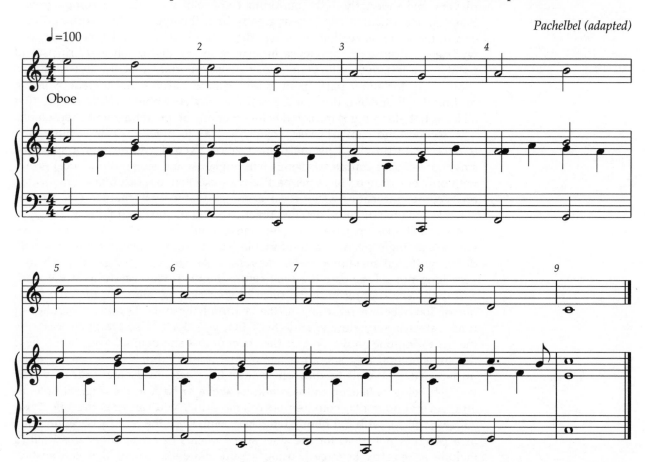

If, when you check your answers to this test, you find you have confused sharp and flat intonation, write in the correct solutions and play the track again; listen particularly for the dull effect of the flat notes and the shrill effect of the sharp notes and compare these with your own results in the vocal scale exercise described on the previous page.

The passages in the next test are reasonably easy to read in score. Try to imagine the sound of each extract before you listen to the recordings. As in the music above, the errors of intonation are mostly quite prominent, some being over a quarter of a tone sharp or flat. You may well know the first melody, which should help you to spot the locations of the errors.

Locate and describe three errors of intonation in each of the following passages.

Locate and describe four errors of intonation in each of the following passages.

Locate and identify five errors of intonation in each of the following passages.

Track 46

Haydn

Violin

Track 47

Orff

Trombone

Spot the Mistakes

Identifying and correcting mistakes in music is a skill that is particularly useful if you participate in, or direct, group music-making of any kind. Be aware, though, that these tests concern only errors in pitch and rhythm. Many other things can go wrong in ensemble performance, from a lack of unanimity in intonation, attack, phrasing and note-lengths, to the total failure of the players to listen to one another. However, if you can correct inaccuracies in pitch and rhythm quickly, at least you will have spare capacity to deal with all of these matters, as well as with the music-stand collapsing, the second oboist not arriving, and everything else that the hapless musician is expected to cope with.

The way to achieve success is to read the score accurately, building a 'sound picture' in your head before you actually hear the playing. In this sort of exercise, it is important that you try to absorb as much detail from the score as possible—a hazy notion of the general contours of the music is not going to help much. Put this into practice by singing the following tune by John Hilton (1599–1657). Go through it several times and check your pitch against an instrument.

This melody was designed to form the three-part round printed in full on page 39. Notice the simple harmonies produced by the counterpoint when all three parts are sounding. If you are working in a group try it in canon, each part starting four bars after the preceding one. You might also be able to do this by yourself if you have access to a multi-track tape recorder or sequencer.

Once you feel you know the tune, listen to the version on Track 48 while you follow the score below. Try, at least, to locate the six errors by circling them and, if you can, write what was actually played above the note or notes concerned. Here are a few tips you may find useful in this type of test:

❏ The first and last notes of the piece will not be altered, since you need these as reference points.

❏ Pitch alterations will only ever affect one printed note at a time, but rhythm alterations will always involve at least two consecutive notes (think about it: if one note is changed in length, the adjacent one will also have to be adjusted so that the overall number of beats in the bar is not changed).

❏ Circle notes clearly, so that there is no doubt which ones you mean.

❏ If you give the letter names for changed pitches, don't forget any accidentals needed and, if there could be any doubt, add an arrow to show whether the note you have named is higher or lower than the one printed.

As in previous chapters, transposing instruments are printed at concert pitch. Play the recordings as many times as you need in order to be confident in your answers but ultimately aim for no more than five playings of each test. With contrapuntal music like this you might find it best to correct one part only on each hearing, then use the other two playings to go back to any bars you missed and to check the whole composition.

 Track 48

Test 26

Indicate and correct six errors of pitch or rhythm (there are two in each part).

Hilton: 'Come follow me' from Catch that Catch Can, *1652 (originally for voices)*

In all of these tests, when you get any of the alterations wrong, play or sing the version you gave; then play or sing the version given in the Answers; finally, listen to the passage in context on the CD once more. It is much more useful to hear and understand the difference between what you wrote and what was played than just to mark your answer wrong and pass on to the next test.

The next piece is a Renaissance ballett in a much more homophonic (chordal) style. Listen to the 'vertical' aspects of the music (i.e., the harmony) as well as to the linear aspects. For example, if the lowest part played G in the second bar, you should hear a minor triad instead of the printed major third. If it played A, for instance, then there would be a noticeable discord. Always check that what you write matches what you hear in the harmony.

[39]

Before you listen, read through the music carefully. Even if you find it difficult to imagine the sound of the chords, you can still do some useful preliminary work. Notice that the chords are almost all major triads in root position and that bars 12–14 are the same as bars 4–6: both sections of this little binary piece end with the same perfect cadence pattern. The key is F major, apart from bars 9–11. At this point, the music briefly passes through D minor, although the F sharp in bar 11 indicates a *tierce de Picardie* at the cadence. This D major chord is followed immediately by an F major tonic triad: not unusual for the period (this was written in the late Renaissance) but these two chords are not close relatives in tonal music, so you should be ready for the surprise.

When you read through, try to get an impression of the rhythm. Notice the fast speed: the metronome mark not only indicates 56 bars per minute, but also shows that it will be played fast enough to have a feel of 'one in a bar'. Note the places where the parts don't move entirely together. Also be prepared for the syncopation in the trumpet at bar 10, and the hemiolas at the end of each of the two sections—you should not then be taken by surprise if you hear a little rhythmic disruption at these points when you listen to the recording.

Track 49

Indicate and correct six errors of pitch or rhythm (there are two in each part).

Holborne: 'Change then, for lo she changeth', published 1597 (originally for voices)

Did you spot the chromatic note? Most notes that are 'foreign' to the key should stand out but when, as here and in Test 26, the accidentals simply cause passing reference to closely related keys they can be overlooked. If you did miss them, listen to both passages again, and notice how raising the fourth (sharpening it, or making it a natural if it is currently flat) leans the tonality up to the dominant. Similarly, lowering the seventh (flattening it, or making it a natural if it is currently a sharp) causes the tonality to sink down to the subdominant.

The next extract is part of an allemande by Bach. We have chosen a two-part piece to ease the note-reading problems, for gone now are the conjunct lines of Renaissance polyphony. Bach's sweeping contrapuntal melodies span a wide range, with many expressive, but difficult to read, intervals. Once again, in your preliminary study of the score, look for 'signposts'—the repeating figures, imitation and the sequential repetition of the whole of bar 3 in bar 4. Don't be intimidated by the accidentals. As you might expect in this style of music, the only keys used are the tonic, dominant and (briefly) relative major. However, don't overlook the *effect* of accidentals in these long bars: the sharp in bar 7 (treble stave), for example, applies to every G throughout that bar.

Track 50

===================================== *Test 28* =====================================

Indicate and correct six errors of pitch or rhythm (there are three in each part).

Bach: Allemande from French Suite No. 3, BWV 814, 1722-25 (originally for harpsichord)

If you have come across the term 'trio sonata' you will know that, confusingly, it is a piece of Baroque chamber music for four players (see page 110). This is nowhere near as strange as the next extract, though, which is from a trio sonata for only one performer. It is, in fact, the opening of Bach's Organ Sonata No. 6: the two treble staves are played by the hands while the bass stave is played on the pedalboard by the feet.

You should, by now, be developing a routine for reading the score before hearing the music, so this is the last time we will repeat the reminders. Notice that, although this is fast and looks complex, the rhythms are mostly straight-forward, the modulations are brief and move to two closely related keys, while the texture is only two-part in the first two lines.

The material is largely scale- and chord-based, often just using the primary triads, although decoration sometimes hides this (as in bars 13–17). In addition to the more obvious scale figures, make sure you can hear the quaver scale in the pedals in bars 11–12 continuing as one note per bar from bar 13 onwards. You should also notice the pedal G (in both senses of the word pedal) from bar 21 through to near the end of the extract.

 Track 51

Test 29

Indicate and correct seven errors of pitch or rhythm in this extract.

Bach: Organ Sonata No. 6 in G, BWV 530, first movement, c.1727 (trills omitted)

You may have found the last rhythmic 'error' in this extract a little difficult to correct. If so, it might help to consider how rhythm patterns can be mistimed in various ways, while still not losing the overall pulse of the music.

The two most common ways of dividing a crotchet beat into two notes are (1) two even quavers, and (2) a dotted quaver followed by a semiquaver. The reverse of (2), putting the semiquaver first (the 'Scotch snap'), is rare. You may also find one other possible division in slow music: the double-dotted quaver followed by a demisemiquaver. There are rather more ways of dividing a crotchet beat into three notes:

Track 52

Several of these possibilities occur in the opening of the melody of the aria 'Ich will bei meinem Jesu wachen' from Bach's St Matthew Passion. Listen to the correct version, played on the oboe, as you follow the music:

This is immediately followed by two altered versions of Bach's melody in which the various threefold divisions of the beat have become muddled:

Listen carefully to these patterns and compare them with Bach's original. Play and sing them for yourself, and experiment with them in improvisation, until you feel comfortable that you can recognize them accurately. Work out for yourself different ways of splitting a crotchet beat into four divisions, and also different ways of dividing the dotted crotchet beat of compound time into various patterns of three and four notes.

Track 53

Test 30

Indicate and correct six errors of rhythm (only) in this extract.

Pepusch (1667–1752): Trio Sonata in C, first movement

Indicate and correct seven errors of pitch or rhythm in this extract.

Stefan de Haan (b. 1921): Divertimento on Folk-Songs, *(i) 'O Vigand' (Flemish war song), 1965*

Indicate and correct six errors of pitch or rhythm in this extract.

Handel: Courante from the overture to Theodora, *1750*

Indicate and correct six errors of pitch or rhythm in this extract.

♩=72

Trumpet

Horn

Trombone

Matthew Locke (c.1621–1677): 'In the Beginning, O Lord' (originally for voices)

Indicate and correct seven errors of pitch or rhythm in this extract.

Giuseppe Maria Cambini: Trio in G minor for flute, oboe and bassoon, Op. 45 No. 2 (c.1785)

Handel, in the excerpt below, has chosen to use short note durations, giving the music a complex, 'black' appearance, although the instruction 'Adagio' ensures that the pulse is very slow. Note-lengths are only relative, though—they don't indicate exact durations. So if you find the score difficult to read, try imagining it notated in notes of twice the given length:

Track 58

Test 35

Indicate and correct five errors of pitch or rhythm in this extract.

Handel: Trio Sonata in D minor, Op. 2 No. 2 (c.1699)

Indicate and correct six errors of pitch or rhythm in this extract (Note: since grace-notes do not have any specific duration, you should not expect these to be altered in length—nor should you expect changes in other types of ornament).

Schubert: Trio in B flat, D 581 (1817)

[51]

Indicate and correct five errors of pitch or rhythm in this extract.

Reger: String Trio, Op. 141b (1915)

Aural and Stylistic Analysis

Prelude to Part II

At first sight, the scope of this second part of the book may seem daunting. Yet, as you work through the chapters, you should find that much of what you have learned about one style can help in your understanding of music that you thought was radically different. As you progress through the book, try to understand those basic analytical concepts which you can apply to the music of many different styles. If you come across an unfamiliar term, check the meaning in a dictionary of music, then look it up in the index of this book and listen to the musical effect to which the term refers in different styles of music.

Always describe what you hear rather than what you expect to hear. There is little point in describing an extract from a piano sonata by Mozart in terms of textbook generalizations such as 'melody-dominated homophony' or 'Alberti bass' if you are listening to two-part counterpoint. If you cannot remember a technical term such as 'augmentation', simply describe what happens—'the tune is repeated but with all the notes doubled in length'.

Repeat the extracts as many times as you need in order to feel confident in answering the questions. In examinations, the type and number of questions will be designed for the three repetitions you are given. Here we have included some longer tests which will undoubtedly need more playings so that you can understand how short extracts relate to their contexts in complete sections or movements. In all cases, though, do get used to pausing for about one minute between playings, and try to memorize the salient features of the music so that you can recall these in the silences.

Finally, you should realize that, while we have included many of the basic elements of a number of different musical styles, a book of this size cannot include representative examples of every important musical trend and composer. Take every opportunity to listen with perception to a wide range of music, using the resources provided by radio stations, anthologies with recordings and collections such as the extracts on disc that accompany some music magazines.

Identification

In addition to the types of question in the tests, you will sometimes be asked to identify the composer, style, period or date of an extract. Practise this skill by random 'dipping' into the accompanying recordings—some CD players include a 'random play' feature that you can use for this purpose. You can then check your answers against the identification provided in the list of CD tracks.

When identifying an extract, always consider *all* of the evidence. A slow piece with foreign words sung by an unaccompanied choir will not necessarily be Renaissance church music. It may be a chorus from a much later opera, a motet by a Romantic composer such as Bruckner, or an excerpt from a 20th-century Requiem. Consider all of the parameters, including melodic, harmonic and rhythmic style and the compositional techniques employed, before deciding.

Remember that the earliest music in these extracts is from the late Renaissance. It is a waste of effort to suggest anything earlier. However, try to be specific by appending 'early' or 'late' to the musical period that you do suggest.

No one will expect you to give the precise date of a piece you have never heard before. When suggesting dates, aim to be within 25 years either side of the actual date, but try to avoid such impossibilities as ascribing a chorale by Bach to 1775 or a piece of 'free jazz' to 1935. Beware of the trap of describing a date as '18th century, about 1850': in English, 1850 is in the *19th* century, just as 1993 is in the *20th* century. Finally, always try to suggest the name of a single composer. You will receive credit for a plausible, if incorrect, suggestion, but you will not be rewarded for guessing at a list of possibilities.

Folk Music of the British Isles

There are as many definitions of folk music as there are dictionaries of music. For present purposes we will concentrate on music which has evolved in the community and has been transmitted by aural tradition rather than musical notation. This does not mean that folk music will never be notated, but that any notation (most frequently in the work of folk music scholars) will always come *after* the music has been composed and passed on by ear.

Have you ever tried a party game in which one person whispers a story to another, then the second person whispers it to the next and so on until it reaches the last guest? When the last person relates the story it is usually quite different from the original. Just so with folk music. As a tune travels around the country (or, as is often the case, around the world) it acquires different ornaments, and even the basic structure may be modified to suit changes in musical fashions or the taste of each new performer.

These observations have two practical consequences. Firstly, you must not expect most folk music to be performed as simply and consistently as printed collections of folk music would lead you to expect. In living folk music, each verse is likely to have slightly different music, the regular four-bar phrases of printed collections are likely to be much more irregular, and sometimes it is quite impossible to detect a regular beat—let alone a consistent metre.

Secondly, since folk music travels, it can be difficult to distinguish regional styles. In folk-song anthologies you may well find the provenance of each tune, but often this means nothing more than that the tune was heard by the collector in that place: in fact the performer may be the latest in a chain stretching back many years and leading to a region quite remote from the area given in the anthology. Consider the 'Scotch snap'. Even if it did originate in Scotland, it soon spread to Ireland during the Elizabethan plantations, and thence to the New World: you are as likely to hear this rhythm in a Newcastle pub as you are to hear it at the Highland games. Your response must be to write about what you actually hear rather than what you think you ought to be hearing.

Structures

Most European folk music, and especially that of the British Isles, uses short structures that depend on repetition and simple variation. This is particularly apparent in dance tunes, where the nature of the dance demands clear-cut rhythms and regular sections.

It is a useful convention to identify musical structures in terms of letters: A for the first main section, B for a new section with clearly different material, and so on. Thus, the simple threefold 'sandwich' known as 'ternary form' can be quickly notated as ABA. If a section returns with some significant change, a superscript number is appended to the letter, such as A^1 for a first modification and A^2 for a further change. It is a matter for your judgement whether any difference is sufficiently important to be recorded as a variant in this way. If section A is repeated with, say, just a passing-note to fill a gap of a third early in the melody, then this is of no great significance. On the other hand, if just a single note is altered to change the type of cadence or to introduce a modulation to a new key, then the phrase should be identified with a superscript, since the small alteration has totally changed the function of the phrase.

At least in simpler types of tonal music, phrases are often delineated by a **cadence**. In the majority of cases this is likely to be either conclusive (the perfect cadence) or inconclusive (the imperfect cadence). Since much folk music is monophonic, possibly accompanied by just a drone or a percussion part, you may find it surprising to think of a melodic line in terms of cadences, which are more commonly regarded as a harmonic feature. Nevertheless, the cadences *implied* by a melody are often simple to locate and identify. In the first phrase of the folk dance 'Portsmouth', printed below, you can see that the tune comes to rest on a long A, in the fourth bar. The melody is in G major, and the note A is clearly not the tonic—the ending is inconclusive and the implied cadence is imperfect. If the tune were harmonized, the dominant chord of an imperfect cadence would fit comfortably under this note.

Now listen to the whole of this tune on Track 61. Notice that it is **periodic**: that is, the phrases continue in regular patterns like the first—each begins with an anacrusis (an upbeat start) and each is four bars in length. Make sure that you can identify four clear phrases and that you can hear that the third of these repeats the imperfect cadence of the first phrase.

'Portsmouth' first appeared in print in 1701 in Playford's *The English Dancing Master*. This collection, which ran to 18 editions between 1651 and 1728, is the most important source of popular instrumental music in England of the time.

The recording reflects one possible mode of performance—the use of pipe and tabor (small drum). Equally likely, though, would be performance on such contemporary instruments as the violin, recorder or oboe. For dancing, the two halves of this short tune would undoubtedly have been repeated a number of times, in which case ornaments and variations would have been introduced to sustain interest.

Track 61

Test 38

This is the melody of the first phrase (A) of the folk dance tune 'Portsmouth':

(a) Apart from the addition of a drum part, how does the performance of phrase A differ from the music printed above?

(b) How does the second phrase relate to phrase A?

(c) Compare the rhythm, melody and tessitura (average range of pitches) of the third phrase with phrase A printed above.

(d) Which previous phrase is repeated to form the last phrase of the tune?

(e) Using your answers from questions (b) to (d), state the phrase structure of this dance, using letters and (if necessary) superscript numbers for any variants.

(f) (i) Which of the following rhythms is played by the drum throughout most of this extract?

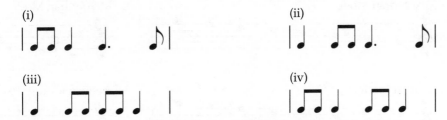

(ii) Where is the only place where this pattern is varied?

Track 62

'The Jig of Slurs' on the next track is a piece of Scottish folk dance music that extends this same idea of short, regular phrases into a more complex structure. One of the most common ways of providing variety in longer pieces is to modulate to a new key. You should hear this clearly in 'The Jig of Slurs', especially if you listen carefully to the bass.

The music on this track falls into pairs of regular eight-bar phrases as follows:

A	A	B	B	C	C	D	D	A¹	A¹
0"		13"		26"		39"		52"	

Each pair of phrases is 13 seconds long and the figures indicate the start times in seconds for each pair. Listen several times until you can recognize all of these phrases by ear alone, then answer these questions:

(a) At what point does the music first move into a new key?

(b) How is this new key related to the key of the opening?

(c) How does the piano bass of A¹A¹ differ from the piano bass of AA?

(d) In what metre is this music?

(e) Comment briefly on the rhythm of the fiddle part, explaining how rhythm is used to clarify the phrase structure of the music.

Tonality and Modality

Nowadays **tonality** usually refers to the way in which music is based upon major and minor scales so that one note, the tonic, acts like a magnet to which the music is constantly attracted. Movement away from this magnet, particularly in the case of modulation, creates variety and a degree of tension which is resolved when the home tonic is regained. Tonality is often contrasted with **modality**, the former being thought of as a modern phenomenon and the latter as applying to pre-Baroque music. But this is an over-simplification. Renaissance music (especially dance music) was sometimes written entirely in the major and later styles may often be very modal (convince yourself by listening to *Sgt. Pepper*). In fact, the so-called modes are largely a theoretical construct and major and minor scales are just special cases of modality.

Folk music of the British Isles freely mixes a variety of modes. The most common are the major, Dorian, Mixolydian and Aeolian, all of which are also widely found in pop music and jazz.

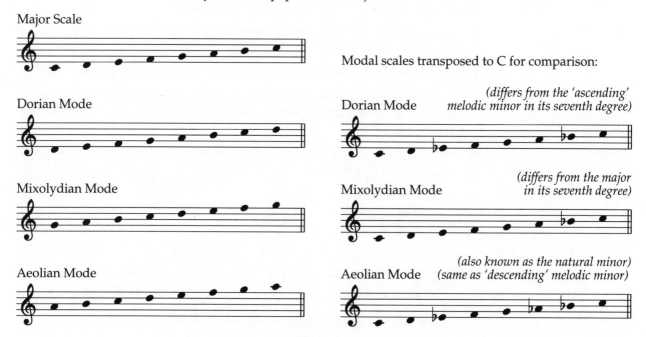

Major Scale

Dorian Mode

Mixolydian Mode

Aeolian Mode

Modal scales transposed to C for comparison:

Dorian Mode — *(differs from the 'ascending' melodic minor in its seventh degree)*

Mixolydian Mode — *(differs from the major in its seventh degree)*

Aeolian Mode — *(also known as the natural minor) (same as 'descending' melodic minor)*

Play and sing these scales, noting the particular 'flavour' of each one: the flat seventh of the Mixolydian mode, the flat third and seventh of the Dorian mode, and the descending melodic minor (or natural minor scale) quality of the Aeolian mode with its flat third, sixth and seventh. Note that modal melodies, like tonal melodies, do not necessarily cadence on (or even end on) their first degree.

Describe the music on each of the following tracks by using one of these terms:

major key   minor key   Dorian mode   Mixolydian mode   Aeolian mode

(a) 'The Four-Loom Weaver' on Track 63.

(b) 'Mickey Doherty's Highland' on Track 64.

(c) 'Fairer than the White Rose' on Track 65.

(d) 'Leaving Glasgow' on Track 66.

'Mickey Doherty's Highland' comes from County Donegal and features some of the characteristic instruments of Irish folk music. The melody is played by violins (usually known in folk music as 'fiddles') and is accompanied by the *bodhrán*, a single-headed drum struck with a 'tipper' held between the fingers and using a swivelling movement of the wrist. Towards the end of the extract, the soft sound of the union (or *uilleann*) pipe can be heard. This is an indoor bagpipe, blown by elbow-operated bellows. Unlike the Scottish Highland pipes, it has the facility to change the pitch of the drones through 'regulators' operated by the heel of the hand while playing. This piece also features the rhythm pattern of semiquaver–dotted quaver, shown at *(y)* below. This is known as Lombardic rhythm, or the 'Scotch snap', and is common in all gaelic folk music.

'Mickey Doherty's Highland' begins with a solo on the *bodhrán* and then continues in repeated four-bar sections, following the pattern AABBAABBAA. The skeleton score below shows the introduction and A section:

(a) Identify the rhythm played by the *bodhrán* at *(x)*.

(b) On what note does every four-bar phrase of the melody end?

(c) Identify the rhythm played by the fiddles at *(z)*, just before the last note of the phrase.

(d) Comment on the texture of the fiddle parts in this extract.

(e) When the repeated phrase A appears for the final time, the pipes and a mandolin enter. How do their parts emphasize the modality of the music?

It is not always possible to identify the use of one particular mode in folk music, particularly as the impact of tonal music gradually encouraged new generations of performers to introduce such techniques as sharpening the seventh degree of a mode to bring it closer to the major or minor scale. In addition, some folk music draws on the notes of more than one mode anyway. Listen to 'Dives and Lazarus' on Track 67 and you will hear that the major thirds and sevenths of the first half are flattened at the end. In fact, the precise distinctions between major and minor intervals that we are used to in the tempered scales of Western art music are often blurred in folk music. In particular, the third, sixth and seventh of the major scale—the very notes which differentiate the common folk music modes from one another—are frequently sung or played flat, just as they are in the blues, jazz and some types of popular music.

This phenomenon puzzled folk-song collectors in the early 20th century, like Cecil Sharp and Percy Grainger, although the explanation is quite simple. Our modern system of intonation (the precise tuning of notes within the scale) was not established until the time of Bach, in the 18th century. This system, known as 'equal temperament', essentially compromised the pitches produced naturally by stretched strings and columns of air in order to allow fixed-pitch instruments (particularly keyboard instruments) to modulate freely between all major and minor keys. This compromise involves making the intervals of every scale precisely the same distance apart and this could only be done by nudging certain notes away from their acoustically natural pitches. The three notes to be most affected are the third, sixth and seventh of the major scale, which are all a little sharp in the equal temperament of art music.

Folk musicians, who rarely use keyboard instruments, have had little need for equal temperament, and it should therefore not be a surprise to find these flatter versions of notes coexisting with their modern counterparts. If you have ever sung in, or directed, a choir you will know that, to this very day, thirds, sixths and leading notes are the most difficult to get in tune, because the untrained voice still prefers to sing them flatter than the pitch that equal temperament demands. It is also probable that the natural tendency to flatten these notes (often by less than a semitone) survived in the copious amount of British folk music that was carried by the settlers to America. There the style merged with Afro-American musical traditions in the creation of the blues and thus became the origin of the 'blue notes' that are such an important feature of jazz and popular music. The use of 'blue notes' in folk music is most obvious in the context of music in a major key, as the next test will show.

 Track 67

=========================== *Test 42* ===========================

Listen to the following verse from an English folk-song:

1. As it fell out upon a day
2. Did Dives make a feast,
3. And he invited all his friends
4. And gentry of the best.

(a) Which line cadences on the leading note of the major scale?

(b) On which syllable can you hear a flattened seventh?

(c) On which syllable can you hear a flattened third?

(d) Describe the texture of this music.

Pentatonic and Hexatonic Scales

Sometimes folk music omits one or more notes of a scale. When you listened to 'The Jig of Slurs' on Track 62 (page 56), you may well have heard the key centre shift away from the tonic at the start of section B but have been uncertain what new key had been reached. In fact, there was no clear modulation in a classical sense. The pedal bass and the opening fiddle figure simply, but firmly, shifted up from D to G. The melody, however, never used the fourth note of the major scale so, in the G major section, there was no C natural to indicate conclusively that the realm of D major had been left—not, anyway, until one eventually appeared in the accompanying parts when harmonic movement started to be introduced later in the extract.

When a note of the scale is omitted, it is frequently either the fourth or the seventh degree. These are the very two notes which, in a classical sense, are needed to define basic modulation—sharpening the fourth usually takes the key to the dominant, while flattening the seventh often takes the key to the sub-dominant. Folk music sometimes prefers to be much more ambivalent and omits one or both of these notes. If all seven notes are not present, it is often difficult to identify a precise key or mode of a piece, and it becomes more convenient to think in terms of the number of notes of the scale actually used. A six-note scale (usually omitting either the fourth or seventh) is called **hexatonic** while a five-note scale (usually omitting both) is known as **pentatonic**. In the British Isles the latter is almost invariably the combination of tones and minor thirds that match the pattern of 'black notes' on the piano—they have been transposed to start on C in the example below. Notice that, in terms of C major, it is those same degrees of the fourth (F) and seventh (B) that are omitted:

There are other permutations of five intervals, forming different versions of the pentatonic scale that are more common in other parts of the world, as will be discovered in the next chapter. However, the anhemitonic quality (lack of semitones) of the 'British pentatonic' scale should always make it recognizable.

 Track 68

================================= *Test 43* =================================

Listen to the Scottish folk-song, 'Wha Wadna Fight for Charlie?' on Track 68. The text of the first four lines is:

    1. Wha wadna fight for Charlie? Wha wadna draw the sword?
    2. Wha wadna up and rally at the royal Prince's word?
    3. Think on Scotia's ancient heroes, think on foreign foes repelled,
    4. Think on glorious Bruce and Wallace, who the proud usurpers quelled.

(a) The song begins with the following figure:

    On which note does every line of the song end?

(b) What is the total range spanned by this song?

(c) On which word do you hear the rhythm known as a 'Scotch snap'?

(d) On which words does the singer introduce pauses into the pulse? What is the significance of these pauses?

(e) The extract continues for two more lines after the four lines given above. Describe the phrase structure using letters and numbers, and then name the form of the entire song.

(f) Which of the following terms best describes the scale on which this song is based?

    Mixolydian   major   Dorian   pentatonic   Aeolian   hexatonic

Texture and Harmony

Most of the music we have heard so far has been **monophonic** (a single melodic line, either without accompaniment or with the support of just percussion or a simple drone). For harmony we should go to the 'Land of Song'—Wales! But do not expect harmonized folk-song to conform to the norms of four-part hymns with 'correct' harmonic progressions. Track 69 begins with an ancient carol tune,

'On This Day's Morning', sung with improvised harmony and recorded in 1967 at a Congregational chapel in Montgomeryshire (now part of Powys). Follow the skeleton score below as you listen and notice how it begins with a single voice answered by male-voice harmony (rather like the call and response of some African music). Notice, too, the consecutive octaves between the outer parts in bar 3 and the bare fifths of the dominant chords. The harmony is entirely diatonic (though this is not true of all Welsh harmonized song) and the texture is entirely **homophonic**—the parts all move together in the same rhythm.

In the third line listen for two cadences, imperfect on *Bosra* and perfect on *Seina*. Cadences usually have a weak–strong pattern of accents, but both of these cadences reverse this order and end on weak beats (the notes marked with pause signs)—these are known as **feminine** cadences.

Now compare this with Steeleye Span's recording of 'All Around My Hat' on Track 95. Although the melody is traditional, the arrangement is in a folk-rock style and was in the top ten of the charts in 1975, just eight years after the Welsh carol was recorded. You will hear that the arrangement starts with just the same type of rugged harmony, with prominent consecutive fifths in the lower parts and no qualms about disregarding harmonic 'rules' when the simple, melodic part-writing demands that phrases should end on second inversions.

 Track 69

Test 44

Follow this skeleton score of the first part of the Welsh hymn, 'On This Day's Morning' as you listen to the recording:

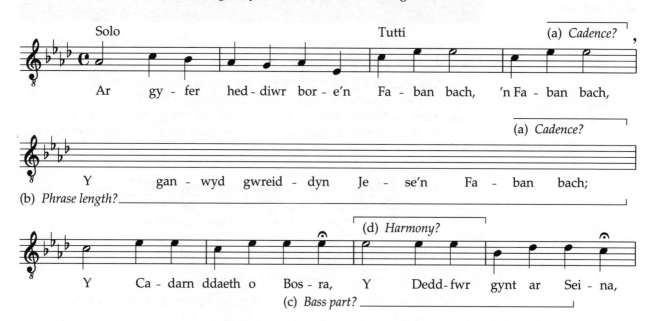

Translation:

On this day's morning, as a tiny Child
The root of Jesse was born, a tiny Child;
The Mighty came from Bozra, the Lawgiver once on Sinai …

(a) Compare the cadence in bar 4 with the cadence at the end of line 2.

(b) Comment on the phrase length of the second line of music.

(c) Describe the bass part in the section marked (c) in line 3.

(d) Describe the harmony in the bar marked (d) in line 3.

(e) What happens after the end of the printed extract above?

(f) Describe the choral texture in this extract and explain how the part printed above relates to this texture.

In this part of the book you will not be expected to identify the chords in a passage of music (as is the case in Part I), but you should be able to distinguish the principal types of chords, such as primary triads, sevenths, and so forth, and recognize different types of cadence. You should also be able to recognize if chord progressions are **functional** or not (i.e., if they serve the function of defining a key as well as just thickening the texture in a pleasing way).

The cradle song on the next track, like 'On This Day's Morning', is **diatonic**. In other words, it uses only the unmodified notes of its key, without any chromatic alterations.

 Track 70

Listen to the cradle song on Track 70. There are two verses, each of which divides up into four clearly defined musical phrases corresponding to the four lines of the Welsh text:

Verse 1

1. *Mi gysgi di 'maban, mi gysgi di'n braf,*   You'll sleep my baby, you'll sleep softly,
2. *Dy wyneb mor dawel â diwmod o haf,*   Your face as tranquil as a summer's day,
3. *Dy fysedd yn llacio wrth ollwng fy llaw,*   Your fingers slacken as you let go my hand,
4. *Mi gysgi di 'maban, a'r bore a ddaw.*   You'll sleep my baby, and the morning will come.

Verse 2

1. *Mae'r pwll mawr yn dduach na dwr corsydd mawn,*   The big pool is blacker than peat bog water,
2. *Bu hwnnw yn gwahodd, do lawer prynhawn,*   It enticed me many an afternoon,
3. *Wna'r barrug ddim codi wrth 'rhen felin blwm,*   The frost won't leave the old lead mill,
4. *A'r dagrau o'r derw sy'n disgyn yn drwm.*   And heavy tears fall from the oak.

(a) Give the verse and line numbers where you hear each of the following:

    (i)   voices in octaves,

    (ii)   voices in parallel sixths,

    (iii) an unaccompanied solo voice.

(b) Give the line numbers where you hear each of the following (these features all appear in similar positions in both verses):

    (i)   three-part homophony,

    (ii)   a perfect cadence,

    (iii) a feminine cadence,

    (iv)   an implied perfect cadence,

    (v)   an implied imperfect cadence.

(c) Comment on the metre of this song.

Folk Music in the Industrial Age

Folk music is essentially a type of popular music—'folk' means 'of the people' as much as the word 'popular' does. Indeed, it would be difficult to make any distinction between the two before the 19th century. However, with the industrial revolution came a great move of the rural population into the towns. Those for whom this brought a modest increase in wealth soon showed a desire to climb the social ladder and seek new ways of being musically entertained. It was largely for them that a new light-music industry emerged, supplying popular material for the home, for brass and military bands and for music-hall singers. As we shall see in the chapter on popular music, this music was professionally composed, taking the lighter forms of art music as its model and departing from both the style and the function of folk music. It was, in fact, music designed to exploit public taste as much as to reflect it. It was also a type of music beyond the reach of the poorest classes, who continued to entertain themselves with music whose text and ethos more genuinely reflected their own community.

The words of even rural folk-song often painted a picture that was sharply at variance with images of an idyllic land of sheep and meadows. Like the sea shanties sung on sailing vessels, many songs were used to accompany long hours of drudgery or to provide sarcastic comment on low pay, poor food and tyrannical working conditions—and, indeed, this was encouraged as a harmless way of allowing the workers to 'let off steam'.

In the industrial age, not only does the subject matter of folk-songs change, but also the influences of art and commercial music start to be seen. In 'Poverty Knock' on the next track, you can hear regular phrase lengths, clear major tonality underpinned by functional harmony, and a new instrument of the century—the concertina (invented 1844). You can also see that the underlying theme of protest is an element that has not changed.

🎵 Track 71

Test 46

The music on this track is taken from the first part of an industrial song of the late 19th century, originally recorded in Batley, West Yorkshire, in 1965. After a four-bar introduction on a concertina, the first verse is:

Up ev'-ry mor-ning at five, I won-der that we keep a-live.

Tired and yawn-ing in the cold mor-nin' And back to the drea-ry old drive.

Then follows a second verse with the following words:

A	O dear we're goin' to be late;
B	Gaffer is stood at the gate.
C	We're out of pocket, our wages he'll dock it,
D	We'll have to buy grub on the slate.

And finally a chorus:

> Singing poverty, poverty knock,
> Me loom is a-sayin' all day,
> Poverty, poverty knock,
> Gaffer's too skinny too pay.
> Poverty, poverty knock,
> Keepin' one eye on the clock.
> And I know I can guttle (*eat*) when I hear me shuttle
> Go poverty, poverty knock.

(a) In verse 1, how does the singer decorate the first note of 'yawning' (bar 5)?

(b) Compare the melody of verse 2 with that of verse 1.

(c) The musical structure of the verses is represented by the letters ABCD above. Use these letters to show how the eight lines of the chorus are all derived from these same four lines of music.

(d) Describe the vocals in the chorus as precisely as you can.

(e) From which part of the song is the concertina introduction taken?

(f) The first bar printed above is harmonized with a chord of F. How is this chord modified in bar 2 and what chord is used in bar 3?

(g) Comment on the harmony of the entire song.

Sometimes verses are much more radically varied, particularly in unaccompanied songs where the scope for improvisation is not limited by harmonic progressions. Such **monophonic** folk-songs are also likely to be sung in a much freer rhythm, and to feature vocal ornamentation, so that no two verses (and no two performances) sound the same. This can be heard in the much earlier industrial song, 'The Four-Loom Weaver', which dates from just after the battle of Waterloo (1815). Whereas 'Poverty Knock' was a song about the harsh conditions working on the power looms in textile factories, 'The Four-Loom Weaver' is a song of an even poorer class—the hand-loom operators whose livelihoods were reduced to a pittance by the industrial processes of the 19th century.

Track 63

Test 47

The music below is the first verse of 'The Four-Loom Weaver', an unaccompanied song in the Dorian mode.

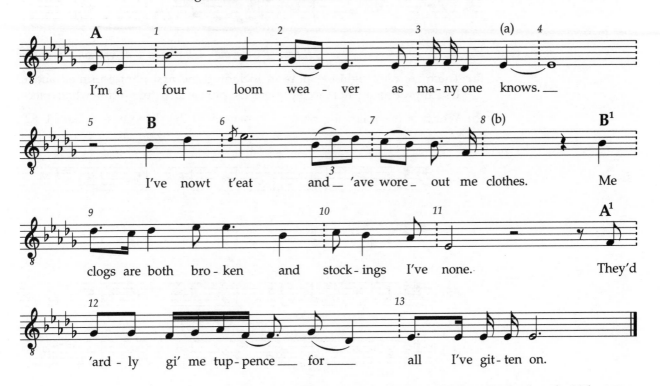

The Four-Loom Weaver, Northern England, early 19th century

The words of verse 2 are:

A   Owd Billy a'Bent 'e kept tellin me long,
B   We met 'ave better times if I'd nobbut 'eld me tongue.
B¹ Well I've 'eld me tongue 'till I near lost me breath,
A¹ An' a feel in me 'eart that I'll sune clem to death.

(a) How does the singer decorate the note marked (a) in bar 3?

(b) Lines 1, 3 and 4 of each verse end on the first degree of the Dorian mode (E flat). On what note does line 2 end, at the point marked (b) in bar 8?

(c) Both verses have the musical structure ABB¹A¹. Which of these four phrases is most radically varied in verse 2?

(d) Describe two ways in which the singer imparts greater poignancy to the last line of verse 2 as compared with the same line in verse 1.

The final example in this chapter is another Dorian mode melody, played by a flute and accordion and accompanied by a harmony part played on the piano. The flute and accordion do not play quite the same notes—each decorates the melody individually, so that the two parts seem to shadow one another, rather than playing in strict unison. This is known as **heterophony** ('difference of sounds') and is a feature of traditional music from a number of cultures, particularly of Greece and of Far Eastern countries.

Test 48

Here is the first eight-bar phrase of this melody from the Isle of Skye:

'Leaving Glasgow', Dunvegan (Isle of Skye), Scotland

(a) There are four eight-bar phrases including the first phrase printed above. Use appropriate letters to represent the phrase structure of the whole piece.

(b) Which of the following patterns is played by the piano bass in bars 1–8?

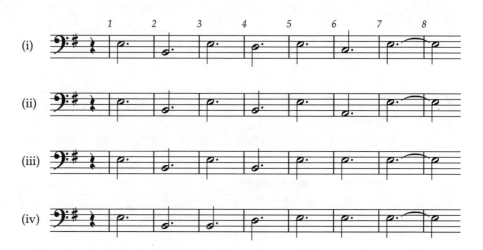

(c) How do the types of chords used in bars 2, 4 and 6 differ from the types of chords used in the rest of this first eight-bar section?

(d) What cadence occurs at the end of the whole tune?

Folk music continues to flourish today, although the term now also embraces contemporary political commentary by singers such as Billy Bragg, and such composite styles as the folk-rock of Fairport Convention and the thrash-folk of The Pogues. It is, however, difficult to talk of a modern 'British' folk tradition because of the pervasive influence of American music, particularly through singers such as Bob Dylan and Joan Baez, genres such as Vietnam War protest songs ('Where Have All The Flowers Gone?' and 'We Shall Overcome'), folk-pop community songs like 'I'd Like To Teach The World To Sing' (The New Seekers) and the whole area of American country music (the 'hillbilly' origins of which are, themselves, distantly related to British folk music). In our modern multi-cultural climate, traditional music (often called 'roots' music) from many other parts of the world also adds to the rich diversity of folk music that can be heard today—from Bulgarian partsongs and Catelan folk dances to Tex-Mex, Cajun and Zydeco. This blurring of the boundaries, so typical of all types of late 20th-century music, takes us beyond our working definition of folk music and on into areas that require chapters of their own: world music and popular music.

World Music

We can think of world music as being like a group of languages. Each society has its own principal music, and members of that society respond to it with a common understanding, in the same way as they communicate through their spoken language. In complex societies such as our own, there may even be several parallel types of music serving different purposes. In listening to the following extracts, however unusual they may sound at first, it is important to remember that music reflects each social group in its values and aesthetics. For example, in our own society we take it for granted that music should be an enjoyable auditory experience. Most of it involves a group of musicians 'entertaining' a group of listeners. Elsewhere the purpose of the music may be quite different. Consider Tibetan Buddhist chanting or the shamanic healing songs of Venezuelan Indians. These musics are not 'enjoyable' in our definition of the word; some might even argue that they're not 'music' at all. However, they are absolutely indispensable to the ways of life of the respective communities. Music may require quite a different response from us as listeners. You would find it difficult to sit passively at a musical gathering in Ghana—you would soon be persuaded to join in and sing, clap, dance or play, but if you were to respond to music in the same way in the concert hall and clapped along in time with a Mozart symphony you'd quickly be directed towards the exit!

Just as languages borrow words from one another (e.g., 'gong' is originally a Javanese word) so different types of music influence each other, often borrowing elements of style and even instruments. Sometimes a whole society becomes bilingual to adapt to new circumstances, such as the Asian community in Britain. Some similarly become 'bi-musical', using their native music and imported Western music for different purposes. There are North American Indians who carry on their tradition of personal songs received in dreams from supernatural beings, or passed on by inheritance, while at the same time being devotees of country and western! In Java young people enjoy gamelan as much as American or Indian pop music.

Each culture has its own musical system and values, but why did it develop in such a way? Why isn't music 'the universal language' as the old cliché goes? There is no simple explanation, but some ideas we can rule out straight away. For example, there is no evidence that genetics plays any part in musical evolution. It is true that there are certain similarities between African, Caribbean and black American music, but this is because of a shared African cultural heritage, not because of physical heredity. There are members of non-Western societies who have become famous musicians in the field of Western classical music and similarly there are Europeans who have become accepted as excellent performers of Asian or African music. Like learning a language, anyone can learn to play any music, though to become fluent in a 'foreign' music, to speak musically without an accent, requires special talent and effort.

Is there, then, anything that all these different types of music have in common? It seems that all cultures use music to transform ordinary everyday experience; anything from trance in a tribal ritual to the emotionally uplifting effect of a symphony orchestra concert. There are a few societies that don't have musical instruments but everywhere people sing, and they don't 'just sing'; they would always sing *something* that they identify as a song or piece. Everywhere people can recognize a tune, a pattern of notes, whether they are high or low. Probably the most common melodic interval in the world is the major second. Everywhere people will recognize rhythmic patterns, whether metrical or non-metrical, and know instinctively how they relate to movement or dance steps.

[65]

Oriental Music

The Oriental world is a complex network of interacting cultures. Firstly there is the subcontinent of **India**, which exported Buddhism to China and Japan along with other cultural elements. India has two main traditions of classical music: **Hindustani** (North) and **Karnatic** (South) as well as many different folk styles and popular music, the latter having reached mass audiences through the thriving film industry. In Britain there is Punjabi pop music called **bhangra**, a very distinctive style and youth culture which has developed here using a curious blend of Indian drums and percussion, congas, guitar, mandolin, saxophone, and keyboard synthesizers.

Secondly there is the **Malayan** area, which includes southeast Asia and Indonesia (Java and Bali are especially noted for their music). Here there are ensembles made up of many types of xylophones, metallophones, tuned gongs, zithers and drums.

China is the third main area, large and highly influential from the earliest times. Musical styles and instruments—including large ceremonial orchestras, board zithers *(ch'in)*, bamboo mouth-organs *(sheng)* and lutes *(pi'pa)*—spread thousands of years ago, along with many aspects of culture and language, to Korea, Japan, Thailand, Laos, Cambodia and Vietnam.

Track 72

Test 49

Here is a traditional Chinese melody called 'The High Moon' dating from the T'ang dynasty (618–907AD). It describes the Emperor's dream in which he meets the Lady of the Moon with her beautiful attendants dancing, appearing and disappearing through the clouds. The instruments are the *yang-qin* (Chinese dulcimer), *di'zi* (bamboo flute), *pi'pa* (Chinese lute) and Chinese percussion.

(a) Is the music mainly (i) homophonic, (ii) heterophonic, or (iii) polyphonic?

(b) What scale is being used?

(c) The percussionist plays finger cymbals and drums. Explain the difference in the way that the two instruments are used.

The traditional folk-songs of **Japan** and music for small ensembles of *koto* (zither), *shamisen* (three-stringed lute) and *shakuhachi* (bamboo flute) are based on two scales, one with semitones (the *in* scale) and one without (the *yo* scale). The interval of a fourth is important to the structure of both. Like the major scale each one can be viewed as two identical tetrachords. Here are the two scales with their auxiliary notes in brackets:

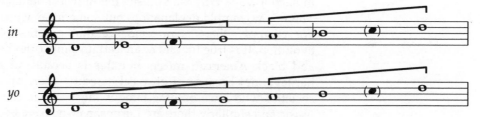

The Japanese aesthetic favours a wide range of tone colour in music. They especially like unpitched sounds mixed in with melodic lines, such as the very breathy sound possible on the *shakuhachi* or the hard twang made by the large ivory plectrum on the *shamisen*.

Track 73

Test 50

The first extract of traditional Japanese music is from a piece entitled *Esashi Oiwake*, the second (very short) extract is from a piece entitled *Kurokami*.

(a) Name the scale(s) used in each of the two extracts on this track.

(b) Describe the interplay of the voice and instruments in the second extract.

The classical music of **Northern India** has a melodic system called *rāg* and a rhythmic system called *tāl*. Within these boundaries the music is basically improvised according to stylistic conventions. A *tāl* is a cycle with a particular number of beats grouped in a certain way, e.g.:

rupaka	7 beats	3+2+2 = 7
jhampa	10 beats	2+3+2+3 = 10
teentāl	16 beats	4+4+4+4 = 16

A *rāg* is a series of notes but it's more than just a scale. Each *rāg* is thought to have a unique personality, expressing a special mood and having an affinity with a particular time of day. In ancient treatises on Indian music there are said to be 22 separate steps in an octave but in practice only seven are used now, much like the Western diatonic scale. These are learned by syllables rather like our sol-fa system, *sa* being the equivalent of 'doh':

1	2	3	4	5	6	7	8
sa	*re*	*ga*	*ma*	*pa*	*dha*	*ni*	*sa*^{1}

In addition there are
flat versions of: *re*   *ga*   *dha*   *ni*
and also a sharp: *ma*

Each *rāg* uses a selection of these pitches, often with pre-learnt melodic phrases. The notes will vary in importance—some may be stressed while others will only be touched upon fleetingly. On a piano the 12 pitches are precise and immovable. When sung or played on a violin they can be made to slide into one another so the 'gaps' become filled in. Such flexibility is used to great effect in Indian melody which is expressively ornamented to a much greater degree than Western music. This sliding between different degrees of the scale is, in a sense, paying homage to the ancient 22 divisions of the octave which have given their name (*sruti*) to the modern subtleties of intonation and ornament in Indian music. You will hear these effects in the *rāg* on Track 74, which is played on the *sitar* and *sarod* (north Indian lutes) accompanied by the *tabla* (a pair of small, tuneable hand-drums).

Track 74

Test 51

The main part of this extract is in fast *teentāl* (16 beats).

(a) How is the melodic phrase treated in this extract?

(b) Name the three notes of the drone heard at the beginning, using either the degrees of the scale (second, third, fourth, etc.) or Indian syllables.

(c) What is unusual about the note *ga* (the third degree of the scale) in this *rāg*?

Instruments, like musical ideas and styles, move around the world. A violin is featured on Track 75. It was introduced into India at the end of the 19th century and is now firmly rooted in the **Karnatic** tradition of Southern India.

Track 75

Test 52

(a) In this *raga* (the Karnatic name for *rāg*), which of the following notes is omitted? (Numbers and names correspond to the degrees of the major scale).

1	2	3	4	5	6	7	8
sa	*re*	*ga*	*ma*	*pa*	*dha*	*ni*	*sa*^{1}

(b) Of the remaining pitches, which are sharpened and which are flattened?

The gamelan music of **Indonesia** is based on a tonal system quite unrelated to the chromatic scale. There are two scales: *slendro* and *pelog*. *Slendro* has five notes which divide the octave into roughly equidistant intervals. *Pelog* has seven notes and a variety of intervals ranging from (approximately) a semitone to a minor third, though in practice never more than five or six are used in any one piece. Once your ears become accustomed to this 'non-tempered' tuning the two scales sound quite strikingly different.

The gamelan is an orchestra consisting mostly of tuned gongs and metallophones. The word applies to the instruments, which are made and tuned together and then housed in a special place, rather than the musicians who come to and depart from the gamelan empty handed. There are many different styles of gamelan: classical and ancient ceremonial styles, contemporary music, folk styles (often played on bamboo instruments), pop and fusion; there is endless variety to be found in Java, Bali, Sunda and Sumatra. The music isn't notated and Indonesian musicians develop an extraordinary aural awareness and memory from an early age. It is expected that most children learn to play gamelan to a high standard and most continue to do so throughout their adult life, especially in Bali. There are few professional musicians in the Western sense: performance is more something that you do for the honour of the village or the temple. The exquisite masked dancer or brilliant musician you see performing one night might be a rice farmer or hot-food vendor by day.

Track 76

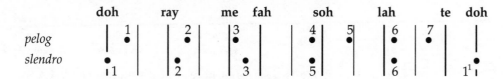

There are two excerpts of gamelan music in contrasting styles on this track. The first is Javanese and the second is Balinese. Describe the differences between them in terms of:

(a) instrumentation,

(b) timbre (tone-colour),

(c) dynamics,

(d) rhythm and tempo,

(e) the scale or scales used *(pelog* or *slendro)*.

The Middle East

In many parts of the world, musicians are looked down upon as rather peculiar. In medieval Europe musicians had a low status and were often thought to be in league with the devil. The devil himself is sometimes pictured as a violinist. Instrumental virtuosity and creativity were ascribed to the supernaturally tinged idea of talent. Nowadays in the West we tend to value music more highly, but this is not so everywhere. In Middle Eastern Muslim societies music is viewed with a kind of ambivalence; simultaneously loved and feared. The Koran warns believers to avoid certain kinds of music that can incite frivolous or lewd behaviour (the extreme in unacceptability would be the sort of ensemble music for belly dancing), and all music must be kept well away from centres of religion, with the exception of recitations from the Koran which are normally sung or chanted. There are no concerts in the mosques.

Middle Eastern societies nevertheless have a great deal of music and they are very good at it. Somehow they have managed to reconcile their religion's disapproval of this form of 'indulgence' with their desire to have music. In classical music in Tehrān (capital of **Iran**) there are professional and amateur musicians but, unlike the West, the well-trained and artistic amateur has a higher social status than a professional. This has to do with the notion of freedom: the professional musician is obliged to fulfil the wishes of his patron, whereas the amateur who plays to his friends or for his own pleasure can make the important decisions for himself; which scale to use and the duration of the performance. This is significant because music is improvised on a mode, or *dastgah*, and each one has its own special mood or character. The choice of *dastgah* will reflect the musician's mood at the time.

Track 77

Test 54

There are two extracts from Middle Eastern music on this track. The first is a composition for an Arabic bamboo flute and two drums. The *dastgah* used in this is similar to a major scale but with slightly flattened thirds and sevenths.

(a) What interval is being played by the flute at the beginning of this melody?

(b) Which of the following two-bar drum rhythms is used in this extract?

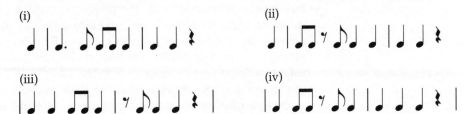

In the second extract on this track you will hear *Sama'i Thaqil*, a classical form of improvised music for the *ud* (a long-necked Arabic lute) and *darbouka* (a vase-shaped hand drum made of pottery or metal).

(c) What is the metre of this music and on which beats do the accents fall?

There are many influences to be found in the music of modern **Israel** for, though it is seen as the homeland of Judaism, the Jews are ethnically a very diverse people with large communities in Yemen, India, the USA, Ethiopia (the *Falasha*) and Europe. The ancient traditions of biblical cantillation and *piyutim* (the chanting of prayers) use scales which are part Western and part Oriental. One scale, called the *Ahavoh-Rabboh* mode, has a particular mournful flavour characterized by an augmented second between the second and third degrees (E–F–G sharp–A–B–C–D–E). There are many examples of this scale to be found in Jewish secular music. Think of the well-known song 'Hava Negillah':

While biblical cantillations are purely vocal, Jewish folk-songs are almost always accompanied by piano, small ensemble or orchestra.

Track 78

Test 55

After a short introduction you will hear four verses of the song 'Haveinu Shalom Aleichem'. Each verse consists of four phrases.

(a) How is the introduction related to the verses?

(b) Describe the choral texture of each verse.

(c) What happens to the tempo? Does it remain constant?

Africa

Mention the music of **Africa** and most people immediately think of drums. This is the common perception but it is by no means the complete picture. There is certainly an immense variety of drums: different designs and methods of construction, different types of ensembles. Further investigation also reveals a wealth of other instruments: flutes, harps, thumb-pianos, xylophones, horns, voices, bells and rattles. The mass impression of African drumming is often a negative one: a music so monotonously repetitive as to dull the senses, or else so rhythmically complex as to be incomprehensible. Many Europeans cannot find anything 'musical' about the sound of a group of drums, but this reflects a natural ethno-centric bias. We are more used to training our ears towards harmony and structures with considerable variety, but there are Western composers such as Steve Reich who have thoroughly explored the effects of repetition and very gradual change, and have been profoundly influenced by this music.

The continent of Africa can be divided into two main cultural areas. The North, which borders the Mediterranean, is traditionally Islamic and has strong links with the Middle East. The music is a part of the Arabic culture. The vocal style is highly ornamented and many public occasions are accompanied by a familiar ensemble of drums and strident oboe-like double-reed instruments. Africa south of the Sahara desert is quite different and home to many ethnic groups, all with their own ideas about music: how and when it should be played and what its purpose is. The singing of the Ba-Benjellé pygmies of Central Africa has little in common with the music of the Ewe people of Ghana, which is different again from the *griot*, or praise-singer in the Gambia. Even within one country the residents of one village may hear the music of the next village as strange and foreign and reveal their prejudices in subtle ways. For instance they might say that people from over there 'have only one way of playing, whereas we have many'. In other words, 'all their music sounds the same to us'!

One feature more or less common to all sub-Saharan African music is the emphasis on rhythm, which is far more intricate and subtle than the rhythms of most European music. Listen to Track 79 and notice the way the drum parts cross each other, loosely woven together within a medium-tempo duple time.

 Track 79

Test 56

(a) Which **two** of the following statements best describe the vocal parts?

> sung in parallel fifths   sung in parallel tenths   sung in unison
>   using call and response technique   contrapuntal

(b) There is a break in the rhythm towards the end of this extract. Describe the relationship between the rhythm of the music before this break and the rhythm after it.

Flamenco

In certain areas of the world there seems to be a preference for certain tone colours. For example in Indonesia, South East Asia and China there is a great feeling for metal percussion; gongs, chimes and cymbals of all types. In Java certain old gongs are so revered that they can't even be played! Throughout the Middle East and North Africa one can hear drum and double-reed ensembles, the harsh, plangent sound of the latter influencing the preferred vocal timbre, which could be described as 'strained' or 'intense'. This preference reaches into southern **Spain** where gypsies perform in the flamenco style.

Like Indian classical music, flamenco is improvised within a definite stylistic framework. The actual sound of flamenco—the virtuoso guitar, the emphatic rhythm and anguished vocal delivery (*canto hondo*)—is unmistakable.

 Track 80

Test 57

(a) Is this music in $\frac{3}{4}$, $\frac{4}{4}$, $\frac{5}{4}$ or none of these metres?

(b) The first guitar chord is A major. When the pitch changes, how do the two other chords relate to this chord? (You may name the chords, if you prefer.)

(c) A second guitarist starts improvising on a scale based on the note A. Which of the five-note patterns below does this scale use?

The Caribbean and Latin America

Island nations usually have the greatest cultural diversity. This is understandable as populations have evolved in relative isolation, separated by water from other cultures. One type of ensemble associated with the Caribbean, and enormously popular in Britain, is the steel band. This music originally came from **Trinidad** and a few other small islands where the USA had army bases during the Second World War. When the war was over the Americans left behind huge quantities of oil drums, so the inventive and resourceful Trinidadians discovered that the best way of disposing of them was to recycle them as musical instruments! In **Jamaica** the predominant national music is reggae; in the **Dominican Republic** *merengue*—an ultra-fast, accordion-led dance music—is very popular, and in **Cuba** one can hear everywhere the African-influenced rhumba, Hispanic folk music, and the sophisticated modern Latin dance music called 'salsa'.

Steel bands are made up of a number of 'pans' (the cut-off tops and bottoms of oil drums) which are hammered into tuned indentations. They come in four basic sizes to give a complete melody/harmony range to the ensemble, and they are usually accompanied by some extra percussion or drum kit. The four sizes are *ping pong* (soprano), *guitar pan* (alto), *cello pan* (tenor) and *boom* (bass).

Steel bands can be very versatile and are often heard playing arrangements of pop songs, TV theme tunes and even Classical symphonies! Traditionally, however, they play calypso which is a lively, syncopated form of Caribbean music associated with the street processions of the pre-Lenten carnival. Calypso-derived songs like 'Rum and Coca-Cola' and 'Banana Boat Song' became great hits in the USA in the 1940s.

'Yellow Bird' is a traditional calypso tune. Listen to the balance of the different parts: a strong melody line played on the *ping pong*, rhythmic/harmonic support from the inner parts, and a simple bass line. The drummer plays a constant off-beat on the hi-hat.

🔊 Track 81

━━━━━━━━━━━━━━━━━━━━━━━ *Test 58* ━━━━━━━━━━━━━━━━━━━━━━━

(a) On what degree of the major scale does the melody begin?

(b) The next part of the tune is made up of arpeggios. Which of the following chord patterns in G major is outlined by these arpeggios?

(i)		Em		C		D^7		G	
(ii)		Em		Am		D^7		G	
(iii)		G		D^7		D^7		G	
(iv)		Am		G		D^7		G	

(c) In which of the following rhythm patterns is the bass of this section?

(i)　　　　　　　　　(ii)　　　　　　　　　(iii)

(d) This extract falls into six four-bar phrases. Describe the structure using letters, with superscript numerals to indicate any variants (e.g., ABACAA^1).

The samba is another type of street music for the pre-Lenten carnival—always a time to inspire prolific musical activity (see page 75). It is from **Brazil** and is associated particularly with the festivities of Rio de Janeiro. Since 1928 the processional samba groups have been formally organized into 'schools' which compete for prizes (cash and recording contracts) awarded by a selected jury. Because the practitioners of samba are normally the very poor residents of the hillside slums around Rio (*favelas*) the spirit of samba is intensely competitive. A samba consists of a choral melody with instrumental accompaniment which is quite European in character, but the street version for the carnival is dominated by the *batería*, a group of percussion instruments which play syncopated patterns over a steady binary pulse provided by the *surdo* (bass drum).

[71]

In 'Simpatia e quase amor', a song of unrequited love, the chorus is in two parts; male and female.

(a) What is the harmonic device used in the guitar accompaniment at the beginning?

(b) What is the compositional device used in the vocal parts of the first section?

(c) (i) What happens to the vocal melody when the tempo picks up?

(ii) What happens to the vocal melody at the end of the extract?

(d) How many instruments are playing in the fast section and what are they? You may use English terms to describe them.

The Music of the Andes

Moving west from Brazil, the folk music of the Andean culture is practised in much of Bolivia, Peru, Ecuador, Chile, and a small part of Argentina. This music has its roots in the great pre-Colombian civilizations such as the Incas, but since the arrival of the Spaniards in the 16th century it has become steadily European-ized. The ancient non-tempered tritonic (three-note) scales that archaeologists have discovered from old musical instruments were gradually replaced by diatonic scales. The mestizo population adapted their traditional flutes, such as the *zampona* (panpipes), as well as learning to play clarinet, harp, guitar and brass band instruments.

In the next extract you will hear two *quenas*, traditional flutes which are made from bone, clay, wood, or now more commonly, bamboo. The accompaniment is provided by guitar and *bomba*—a bass drum made from a section of hollowed out tree trunk with goatskin at each end.

The form of this extract is an introduction followed by an AABB pattern.

(a) Section A begins on the note B played by the first *quena* (flute). What chord is outlined by the *quenas*?

(b) How do the melodies of the two flutes relate to each other in section B?

(c) Which two degrees of the scale are emphasized by the guitar?

Eastern European Dances

In this chapter we have concentrated mainly on music from Asia, Africa and America. However, the continent of Europe is also home to a rich diversity of folk traditions, many of which have for centuries influenced the styles of Western art music. With the end of the cold war we have greater opportunity than ever before to encounter both the folk and art music of Eastern Europe. You can get some idea of the diversity of styles in Poland, Central Europe, Russia and Romania by taking a sneak preview of Tracks 44–50 on CD 2.

Jazz

At the end of the previous chapter you saw how the movement of populations has produced cultural diversity, generating new styles and genres when different musical traditions come into contact with one another. One of the richest of these interactions has been in the USA, particularly in the southern states, where a combination of influences from Africa, Britain, France and Latin America has produced two of the 20th century's most important styles of music—jazz and the blues—as well as countless related genres. All of these had an enormous influence on the direction of popular music throughout the century.

The Pre-Jazz Era

Jazz originated in the southern states of the USA during the early years of the 20th century. Many of its features arose from an amalgam, over a long period, of the musical traditions of the two principal populations in the region, the Scots-Irish settlers and the less willingly imported African slaves. Folk music was generally less susceptible than art music to the changing tastes of fashion, and never more so than in the remote and rural populations of the USA. However, over a 200-year period, the rhythmic vitality and melodic formulas of African music became inextricably merged with the formal patterns and harmonic bias of European music. After the abolition of slavery in 1865 it is possible to see the increasing influence of Western music (particularly in harmony and choice of instruments) on a newly emerging Afro-American music, resulting in hybrid forms such as **gospel** (originally a combination of white hymnody and the spiritual) and **ragtime** (the syncopation of minstrel songs superimposed upon the Western military march). The period from about 1865 to 1918 is often called the 'pre-jazz' era, and it is important to realize that the music of this time is not jazz. It was, however, the age in which the roots of both blues and jazz (and thereby much of modern pop music) started to develop.

Ragtime

Ragtime simply means 'ragged time'—principally, the continual syncopation of a melody against a regular bass which forms the most characteristic feature of the style. It is likely that the syncopated melody line derives from the playing technique of the banjo, an instrument most probably of West African origin that became increasingly popular in 19th-century minstrel shows. Ragtime, however, is essentially a type of piano music, although rags were also performed on the banjo, played by bands and some were even sung. The first piece to be published specifically as a rag appeared in 1897 (William H. Krell's *Mississippi Rag*), this date marking the start of ragtime's 20-year period of greatest popularity.

Ragtime was heavily dependent upon Western influences, particularly in the use of simple, functional harmony with regular cadences and modulations to closely related keys. This was almost invariably outlined by a left-hand 'vamp' accompaniment in duple time, consisting of single notes (or octaves) on down-beats alternating with triads on the intervening quavers. The left-hand leaps were later to become wider and wider, developing into the impressive 'stride' style of jazz pianists such as Fats Waller.

This foundation was borrowed directly from the style of the march and related popular dances, such as the quadrille and military two-step. Indeed, there is surprisingly little difference between Sousa's immensely popular marches of the 1890s and early ragtime of the period. The musical form of ragtime shares that of the march: the most popular structure being four repeated 16-bar 'strains', separated by clear cadences, in the pattern AABBCCDD, or variants such as AABBCCA. Like the 'trio' of a march, the C section is often in the subdominant and some rags, like some of Sousa's marches, happily end with the final strain in this key—the grand subdominant recapitulation *sounds* like a tonic, and earlier sections then seem to be a dominant preparation for it. The importance of the subdominant in jazz and popular music is a theme to which we shall return.

Further features borrowed from the march include short introductions and occasional four-bar links between sections, as well as much passing chromaticism in the melodic line. The functional harmony is also often decorated with chromaticism, almost always used only for colour—chromatic passing-notes in the bass, secondary dominants (especially V^7 of V at cadences) and diminished sevenths (particularly as arpeggios) were all favourites.

Track 84

You can see many of these features in the first strain of Joplin's rag, *The Strenuous Life* printed under Test 61 below. As you listen, notice the left-hand style, the periodic phrasing (each of the four-bar phrases ends with a cadence) and the chromatic double auxiliary, followed by chromatic passing-note (D sharp) in bar 3. The left-hand motif that fills the remainder of bar 4 is a small but significant feature. If the piece were played by a military band, you could doubtless imagine the trombones thundering in on this figure—and that would be appropriate, since 'bass runs' of this sort were an integral part of the military march. Its real significance, though, lies in the fact that it is a moment for a new voice to attract interest in the texture at a point when the main part has reached a natural break. The idea of the solo 'break', which would later extend well beyond the limits of a single bar, became one of the most characteristic features of jazz over the following decades.

As you listened to this extract, and noticed the many features borrowed from the march, you were probably most aware of the syncopated rhythm of the right hand. Although **syncopation** was inherent in much existing Afro-American music, this was the novelty seized upon by white audiences and the feature that caused ragtime to become the sensation of the age by 1900. The most characteristic rhythm is the tie across the middle of the bar, leaving the third quaver unarticulated in nearly half of the bars in this extract. Almost as common is the rhythm first heard in bar 3—this is one of three possible ways of grouping two semiquavers and a quaver (see page 44), but the one that is least common in European art music. To these should be added a technique which appeared in later rags, in which cross-rhythms are created by the reiteration of three-note melodic cells within four-note rhythmic groups, as in Northrup and Confare's *Cannon Ball: A Characteristic Two-Step* of 1905:

This type of rhythmic dislocation is a feature that may remind us more than most that the complex cross-rhythms of West African music were still, albeit in simplified and Westernized form, one of the roots of this new music.

Scott Joplin (1868–1917), an Afro-American pianist trained in the Western style, is the composer now most readily associated with ragtime, although James Scott and Joseph E. Lamb were equally famous at the time. During Joplin's short life, ragtime was widely and rapidly disseminated. Unlike jazz, it was easy to notate (even if, like all notation, the score cannot reflect the more subtle aspects of performance) and it thus benefitted from the cheap, mass music printing available at the time. It also coincided with the period of the automatic 'player piano' (operated by a roll of punched paper) and of the earliest gramophone recordings. Ragtime was therefore in a position to be a strong influence on early blues composers such as W. C. Handy (even though he described ragtime as 'rhythm without melody'), early jazz musicians such as Jelly Roll Morton and Louis Armstrong, and European composers, such as Debussy and Stravinsky. After about 1915, ragtime took on a $\frac{4}{4}$ metre, with either a heavy walking bass or additional left-hand syncopation, and started to use 'blue notes'. By then, though, its hey-day as one of the principal types of popular music at the turn of the century was over and the jazz era proper was beginning.

The music below is an incomplete score of the first strain of Joplin's rag *The Strenuous Life* (the left-hand part has been omitted after the first line). All of the questions relate to this music.

Scott Joplin: The Strenuous Life

(a) How is the bass figure of bar 4 treated in bar 8?

(b) In what other way is the end of line 2 different from the end of line 1?

(c) How does the end of line 3 relate to the end of line 1?

(d) Describe the harmonic progression leading up to the final cadence.

(e) Give the locations of one example of each of the following (describe beat numbers in terms of 4 quaver beats per bar):

   (i)   A diminished seventh,

   (ii)   A chromatic descent in the bass,

   (iii)   The dominant seventh of the dominant.

Traditional Jazz

The early history of jazz is inextricably linked with the region in the south of the USA around New Orleans which was, until 1803, a French territory. The term **Dixieland** is sometimes used as a synonym for traditional jazz, although it strictly refers to jazz in the New Orleans style played by white musicians. Dixie *is* New Orleans—the term most probably arose when a local bank issued a ten-dollar note carrying the French number *dix*. The word jazz itself (originally 'jass') probably derives from the French Creole word *jaser* ('to gossip') and it is no coincidence that the earliest jazz bands used the instruments of the French military bands that had been so popular in the 19th century—particularly cornets, trombones and clarinets (but not yet saxophones).

Small bands of Afro-American musicians played at pre-Lenten festivals such as *Mardi Gras* (Shrove Tuesday) and at the grand funerals which were the lifetime's ambition of even the poorest inhabitants of New Orleans. Accounts from the early years of the 20th century relate how a band would play suitably sombre hymns on the way to the cemetery but, on the return journey, would break into ragtime versions of spirituals such as 'When The Saints Go Marchin' In'—treated very freely, not least because the music was played from memory. Many types of contemporary popular music were also given a jazz treatment by such bands—piano rags, marches, dances and, above all, blues songs.

It is likely that the varied membership of these very early jazz bands played largely the same melodic line in heterophony, perhaps with banjo or piano for harmonic support. Before long, ensembles were consolidated into a typical group of three melody instruments (clarinet, trombone and cornet) with a rhythm section of piano and banjo, sometimes with string bass and drums. A distinctive rôle for each instrument gradually emerged, the cornet frequently taking the lead, with a clarinet providing an agile descant and a trombone filling every available break, often providing motifs in dialogue with the main melodic line. Collective improvisation like this required much greater harmonic awareness from the players, although the emphasis remained on the linear elements of music and the result was the three-part New Orleans polyphony that can be heard in the opening of the next extract. Listen to this and notice how the rhythm section keeps to a very four-square harmonic backing, fulfilling a similar rôle to the continuo in Baroque music.

Track 85

Most jazz consists of improvised variations on a theme and its associated harmonies. The theme is often either a 'standard'—typically, a popular song with a harmonic pattern that particularly lends itself to variation—or a classic harmonic progression, such as the 12-bar blues. Standards are often written out in the form of a 'lead sheet' (melody line plus chord symbols) although experienced jazz musicians memorize a repertoire of standards and generally don't play from music at all. Jazz is therefore rarely notated in full and many jazz musicians would say that the lack of notation is important if the music is to sound spontaneous. This ideal has sometimes to be compromised, particularly where a large band makes collective improvisation impossible, but even in these circumstances it is usual to have a string of solo sections which can, of course, be improvised. *Muskrat Ramble* dates from the transitional time when jazz was moving up the Mississippi—quite literally, on the paddle steamers that plied between the great jazz cities of New Orleans, Memphis, St Louis and on up towards Chicago. Jazz in Chicago saw much more emphasis placed on the soloist, and this is already reflected in this early Louis Armstrong recording. The first two strains are typical of New Orleans polyphony, although even here Armstrong's cornet playing is well to the fore, but after this each strain features a solo player, accompanied only by the small rhythm section.

The influence of ragtime is obvious. The piece consists of similar 16-bar strains, in the pattern $ABB^1CC^1A^1A^2$ (the first four are recorded here), each containing four clear phrases which mostly terminate in conventional cadence patterns—although you should notice some attempt to 'paper over the cracks' by rhythms that drive through the cadence, by phrases that start early, and so forth. The cornet part also betrays its ragtime origins, with the third beat of every bar in the printed extract receiving the customary tie over from the previous note to produce syncopation. Then why is this jazz and not ragtime? The answer lies partly in the improvisatory quality, but mainly in the rhythm: play or sing the individual lines of the opening *exactly* as printed and then listen to the recording.

Louis Armstrong (1900–1971) was one of the most influential figures in jazz. He established the highest of technical standards from an early stage, and had the ability to find fellow musicians who could support his own virtuoso style. His trumpet playing spanned a colossal three-octave range and encompassed a seemingly endless range of timbre and attack. Armstrong's reputation also lies in his subtlety of rhythm and phrasing, freeing jazz from the rhythmic strait-jacket of its early years. Listen to the rhythmic spring in this extract, and to the flexibility of Armstrong's solo in the last strain, where you will also hear his characteristic wide vibrato decorating long notes. This extract is taken from the original recording of 26 February 1926 and has been digitally reprocessed to improve the quality. Louis Armstrong had been engaged as a 19-year-old cornet player in the band run by 'Kid' Ory, composer of this piece, in Chicago in 1919. Now it was Ory's turn to play trombone for Armstrong in this vintage recording.

This extract consists of four 16-bar strains of music. The cornet part of the first strain starts as follows (only the rhythm is shown for bars 7 and 8):

Edward 'Kid' Ory: Muskrat Ramble

First strain (tutti)

(a) How does the quaver rhythm of the cornet part in bars 1–8 differ from the quaver rhythm printed above?

(b) The music above starts in the key of A flat. What key is reached in bar 8?

(c) In the eight bars that follow the music above:

    (i)   How does the clarinet part differ from the part it had in bars 1–8?

    (ii)   How does the harmony differ from the first eight bars?

Second strain (tutti)

(d) The cornet plays the figure printed below at the start of this section. What melodic feature does the trombone play beneath this and what do you notice about the rhythm of this trombone part?

(e) The harmony of line 1 (bars 1–4) is essentially: | V | V | I | I | How do lines 2, 3 and 4 compare with this?

Third strain (trombone solo)

(f) How is the accompaniment figure shown in question (d) modified in this strain?

(g) Apart from the cornet and clarinet, which instruments accompany the trombone solo in this strain?

(h) What special effect is used by the trombonist in this strain?

Fourth strain (trumpet solo)

(i) How is the rigid 16-bar structure of this piece disguised at the beginning of this section?

(j) At the midway point of this strain, the trumpet leaps to a dissonant high note. How is this note related to the underlying harmony?

(k) To which of the previous three strains is the harmony of this strain related?

The struggle for an identity separate from popular music has been one of the enduring problems of jazz. At times it has been a minority interest, on a par with specialist enthusiams such as chamber music or Anglican church music, while at other times it has been close to becoming the 'hit' music of its age.

Within five years of giving the first 'public' performances of jazz, and of making the first jazz recording (New York, 1917) The Original Dixieland Jass Band was playing commercial foxtrots with carefully composed instrumentation, and no hint of improvisation, because the public preferred 'refined' dance music to the raw edges of genuine jazz. One of the reasons was undoubtedly the advent of recording. Once a piece was known in recorded form, this was the version that was expected to be heard. True jazz performers, on the other hand, continued to regenerate their material every time they played it—there are countless different versions on record of the great jazz standards, and these represent only a fraction of the improvisations that were heard in live performance.

One particular commercial enterprise which deserves attention was the rise of **orchestral jazz**. Sousa had included ragtime, scored for the full resources of a military band, alongside his own marches when touring in the early years of the century. Don Redman (writing for the Fletcher Henderson Orchestra) and Ferdinand Grofé (the arranger for Paul Whiteman's Orchestra) were both scoring for complete orchestras, including strings, from the 1920s onwards. Their scores, although intended primarily for dancing, included many jazz-like elements, and became the new style in popular music of the time—the acceptable face of jazz. It was Whiteman who commissioned *Rhapsody in Blue* from the popular song-writer George Gershwin in 1924—a work which introduced many of the public to features of jazz, yet which is totally unjazz-like in its imperviousness to improvisation (the vivid orchestration, in both the original band version and the later orchestral version, is by Whiteman's arranger, Grofé).

Swing

Jazz bands, if they were to survive the economic depression of the 1930s, were also obliged to play in larger venues and to increase their resources accordingly. This was done by developing the solo lines of traditional jazz into complete instrumental sections, each capable of providing the five or six parts required by the increasingly rich harmony used. Thus Duke Ellington's band was, by 1940, employing a **horn section** of 3 trumpets and 3 trombones, a **reed section** of 4 saxophones (2 alto, tenor and baritone) plus clarinet, and a 4-piece **rhythm section** of piano, guitar, string bass and drums.

These ensembles were known as **big bands** and many played arranged music, later to be known as 'swing', written in imitation of improvisatory jazz—although the bandleader (or other star soloist) still had the opportunity to improvise over the top of the ensemble, or in solo 'breaks'. Equally important, however, were the possibilities for the arranger to use antiphony between the sections and to employ a blazingly powerful tutti.

Swing generally aimed for a smoother tone than traditional jazz, the type of ensemble encouraging blend, rather than individual colour. Harmony became more complex: a favourite technique was the use of 'substitutions' in which the plainer chords of standards were replaced with secondary 7ths, 11ths, 13ths, added 6ths, minor 9ths, minor subdominants and half-diminished 7ths (the 'Tristan' chord, as in bar 8^3 on page 134: F–C flat–E flat–A flat). Resolutions of such discords were often unconventional in terms of 'classical' harmony. Rhythm became less rigid, with various triplet groupings freely combined with elaborate syncopation and the technique of melodic variation gave way to variations built on a set chord pattern. When this progression remains essentially unchanged throughout, it is called a 'head' arrangement (i.e., the harmonies remain as they were at the head of the music). Listen to *Mysterioso* by Artie Shaw (b. 1910) and identify the 12-bar harmonic pattern, which is repeated three times in the extract.

⊙ Track 86

You may have recognized this as the **12-bar blues**, the chord pattern which, in one of its most common forms, is I–I–I–I IV–IV–I–I V–IV–I–I (one chord per bar). If you didn't recognize it, try to memorize its distinctive sound, because this is one of the most frequently encountered progressions in both jazz and popular music. The move to the subdominant, after an initial four bars of tonic harmony, should strike you as the most recognizable feature. The last line is sometimes just a simple V–V–I–I progression and there are, of course, other variations of the pattern, some even extending it to 16 bars in length. The immediate origins of this progression lie in the emergence of the blues as a modern folk music around 1900, although it probably developed long before this, during that rich interaction of Scots-Irish and African traditions in the south of the USA. You should also have noticed another blues influence in *Mysterioso*—the prominent use of 'blue notes', particularly the flat third and flat seventh, previously encountered in the chapter on folk music.

The impact of the blues on jazz and popular music is of enormous importance. It takes these styles much further away from Europe than the Western-influenced music encountered so far. The 12-bar blues is the antithesis of classical harmonic procedures. It is a 12-bar form, not 8 or 16. Its prime harmonic direction is to the subdominant—the dominant seems almost incidental. This difference is encapsulated in the last line of the progression: V shifts down to IV (you can hardly say it resolves) before ending on I. Just as chord V is the linchpin of classical harmony, so classical melody depends on the directional tendency of the leading note as well as on the third of the scale as the chief differentiator between major and minor. And it is precisely these two notes which are deliberately blurred into ambiguity in the blues scale.

◉ Track 86

Test 63

The recording is of the first three sections (identified here as A, B and C) of *Mysterioso* by Artie Shaw. This is the bass part of the start of section A:

Slowly, with a good beat

(a) How does the performance of this bass part differ from the printed music?

(b) A two-note motif is heard above the bass part. On which instrument is this motif played and which of the following rhythms does it use?

(c) Section B is based on the motif printed below. Two of these three parts are played by clarinet and guitar. What instrument plays the third part?

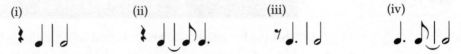

(d) What instrumental effect is used on the last note of this motif?

(e) How does this motif relate to the two-note motif in section A?

(f) The end of section B is heralded by a change in the presentation of this motif. Describe this change.

Section C features a clarinet solo played by Artie Shaw, which begins as follows:

(g) What change is needed to the pitch of the note marked with a cross in order to indicate what was actually played?

(h) Describe the technique used by the clarinettist on the last note printed above.

(i) On what harmonic progression is section C based?

(j) Briefly describe the bass part throughout sections A, B and C.

Although the extract on Track 86 was recorded by one of the great band-leaders of the swing era, you will undoubtedly have noticed that it is not big-band jazz. The recording was made in 1945 by Artie Shaw and The Gramercy Five, and is in a tradition that was one of the jazz musician's answers to the strait-jacket of swing—the use of a small group of soloists from the band to keep alive the improvising jazz ensemble. Benny Goodman and Tommy Dorsey were two others who also developed the 'band within a band' concept mostly, like Artie Shaw, for the purpose of recording.

This more intimate style of jazz also become popular in France. Two of the very few non-American musicians to achieve a world-wide reputation in jazz had worked together from 1934 as the nucleus of a quintet, The Hot Club of France, that achieved enormous success in both recording and live performance. These were the Belgian gypsy guitarist, Django Reinhardt (1910–1953), and the French jazz violinist, Stephane Grappelli (b. 1908), who had met while playing in the same band at the Hotel Claridge in the Champs-Elysées in Paris. Their music was small-scale, lyrical jazz, almost romantic in quality.

The guitar and violin are not instruments you might associate with jazz, and the next extract is therefore a good illustration that jazz is a style of playing, not a period or genre with clearly defined boundaries. The classically trained Grappelli and the largely self-taught Reinhardt might also seem an odd couple to produce one of the most famous partnerships in jazz. However, their solos on Tracks 87 and 88 show how each had a unique understanding of his own instrument yet perfect rapport with the other's virtuoso technique. This was all the more astonishing in Reinhardt's case, since his left hand had been badly damaged in a fire, causing him to develop a unique fingering style using only two fingers for much of the time. *Undecided* was recorded in London on 25 August 1939, immediately before the outbreak of the Second World War, and is a jazz version of a popular song by Charlie Shavers that had become a hit earlier that year in a performance sung by Ella Fitzgerald. Its strong, simple chord pattern quickly led the song to become a popular jazz standard.

🔊 Track 87

================ *Test 64* ================

This track consists of a guitar introduction followed by variations on the **changes** (the jazz musician's term for a harmonic progression) printed under question (f) below. Listen to just the introduction first and follow this outline score:

(a) How is the note B in bar 1 decorated?

(b) How do bars 3–4 and bars 5–6 relate to the first two bars?

(c) Describe the pitches represented by the rhythm given from bar 6⁴ to bar 8.

Now listen to the whole of the guitar part on this track. The original song, *Undecided*, is based largely on the following opening:

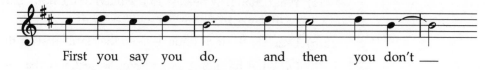

First you say you do, and then you don't ___

(d) How is this motif used by the guitarist?

(e) What accompanying instruments enter after the introduction?

(f) After the introduction Django Reinhardt improvises on the chord pattern of the original song:

1	2	3	4
D	D	G⁷	G⁷

5	6	7	8
E⁷	A⁷	D	D

This is heard four times. The second and fourth appearances follow this pattern reasonably precisely, although even they are varied with ninth chords and 'blue notes'. Follow the chord pattern carefully as you listen and explain:

(i) How bars 7–8 differ from the printed pattern on the first time through.

(ii) How bars 5–8 differ from the printed pattern on the third time through.

(g) To what key does the music modulate after the fourth time through (as the violin enters), ready for the entrance of the vocalist?

 Track 88

Finally, listen to the violin 'break' on Track 88. This is taken from later in the recording, after the vocal section. It starts as follows:

(h) Explain how the notes marked *(x)* and *(y)* are decorated.

(i) Explain as precisely as possible how Grappelli decorates the C major triad indicated by the diamond shaped notes in the bar marked *(z)* above.

(j) Apart from key, what are the main differences between the solo on this track and the guitar treatment of the same chord pattern that you heard on the previous track?

Bop

The Second World War, which temporarily split The Hot Club, leaving Grappelli in England and Reinhardt in France, also sounded the death-knell of the big band, which proved too expensive to tour in the austere years after the war. Glenn Miller, one of the most famous of the big-band leaders (albeit of essentially a dance band, with comparatively little jazz input) died in a mysterious plane crash in 1944. Artie Shaw had technically quit at the height of his success before the war—the recording on Track 86 was made in 1945 during one of his 'come-backs', of which he had nearly as many as he had wives (there were eight of the latter). Both of the leaders of the jazz world in the early 1930s had also lost some of their pre-eminence. Louis Armstrong had turned more towards films and popular songs (recording both with Bing Crosby) and after the war was another to explore small-scale jazz with the formation of his All Stars, a New Orleans style sextet with whom he worked until his death. Duke Ellington suffered from continual problems with changing personnel in his band and a consequent inability to recapture the best of his pre-war style.

As important as these circumstantial reasons, though, was the crisis that had beset the musical direction of jazz with the popularity and commercialism of the swing era. As a reaction to this, some turned back to the music of the past—there was a distinct traditional jazz revival in America during the war years, mostly involving the recording of older musicians playing in the New Orleans style, but also spawning the pastiche-based, Dixie-style British bands of Chris Barber, Kenny Ball and Acker Bilk, that continued to find a market for 'trad jazz' through until the 1960s.

The most far-reaching products of this war-time fragmentation of jazz were, however, formulated in Minton's night club in Harlem, New York. Here, the younger generation of jazz musicians such as the trumpeter, Dizzy Gillespie, the pianist, Thelonious Monk and (later) the saxophonist, Charlie Parker were given a free hand to 'jam' (to play without fee, or only for tips). Here they could experiment in a style that left behind what were already recognized as the conventional formulas and clichés of swing. In effect, they started to reverse the principles of Paul Whiteman's 'symphonic jazz'. Instead of adapting the superficial features of jazz to the needs of European music, they started to adapt various aspects of modern art music to the needs of jazz. The results often left both the public and other musicians perplexed. Louis Armstrong described it as 'that modern malice' in a rare moment of criticism of fellow jazz players, and the name given to the style, 'bebop' (or just plain 'bop'), is said to have been bestowed by fellow jazz musicians who thought the onomatopœic title highly descriptive of the only worthwhile sound the music seemed to make.

In bop, the swung rhythms and regular syncopation of the previous generation gave way to fast and furious passage-work, full of cross-accents creating complex polyrhythms between the parts. Irregular phrase-lengths were often part of the style and improvisations explored the less obvious reaches of the original material, sometimes leaving the connection with the original difficult to perceive (as in the example below). The harmonic vocabulary is so rich and the use of passing dissonances so varied that almost any note can appear to be somehow distantly related to the current key or chord (a problem that Schoenberg had grappled with in art music, thirty years earlier). Indeed, as in contemporary 'serious' music, dissonances were frequently left unresolved.

Instrumentation generally returned to smaller-scale resources, although there were big bands playing bop—the best known is probably Woody Herman's band, for which Stravinsky wrote his *Ebony Concerto* in 1945 (a work that has surprisingly little connection with real jazz). More typical, though, was a sextet of trumpet, alto (sometimes tenor) saxophone, piano, electric guitar, string bass and drums. The rhythm section saw some of the biggest changes. Indeed, it is hardly fair to call them that, since all of the instruments now took on a much more soloistic function than the four-square 'vamp' background they had often hitherto supplied, and all took an interactive part in the texture, pointing out cross-rhythms or creating new ones in dialogue with the melody.

Dizzie Gillespie (b. 1917) worked with a number of big bands, including Duke Ellington's for a short time, between 1937 and 1944, after which he formed his own band. Although not initially successful, it became one of the leading jazz bands in the late 1940s, specializing in the Latin-American rhythms of **Afro-Cuban jazz** (sometimes, less happily, called 'Cubop'). One of Gillespie's earliest solos, recorded at Minton's in 1941, included the whole-tone scales, intricate rhythms and complex harmonies that were to feature in bop. Although always a player with plenty of musical trade-marks of his own, he was also famous for the trumpet he used, in which the bell portion was upturned at an angle of some 45 degrees—apparently due to an accident of the sort that can beset brass players. He preferred the sound of the upturned bell, and retained it thereafter.

The recording on Track 89 is the opening of *Anthropology*, a jazz composition by Dizzie Gillespie and Charlie Parker, recorded in New York in 1946. It is based on the popular song 'I Got Rhythm' from Gershwin's musical, *Girl Crazy* (1930). The comparison below of the opening four bars of these shows how, between the first and last chords (both of which have added notes), almost every chord has a substitution of a highly chromatic and dissonant kind. The solo melodic line above this progression is equally typical of bop: it is an example of **thematic substitution**. No hint here of the melodic variation of earlier jazz, it is an entirely new theme designed to substitute for Gershwin's original. This line adds further clashes to the dissonant harmony—the F natural over a B^9 chord in bar 2 forms a flat fifth, a favourite device of bop (the start of the third section even uses a flat fifth in the middle of Gershwin's original dominant chord). Also typical of bop are the almost random accents and short snatches of melody after rests, breaking up the phrasing into irregular periods. Notice the abrupt effect of the end-stopped first and third phrases, finishing on accented quavers (causing a syncopated effect) and followed by rests. Similar techniques were used by **scat** singers such as Ella Fitzgerald, who improvised fast, wide-ranging and often dissonant instrumental-style melodies to nonsense syllables.

🎵 Track 89

===== *Test 65* =====

The music below is the first four bars of a popular song by Gershwin and the first four bars of *Anthropology*, which is based on this song:

Gershwin: 'I Got Rhythm' (refrain)

Dizzy Gillespie and Charlie Parker: Anthropology

The entire extract consists of four eight-bar sections, as follows (the shaded area represents the printed passage above):

1		(c)	2	3	4

(a) Name the two instruments that share the melody line in all four sections

(b) Describe the part played by the string bass throughout this extract.

(c) In what way is the last bar of section 1 (marked (c) on the plan) similar to the last bar of printed music above?

(d) How does section 2 differ from section 1?

(e) What standard harmonic progression underlies the chromatic harmony of section 3?

(f) State which earlier section is repeated to form section 4, then identify the structure of the whole extract using letters with superscript numbers for any varied repeats (e.g., ABB^{1}C, etc.).

(g) Describe, as precisely as possible, the music played by the drummer.

[83]

Cool Jazz, Free Jazz and Beyond

The motor of change in musical style is a constant cycle of development followed by reaction, followed again by development. The **cool jazz** of the 1950s was a reaction to the hot tone of swing and the frenetic pace of bop. Typical of the new style was Miles Davis who, from 1948, was developing a more relaxed, economical approach to jazz, with an emphasis on understatement and a 'laid back' rhythm that sounds almost behind the beat compared with bop. At last the tyranny of quadruple time lost its stranglehold (perhaps the most famous example is the quintuple metre of Dave Brubeck's *Take Five*) and instruments new to jazz started to appear—the flute, oboe, cello, flugelhorn, accordion and (following Gillespie's example) the vibraphone. Latin-American rhythms and percussion instruments also became a feature, following the lead of Gillespie's Afro-Cuban style. Also important was the launch of the LP vinyl record in 1948, freeing recording artists from the restriction to only a few minutes of continuous music imposed by the medium of the old shellac '78' record, and thus enabling long, linked structures to be developed.

Jazz musicians, many now with an academic music training, started to explore alternatives to the major and blues scales—the modes, the whole-tone scale, polytonality, atonality and even serial technique all appeared. Musicians working for the film industry, in and around Hollywood, had the opportunity to be the most experimental—their style is known as **West Coast jazz**. On the East Coast, in the night clubs of New York, the need to 'sell' jazz to an audience produced more conservative music. However, groups such as the Modern Jazz Quartet included such novel ideas as jazz fugues (see pages 107–108) in popular programs that also spanned swing and film music (they are perhaps most recognizable for the stunning solos of Milt Jackson, the vibes player you heard playing for Dizzie Gillespie on Track 89).

Since the war, the language of jazz had become complex, although the music is all the more rewarding to listen to in depth. Reaction set in again in the 1960s as jazz musicians perceived the innovations of a previous generation turning into the clichés of their own. In particular, the basic premise of improvisation over a given harmonic progression was challenged. The saxophonist, Ornette Coleman (the title of whose 1960 LP, *Free Jazz*, provided the name for the new style) said, 'If I'm going to follow a pre-set chord sequence I may as well write out my solo'. The immediate result was much greater emphasis on melodic invention, unaccompanied work being an important part of the style. With this came the opportunity to dispense with a regular pulse and with harmony-dominated structures. In the eyes of some musicians this was, at very long last, the breaking of the ties with two remaining areas of European musical dominance in jazz. A balance was provided by composers such as Gunther Schuller, who sought to fuse jazz and art music into a new style, known as **thirdstream**, following a precedent set many years before in the jazz-influenced works of Milhaud and Kurt Weill. A more productive synthesis finally emerged during the 1970s and 1980s in **jazz fusion**, the integration of rock and jazz techniques. Miles Davis and Chick Corea were using electric instruments (in a style sometimes called 'electric jazz') in the late 1960s, and exposing some of the problems. Rock is capable of being given the subtle and inventive treatment of jazz, but it too easily loses its raw edge, and ultimately its complete character as rock music, in the process. Later, the group Weather Report (whose co-leaders had both played with Miles Davis) had considerable success in creating a more integrated style, although it is inevitable that, in any fusion of this kind, the enthusiasts for one stylistic component will see its principles being watered down by the other. However, the attempt to break down rigid divisions between previously estranged types of music has been a key feature of the late 20th century, and is a topic that will return later in the book.

Charlie Mingus (1922–1979) was one of the most important black jazz musicians of the post-war era. Curiously, his name returns us to the opening theme of the combined Scots-Irish and African roots of jazz, for it is both the pronunciation of, and the old spelling for, the ancient Scottish name of Menzies. Set to learn the cello at school, he switched to double bass because his high-school band was short of bass players. He went on to study with the principal bassist of the New York Philharmonic and after that to play with many of the great jazz musicians encountered in this chapter—Louis Armstrong, Kid Ory, Charlie Parker, Miles Davis and Duke Ellington. *Dizzy Moods* is composed on an altered chord progression (the 'changes', in fact) from a composition by Dizzy Gillespie. It was recorded in July 1957 (although not released until 1962) on the album *Tijuana Moods*, described by Mingus as 'the best record I ever made'.

Track 90

Test 66

The extract on this track consists of an introduction, two choruses, a bridge and a third chorus. A diagram of the introduction is given below. The choruses are each eight bars in length and the start of the bridge can be identified by a change of metre.

Introduction

The sextet is introduced in four short but distinct sections, as follows:

(a) Horns	(b) Bass	(c) Drums	(d) Piano

(a) Describe the texture and harmony of section (a).

(b) In section (b), what interval is mainly used by the bass, and what effect is used before the final note?

(c) Briefly describe the drum solo, naming the instruments used.

(d) What interval is emphasized by the piano in section (d)?

Choruses

(e) (i) What melodic idea links the end of the introduction to the first chorus?

(ii) How is this melodic idea used in the first chorus?

(f) What is the rôle of the piano in the first chorus?

(g) Compare and contrast the second chorus with the first.

Bridge

(h) The metre changes for the bridge, although a regular pulse continues. Describe, as precisely as possible, the rhythm in this section.

Aural analysis gives little time to focus on the more expressive and subjective qualities of music, although these are at least as important in jazz as in any other style. For an epitome of jazz expression, though, do take time simply to *enjoy* the tiny, but intensely personal, bass solo by Charlie Mingus in the introduction of the above extract—the impassioned anguish of its opening and the complete exhaustion of its release. Even if you don't listen regularly to more progressive jazz of this kind, try to notice how often it is used as powerful background music in both film and television drama.

Popular music means 'music of the people' and not, of course, music that is necessarily liked by the majority. The latter may also be the case, but one of the tensions in 20th-century pop music is that 'popularity' can more easily be determined by the skill of promotors, the whims of broadcasters and the power of the music industry than by the people themselves. Commercial interests require the security of a well-tried product and often filter and distort the natural process of innovation and evolution in music that might otherwise be expected.

This was not always the case. The 'people' simply means the 'folk', and many of the pieces in the chapter on folk music could well be described as the popular music of its day—something that art music never was. However, the distinction between popular and art music is far less rigid before the 19th century. Purcell was perfectly happy to write wickedly bawdy catches to go down with the ale in the taverns of London, as was Mozart to supply the insatiable demand for the popular 'German dances' of his time—and Beethoven, as late as 1813, produced his preposterous 'Battle' Symphony: *Wellington's Victory*, complete with cannons and British national anthem to pull in the crowds.

The Popular Style

A distinct style for popular music began to emerge during the 19th century. Although the poorest classes kept alive the rural folk-song tradition, regenerating their material for an industrial age, the new strata of the lower middle class set their sights on the pursuits of the aristocracy—to be entertained by professional musicians and to cultivate leisure interests at home. To fill this demand, a new popular music industry emerged, supplying songs for the music hall, ballads and light piano pieces for the parlour. Models for the latter were early Romantic character pieces such as Mendelssohn's *Songs Without Words*, but the need for more (and lighter) music created a demand that 'serious' composers never filled. Thus appeared the specialist popular music composer. The waltzes of the Strauss family, the excerpts from operas by Balfe, the overtures of Suppé, the marches of Sousa and even the music-hall songs of now-forgotten composers all shared a common aim: the provision of short, tuneful works, perpetuating the simple structures and decorative harmonic style of early Romantic music. Although the style would change many times, the idea that popular music should make an immediate impact and be instantly memorable through the use of bold, clear rhythms and repetitive (often sequential) melodic motifs was established well before 1900. This creation of a new strand of music is nowhere better seen than in the plight of Arthur Sullivan, whose wish to be taken as the serious composer of his day was totally overtaken by the success of his operettas in partnership with Gilbert, and of his popular ballads like *The Lost Chord*.

A more dramatic split from art music is seen after 1900. The impact of ragtime, and later jazz, described in the previous chapter, was the start of a long process in which influences on the popular style swung away from Europe in the direction of Afro-American music. Although the classic 32-bar, AABA structure and use, by now, of late Romantic harmonies dominated popular songs between the wars, devices borrowed from jazz started to appear (syncopation, 'blue notes', added sixth chords), and many of the principal composers were from the USA, notably Irving Berlin, Jerome Kern, Cole Porter and George Gershwin.

Rhythm and Blues

Perhaps the most important change, though, was in the dissemination of new music. By the 1920s, this was no longer principally through sheet music to play on the piano but by record, radio and (from 1927) the musical film. In other words, popular music was no longer primarily for the people to perform but for them to consume—to listen and dance to. The USA, unlike Britain, established a diversity of radio networks which quickly led to a focus on regional tastes. In the south, particularly around Nashville, the modernized folk music of 'country' (first known as 'hillbilly', now called 'country and western') was the standard fare. In other parts of the south, it was the Afro-American traditions of blues and gospel. After 1945 millions of rural whites and southern blacks moved into the cities of the USA, creating a much wider public for their music.

The most important result of this urban interaction was the creation of a new hybrid, rhythm and blues (R & B), in which the driving rhythms of jazz were superimposed on the previously slow blues, creating an exciting and eminently danceable style of music. Typical of R & B is a structure of repeating verses, based on the 12-bar blues (without modulation), taken by a solo singer whose part was replaced by a saxophone improvisation in one of the 12-bar patterns. The accompaniment, in a well-accented $\frac{4}{4}$, was provided by a jazz-like rhythm section of piano, string bass, drums and electric guitar. Any of the instruments might also provide ostinato figures (**riffs**) and a small male-voice backing group would often echo vocal phrases in the form of call-and-response patterns.

Rock and Roll

This new music was slow to make an impact on most white audiences. After the war their popular music still depended heavily on sentimental ballads sung by 'crooners', whose softly murmured singing style was made audible over a lush full orchestra by the use of a microphone. The best known, Bing Crosby, was the highest-selling recording artist of the 20th century up to 1954, with over 300 hits. Meanwhile jazz, so popular in the swing era, was passing through a period of experiment with complex techniques that, however exciting, took it beyond the experience of the general public.

Thus, a post-war generation was growing up with greater spending power than ever before, but with no music to call its own. None, that is, until the advent of rock and roll. This is generally ascribed to the inclusion of the song 'Rock Around The Clock' (Bill Haley and the Comets, 1954) in the rebel film, *The Blackboard Jungle* (1955). Haley's work, though, was just part of a continuing widening of the appeal of R & B to white audiences. In 1954 Bill Haley had also recorded 'Shake, Rattle and Roll'—a song which, like Elvis Presley's first recorded song ('That's All Right, Mama', also 1954), is simply a 'cover' (a recording by a different artist) of an earlier R & B version by an Afro-American.

Rock and roll combined the R & B style with features of country music: the use of several guitars, an extravagant **slap** (percussive) technique on the double bass (later to be replaced by electric bass guitar), a tight rhythm with a distinctive **back-beat** from the drums (accenting beats 2 and 4 on the snare drum) and a singing style that often lost the R & B characteristic of **pushing** (anticipating) the beat—although one of the reasons for Presley's success was his ability to recapture this technique. However, the most important reason for the ascendancy of rock and roll over R & B was simply that it was performed by white musicians, giving it a veneer of acceptability in those often racially prejudiced times. Lyrics were generally purified in the process, although this never stopped reactionary protest at their apparent lewdness. Jazz-like qualities, such as instrumental improvisation, tended to give way to four-square rhythms and the predominance of a vocal line. Most significant, though, was that the music industry suddenly found that it had discovered a gold mine.

Track 91

The extract from 'Blue Suede Shoes' on Track 91 was recorded in 1955 by the song's composer, Carl Perkins (b. 1932). Like Bill Haley, he came from the southern states and could draw on both R & B and country music, in the style that was sometimes dubbed **rockabilly**. It was the first song to achieve success in all three of the pop, country, and R & B charts. The following year the now more famous cover version of the song was made by Elvis Presley—indeed, if you have access to his recording it will make an interesting comparison. Presley once said that he 'couldn't write a song to save his life'—all of his songs were covers of earlier material or were specially composed by professional song-writers, such as the team of Lieber and Stoller. There are many later examples (particularly of solo singers) doing the same, so you should be aware that pop music tends to be associated with the name of its performer, who may not necessarily be the same person as its composer. Even when the performer is the composer, it is most unlikely that he or she will have written more than a melody line and chords to accompany the lyrics. Groups will probably devise their own bass lines and drum parts, but in many cases detailed instrumentation will have been completed by a professional arranger, very often conforming to a 'house style' laid down by the record company's producer.

This song clearly reveals its R & B origins. It is based on the chord scheme of the 12-bar blues (see page 78): listen carefully, and make sure that you can identify two repetitions of the pattern with a four-bar interlude between them. Some of the vocal lines end with guitar **licks** (short solos) and, at the end of the extract, you will hear the start of an **instrumental**—a guitar 'verse' just like the saxophone improvisations that alternated with the singer in R & B. Also listen for the characteristic 'walking bass' of early rock and roll (formed largely of crotchets) that outlines the fundamental harmonic structure.

===== *Test 67* =====

The following is a skeleton score of the opening of this song:

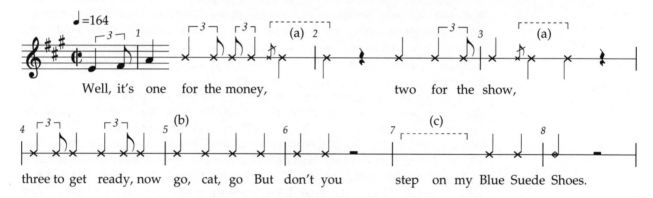

(a) On which degree of the scale does the accompaniment play at (a) above?

(b) How does the note marked (b) in the vocal part relate to the key?

(c) Describe the rhythm set to the words 'step on my', marked (c) above.

(d) State the bar number at which a walking bass starts.

(e) At which bar number do you first hear a change to a new chord?

(f) Describe the melodic outline of the vocal part throughout the extract.

(g) Describe the harmony of the four-bar section between the two repetitions of the complete 12-bar blues pattern (at the words 'Well you can knock me down, step on my face, slander my name all over the place').

Soft Rock

The musical content of rock and roll was novel, but simple. Techniques that were so expressive within the freedom of the blues tended to turn into well-tried formulas in this tightly rhythmic format. Much of the success depended on the style of delivery of the song, and some of the most exciting singers had short-lived careers: Buddy Holly and Eddie Cochran died in accidents, Jerry Lee Lewis and Gene Vincent were involved in scandals, and Presley turned towards Hollywood. Well before 1960, though, the raw edges of rock and roll were being sand-papered by the record industry. White singers from the northern states, and their British imitators like Cliff Richard, were encouraged to look more in the direction of cute lyrics about high school, cars and puppy love than towards the rebellion of early rock. With this came a more polished musical production, professional arrangements and sometimes even symphony orchestra backing.

Typical of the new professionalism is Neil Sedaka (b. 1939). Grandson of a concert pianist and winner of a scholarship to the famous Juilliard School of

Music in New York, Sedaka made his first record in 1956 and can still be heard performing today. The impact of this 'soft rock' style (sometimes called MOR, 'middle of the road') should not be underestimated: only Elvis Presley outsold Neil Sedaka in the years before 1963 and Sedaka was to bounce back with another string of hits in the 1970s. 'Happy Birthday Sweet Sixteen' (1961) has many of the features that brought success in this style—a crisp, up-tempo drum part, vocal harmonies supplied by a backing group (often abbreviated to **bvox**—the word *vox* is Latin for 'voice'), counter-melodies for strings and a final verse (not included here) that modulates up a semitone for climactic effect. The form owes nothing to the 12-bar blues, but follows a much more European structure of repeating 16-bar sections, in the pattern AA^{1}BAA^2. An eight-bar introduction, later modified to form a repeating coda for a final fade, neatly surrounds the entire song. The harmonies depend for their effect on the use of secondary dominants that take the music through a range of related keys, and the melodic line is much more scale-based than the triadic vocal parts of earlier rock and roll. Sedaka also makes use of the increasingly versatile technology by double-tracking his light tenor voice to form a simple harmony part in thirds and sixths.

🔘 Track 92

━━━━━━━━━━━━━━━━━━━━━━ ***Test 68*** ━━━━━━━━━━━━━━━━━━━━━━

After an eight-bar introduction, you will hear two verses, each of which begins with the music printed below. All of the questions relate to the verses.

Verse 1: To- night's the night _____

(a) How is the motif in bars 1–2 above treated in bars 3–4?

(b) Which key does the music pass through in bars 3–6?

(c) How are the starting notes of the first six two-bar vocal phrases related?

(d) (i) Apart from the drum kit, which untuned percussion instrument is featured in this song?

(ii) What rhythm pattern does this instrument mainly play?

(e) Briefly describe how the backing in verse 2 differs from that in verse 1.

(f) (i) How does the final cadence of verse 2 differ from the cadence at the end of verse 1?

(ii) How are these cadences approached in both verses?

British Rock

In 1954, at the end of Britain's austere post-war period, a short-lived craze for **skiffle** suddenly emerged. Skiffle had first appeared in the late 1920s in the poorest areas of Chicago as a simple form of traditional jazz for the amateur. Using elements of blues and country styles, it was improvised music for small groups, featuring a solo singer accompanied by acoustic guitar with (most distinctively) a host of cheap or improvised instruments that almost anyone could provide: comb-and-paper, kazoo, harmonica, cheese-box banjo (made from the circular wooden boxes that used to hold cheeses), tea-chest bass (made from the wooden crate used to import tea, a broom-handle and a single string) and, for percussion, a washboard played with thimbles. The commercial success of skiffle (largely in the person of Lonnie Donegan) was short-lived in the face of the rock and roll onslaught from America. Its importance lay more as a training ground for a new generation of young British amateurs, including Tommy Steele, The Shadows, John Lennon and Paul McCartney.

The Beatles' ultimate rise to fame in 1962 appeared meteoric, although it was actually the culmination of five years spent learning their craft in cover versions (for performance rather than record) of songs by Americans such as Chuck Berry and The Everly Brothers. Significantly, one of their greatest influences was Buddy Holly, who wrote his own songs—rather than Elvis Presley, who did not. Although the music of The Beatles was dominated by the work of Lennon and McCartney, the concept of a group working creatively together, rather than a solo singer accompanied by a backing group, made an immediate and long-lasting impact. So, too, did many things which are more the province of the sociologist than the musician wishing to improve aural perception—the carefully designed suits and haircuts, their near-hysterical cult following and yet an innocent charm which widened their appeal to a record-buying generation of mums and dads. All of these things were avidly exploited by the rapidly growing medium of television.

The early musical style of The Beatles is not easy to distinguish from that of many other groups of their time. They preferred the European 32-bar, AABA, song form to the 12-bar blues, had a good sense of vocal blend with a free mix of solo, unison and chordal vocal textures, and had a gimmick in the interpolation of occasional falsetto notes, sung with a shake of their mop-head hair. The group used the now common format of electric lead, rhythm and bass guitars, plus drums (the less powerful and more cumbersome string bass had been replaced by bass guitar in the late 1950s). Most notable was a tendency to vary the rather predictable harmonic patterns of rock and roll with occasional unusual chords or unexpected progressions. Lennon and McCartney, who both had the skill to create memorable musical lines, soon stopped writing together, although it was agreed to continue publishing songs under their joint names.

From 1965 The Beatles made a conscious change of direction to explore new creative concepts in popular music. Their producer, the classically trained oboist, George Martin, played an ever more important rôle in this. It was he who scored the delicate string quartet backing in 'Yesterday' (1965) and who supervised the carefully layered multi-track recording of *Rubber Soul* (1965)—an album which was devised as a studio production, containing material impossible to reproduce in live performance. The restrained slow ballads and use of unusual textures, such as the *sitar* in the light waltz opening of 'Norwegian Wood' or Baroque keyboard of 'In My Life', were the precursors of a range of experimental techniques used in the albums *Revolver* (1966) and *Sgt. Pepper's Lonely Hearts Club Band* (1967). The latter was designed as a lavish 'concept album'—a collection of related songs from which singles might be drawn, rather than just a haphazard collection of single songs. In this case, the concept was a vaudeville of fantasies from which the listener is finally returned to a very uncertain form of reality. *Sgt. Pepper* begins with applause and an 'overture', and embraces the music hall ('When I'm Sixty-Four'), community songs ('With a Little Help From my Friends'), psychedelic images ('Lucy in the Sky with Diamonds'), a surreal waltz for fairground steam-organ ('Mr Kite'), animal sounds and, in 'A Day in the Life', an aleatoric improvisation by a 40-piece orchestra. This is followed by a colossal E major chord struck simultaneously on three pianos, allowed to resonate for more than 40 seconds before giving way to a 20 kHz tone, above the range of most people's hearing: the album ended with a 'locked groove' on the record, which produced an endlessly repeating loop of a few seconds' noise from the post-recording party—a conclusive return to reality.

The late 1960s was the peak of one of those cycles of creativity and depression that seem to be a feature of pop music. The leading group in the USA, The Beach Boys, similarly turned from their earlier, simple and tuneful 'surfing' songs (such as 'California Girls') to exploring changing metres and new textures. Their album *Pet Sounds* (1966) was written in response to the Beatles' *Rubber Soul* of the same year and pre-dates *Sgt. Pepper* in its use of complex recording techniques, skilful and unusual scoring, novel sounds (including the microtonal possibilities of an early type of synthesizer called the 'theremin', the percussive effects of soft drinks cans and a soda water dispenser, the plucked strings of a grand piano, and barking dogs) and unusual source material, including *a cappella* voices in an arrangement of the West Indian folk tune, 'Sloop John B'. Years later, Paul McCartney was to acknowledge that '*Pet Sounds* was my inspiration for making *Sgt. Pepper* …the big influence'. The success of The Beatles established a world-wide market for British pop music and many other groups followed their model. One such was Procul Harum—their strange name is Latin for 'far beyond these things'. 'A Whiter Shade of Pale' became, along with 'All You Need Is Love' from the Beatles, one of the great songs of the summer of 1967. The lead guitar is replaced by an electric organ, offering a much thicker sound and anticipating the importance of electronic instruments in the following decades. The music owes more than a little to Bach—compare the melody, bass and harmony of the opening with Bach's Aria from his Orchestral Suite in D (the famous 'Air on a G string'). The words are a mix of mystery and whimsy that appealed to the fantastical spirit of the age, and that took pop lyrics further from the clichés of the early years of the decade.

 Track 93

Test 69

This extract consists of an eight-bar introduction, a 16-bar verse and an eight-bar chorus. The introduction begins with the following organ melody:

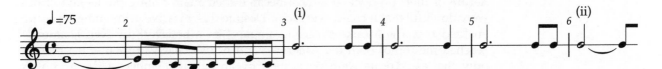

(a) Each of the dotted minims in bars 3–6 is ornamented. Name the conventional ornaments used to decorate the melody at (i) and (ii) above.

(b) Describe the pitches outlined by the bass part in bars 1–4.

(c) (i) What is the predominant rhythm played on the cymbals?

   (ii) How does the drummer signify the transition from the end of the introduction to the start of the verse?

(d) The singer begins the verse as follows:

We skipped the light ___ fan-dan-go ___

On which note of the scale does the short melisma at the end of 'fandango' finish (marked (d) above)?

(e) The chorus starts with the words 'And so it was'.

   (i) Describe the rhythm sung to the words 'And so it'.

   (ii) What does the organ play as these words are sung?

   (iii) How does the singer's note on the word 'was' relate to the harmony?

(g) Name the final cadence of the chorus (at the end of the extract).

(h) How does the harmony of both the verse and the chorus relate to the harmony of the introduction?

Country Music

You may have noticed that the last two tracks seem to owe more to the techniques of Western art music and earlier popular ballads than to any influence of the blues or other Afro-American traditions. This is not the case in all pop music of the 1960s. Groups such as The Rolling Stones turned back to rock's R & B roots to recapture the raw, rebellious energy of singers such as Chuck Berry, five of whose songs they covered in their first successful year. Country music, the other main ingredient in the formation of early rock and roll, also began to re-establish itself as a major genre in popular music. Television and major record companies had attempted to marginalize country music (like jazz) as being a 'minority interest' though this was hardly the case: between 1961 and 1966 the number of American radio stations playing exclusively country and western increased fourfold, to 328. Nashville (Tennessee) became the major centre for the study, publishing and recording of country music—Presley recorded there in the 1950s, as did Dylan a decade later. Despite its title, 'Papa Gene's Blues' on Track 94 is not a blues, but a typical product of this Nashville sound.

The Monkees were a group that provide one of the most vivid examples of the increasing commercialization of pop music. Alarmed by the success of British groups in the USA, NBC TV decided to promote 'America's answer to The Beatles' and, when it couldn't find this answer, it created its own group for the purpose. Two actors and two musicians were successfully auditioned late in 1965, were named The Monkees, and were immediately thrown into a schedule that included weekly television programmes (each containing three new songs), recordings and frequent promotional appearances. Not surprisingly, there was no requirement for the group to write their own songs nor even, at first, to perform them: recordings were made with top session musicians, and the group simply mimed in front of the cameras. NBC were totally open about the artifical nature of their product—it almost became their main selling point—and critics were doubtful that it could ever work. Despite this, massive prime-time exposure ensured that The Monkees' second single, 'I'm a Believer' (by Neil Diamond) reached the top of both the American and British charts in 1966—even though only the lead vocals were performed by an actual member of the group. A second irony was to follow, for it then turned out that The Monkees wanted to perform, and even write, their own songs. 'Papa Gene's Blues' was the first of these, written by Monkees' guitarist Michael Nesmith, who sings the lead vocals on this 1966 recording. Note the characteristic 'chicken' effect of the bent and stopped guitar notes—an effect that can also be replicated on the saxophone.

Track 94

Test 70

The recording on Track 94 is of the complete song, 'Papa Gene's Blues', written, produced and sung by Michael Nesmith. It consists of the following sections:

Intro	Verse 1	Chorus	Verse 2	Chorus	Instrumental	Chorus	Coda
2 bars	8 bars	8 bars	8 bars	8 bars	8 bars	8 bars	2 bars

(a) Verse 1 begins as follows (the same music, but with different words, is repeated later):

(i) What does the backing vocalist sing during the lead singer's melody?

(ii) Briefly describe how the continuation of the vocal melody in bars 2–4 relates to the music printed above.

(iii) Comment on the rhythm and pitches of the bass part in bars 1–3.

(iv) A tonic chord of A major is used in bar 1 of the verse. In which bar does the harmony first change, and which of the following chords does it change to?

    B minor   D major   E major   F sharp minor

(v) How does the second half of each verse relate to the first half?

(b) Each chorus begins as follows:

I have no more than I____ did be - fore, but now

How does the pitch of the notes set to the words 'did before' relate to the pitch set to the word 'now'?

(c) Each chorus ends with the words 'For I love you and I know you love me'. On which of these words does the singer use a chromatic passing-note?

(d) How does the instrumental section relate to the preceding material?

(e) In the final chorus, the words 'I love you and I know you love me' are repeated. What compositional device is used to provide variation in this repeat?

The Folk Revival

Country music was originally a type of American folk music but the increasing dominance of the 'Nashville sound' eventually tended to encourage a slick, more commercial product typified by the songs of Dolly Parton. Nevertheless, the earlier, more authentic country tradition was maintained in parallel with this, in the style known as **bluegrass** (America's nickname for the state of Kentucky). Bluegrass does not exclude new music, but it tends to use traditional techniques such as high harmony parts in thirds (as in the last example) and a line-up of acoustic instruments such as fiddle, guitar, mandolin, banjo, string bass and dopro—a guitar 'amplified' by a simple aluminium megaphone.

Traditionally, folk music meant the music of rural communities, along with more contemporary urban folk-song by singer–song writers such as Woodie Guthrie. All folk music must have been composed by somebody at some time, and the fact that the composer's name is recent enough to be known does not alter the definition of folk as 'music of the people'—indeed, Guthrie placed himself firmly in the folk tradition by opposing any copyright on his songs.

In the 1930s and 1940s there had been considerable interest in this American folk legacy, expressed in the work of the folk-song collector Alan Lomax, and his one-time assistant Pete Seeger. Seeger, unlike Lomax, was primarily a performer—his first group, the Almanac Singers (1940) has included Woodie Guthrie. Seeger went on to become the leading figure in the American folk-song revival, exemplifying his belief in folk music as a living tradition by writing such new folk-songs as 'If I Had A Hammer' (1949), 'Where Have All The Flowers Gone?' (1956), 'Turn, Turn, Turn' (1962) and 'We Shall Overcome' (adapted from a Baptist hymn of 1901). None of these became hits until the 1960s, and then mostly in cover versions by other artists, for Seeger's popularity, along with much of the impetus of this early folk revival, had been severely damaged when his left-wing views were deliberately misrepresented as 'anti-American' during McCarthy's communist purge of the 1950s.

Despite this set-back, the Newport Folk Festival was established on Rhode Island in 1954, and by 1960 had become a major stimulus in the promotion of the folk revival. There could be heard the young Joan Baez singing songs from the 'Child Ballads', a seminal late 19th-century collection of English and Scottish folk-song, made in Boston, Massachusetts, and including more than one hundred songs that had migrated to America with the settlers. Also at Newport, from 1962, could be heard a friend of Joan Baez and Pete Seeger, a young folk musician who was a constant visitor to the now bed-ridden Woodie Guthrie, and a singer–song writer described decades later as 'the most important figure in white rock music'—Bob Dylan. Not only was Dylan a profound influence on the Beatles, the Rolling Stones, the Byrds, David Bowie, and countless others, but he also opened his own folk style to the influences of rock music. Dylan's early songs, like 'Blowin' In The Wind', perpetuated the modern folk style of Seeger and the nasal vocal delivery that some musicologists believe is an authentic part of traditional folk-song. Then, in 1965 Dylan started using a rock band, rather than

[93]

the acoustic instruments of folk, and in so doing acknowledged that if folk is 'the music of the people' then it must reflect contemporary developments in rock music. Pete Seeger was enraged and Dylan was booed by the audience of the 1965 Newport Folk Festival. From this point, an inevitable divison emerged between such new **folk-rock** music and what was perceived as a more traditional folk style, just as a division had emerged between the 'country-rock' of Dolly Parton and others on the one hand, and the more authentic bluegrass style on the other.

The folk revival movement was not limited to America. In Britain, it was led by Peggy Seeger, sister of Pete, and her Scottish husband, Ewan MacColl. Modern British folk was at first closely linked with left-wing politics: the most significant folk record label (Topic) had been established by the British Marxist party, Seeger and MacColl had edited the important collection *Songs for the Sixties* for the Workers' Music Association and modern folk music was, as in America, often associated with social causes such as CND (the Campaign for Nuclear Disarmament) and protest against the Vietnam War. However, by 1969 British folk music was also achieving commercial success. That year saw the release of Ralph McTell's 'Streets of London' and the album *Leige & Lief* from Fairport Convention—a band prepared to present traditional material in a totally rock context. This venture, though, divided the loyalties of the group, and their bass player—interested in a more traditional style of folk—left to form a new band named Steeleye Span (after a character mentioned in the traditional song, 'Horkston Grange').

Steeleye Span became the most successful of the folk-rock groups of the 1970s, and their influence has extended to the present day, since their guitarist later joined the much more radical 'thrash-folk' group, The Pogues, in 1986. *All Around My Hat* was issued as an album in 1975, and the opening of the title track is recorded here on Track 95. The song is traditional, but the arrangement is by the members of Steeleye Span and perfectly combines the quasi-authentic 'improvised' harmony of the first verse (which should be compared to the Welsh hymn on Track 69, page 60) with a simple rock treatment of the second.

Track 95

====================== *Test 71* ======================

The first verse of the music on this track is based on the following traditional song:

The words of verse 2 are:

> Fare thee well cold winter and fare thee well cold frost,
> Nothing have I gained but my own true love I've lost,
> I'll sing and I'll be merry when occasion I do see,
> He's a false deluding young man, let him go, farewell he.

(a) In verse 1, explain how the printed melody is changed or embellished at each of the following places:

    (i) On the word 'green' in bar 3;

    (ii) On the word 'a' in bar 7;

    (iii) On the word 'me' in bar 10;

    (iv) On the words 'wearing it' in bar 12;

    (v) On the word 'far' in bar 15.

(b) Comment on the movement of the lower parts in bar 7 of verse 1.

(c) On what word(s) do you hear the only minor chord in verse 1?

(d) What is unusual about the cadences in verse 1?

(e) On what note of the scale does the bass guitar enter in bar 16?

(f) Comment on the texture of verse 1.

(g) Compare verse 2 with verse 1 in terms of:

    (i) Speed;

    (ii) Melody;

    (iii) Harmony.

Diversification

The years 1965 to 1975 were a decade of rich diversification in pop music. In addition to rock, commercial pop, rhythm and blues, country and various types of folk music, yet more styles started to make an impact. These included the jazz-influenced work of the groups Steely Dan and Weather Report (sometimes known as **jazz fusion**); the development of light shows, projection and other performance effects in the work of Pink Floyd—eventually leading to the spectacular presentation style of Queen; the creation of extended forms in rock opera (such as *Tommy* by The Who, 1969) with its spin-off into the more 'middle of the road' rock operas of Andrew Lloyd Webber; rock versions of art music such as Emerson, Lake and Palmer's version of Mussorgsky's *Pictures at an Exhibition* (1971); the end of the domination of the pop group with the return of solo singers and instrumentalists such as Elton John, David Bowie and Eric Clapton; the increasing use of synthesizers, leading to the 'one man orchestra' and fledgling minimalism of Mike Oldfield's *Tubular Bells* (1973) and the revival of 1950s rock and roll with groups such as Sha Na Na and their British counterparts, Showaddywaddy. In the 'top ten' lists of the early 1970s, you can even find the 58-year-old Perry Como's 'It's Impossible'—an apt title for a piece that was stylistically identical to his hits of the 1940s—and the bagpipers of the Royal Scots Dragoon Guards achieving huge success with 'Amazing Grace'.

Perhaps the most enduring influence of these times was the rediscovery of the Afro-American roots of rock. In the 1960s, the two great traditions of blues and gospel came together in Detroit under the name **Motown** (Detroit is the motor-manufacturing capital of the USA: the name is probably an abbreviation of 'motor town'). From 1969, the term **soul** was used instead of rhythm and blues, and refers specifically to this new style. The most influential soul singers include James Brown, Ray Charles and Aretha Franklin, and the enormous variety of vocal technique that they were able to call upon—melismas, falsetto, sighs and sobs, chanting, shouting, and contrasts between the most mellifluous and most earthy sounds—is one of the most characteristic features of soul and one of the features that had the most influence on pop music generally (you may have noticed a little use of vocal melismas in the recording of 'A Whiter Shade of Pale' on Track 93). Another offshoot of rhythm and blues, with some influence of the local calypso style and with heavy emphasis on the back-beats (beats 2 and 4), had become very popular in Jamaica in the early 1960s under the name 'ska'. As the pulse slowed down it became known as 'rock steady' and eventually, as a heavy and hypnotic bass came to the fore, as **reggae**. Bob Marley and the Wailers had achieved success in Jamaica in the 1960s, but it was not until Eric Clapton's cover version of Marley's 'I Shot the Sheriff' became a hit in 1974 that Marley himself became widely known outside the West Indies. Eventually, reggae developed into **dub** (poetry recited to a reggae backing)—related to **rap** and **hip hop**, in which street talk is similarly superimposed over music, but in these cases usually a disco-style backing. Hip hop, essentially the New York form of rap, is a complete culture—clothes, language and attitude are as important as the music—and technology plays an important rôle in the music, including the use of drum machines, 'sampling' (the digital recording and re-use or transformation of existing recordings) and 'scratching'. The latter gives a creative rôle to the DJ, who can modify the often rather repetitious content of disco tracks by jiggling the record turntable back and forth to create his own rhythmic additions to the mix.

Meanwhile, developments in mainstream rock in the late 1960s started to move away from Britain back to the USA, and particularly to San Francisco, where groups such as Jefferson Airplane and The Grateful Dead were using ever more amplification, newly available electronic instruments such as synthesizers and electronic effects such as guitar distortion to mimic the mind-bending properties of hallucinatory drugs, in the style known as **acid rock**. This ultimately led to the **heavy metal** style of the 1970s, typified by the British group, Deep Purple. Heavy metal tended to be concerned with teenage angst and the occult rather than with the drug-ridden images of acid rock and was more dependent on a powerful guitar-based rock style than on synthesizers, but it shared the same pre-occupation with distortion and brutal over-amplification of the sound. Heavy metal was often a problem for record companies: its long tracks were unsuited to the 'singles' then still popular, and tours of enormous length were needed to market the more expensive album format. Nevertheless, this encouraged live performance which attracted a loyal following of fans with their various rituals of 'head-banging' and playing imaginary 'air guitars' which, in turn, became an important part of the heavy metal experience. The deliberate distortion of the most basic musical parameters of pitch, rhythm and harmony make such music a frustrating (and unlikely) subject for aural analysis. This phenomenon also applies to the **punk rock** style of The Sex Pistols and The Clash in the late 1970s: the social desirability of opening up rock performance to anyone who thinks they might have something to say was rather overtaken by the views of audiences who, after the novelty had worn thin, ultimately did not want to listen to singers who made a feature out of not being able to sing, or guitarists who demonstrated that they could not play.

By the start of the 1980s, many of the trends outlined above had come and gone and yet more were to follow: **new wave** music, the more refined successor to punk rock and typified by Elvis Costello and The Police; the flamboyant dress and music of the **new romantics** such as Culture Club and Spandau Ballet, and the pleasant wallpaper music of the **new age**, with its elements of jazz and minimalism, represented by those virtuosos of the synthesizer, Jean-Michel Jarre, Tomita and Vangelis. Commercial pop continued to be aimed at the lower teenage market, presenting simple material attractively packaged with an eye more to visual effect than to musical content by groups such as Duran Duran, Wham! and Take That. **Disco** music became increasingly important culturally, although the requirement for a totally standard product, even down to different pieces conforming to a set tempo so that they could be seamlessly merged together, gives point to the name **house music** and, in the continual recycling of well-tried ideas, offers little for the analytical ear.

It is important to realize that, for its success, art music tends to rely much more on purely musical content than does pop music. It is a matter of current debate whether or not art music should be played by musicians dressed in long evening gowns, dinner jackets, black tie and tails, or whether the music should be taken out of the formal surroundings of subsidized concert halls and literally into the market place. Ultimately such matters are only peripheral to the music itself. In pop music, on the other hand, the performance (or video) is an inextricable part of an entire package that also includes presentation, lighting, audio and visual effects, dance, social awareness of lyrics, personality and attitude of the performer, and so forth. In this context, the music itself may sometimes be slight in content, making it less suitable for aural analysis, but without diminishing the success of this package taken as a whole. That this is not always true, though, is well illustrated by the final example in this chapter, taken from the 1987 album, ... *Nothing Like The Sun*, written, sung, arranged and produced by Sting (who also plays bass guitar). Sting had been a jazz bass guitarist before becoming a member of the group The Police, who had considerable success in the 1980s with music that drew on a number of traditions, and that is sometimes described as 'white reggae'. Sting, whose real name is Gordon Sumner, went on to develop a career as an actor as well as a solo singer. This album includes contributions from Andy Summers, guitarist of The Police, as well as from two of the leading pop musicians of the age, Eric Clapton and the prolific song-writing guitarist of Dire Straits, Mark Knopfler.

🎵 Track 96

=== *Test 72* ===

Listen to the music on this track and make sure that you can identify the following sections before answering the questions (the top row of numbers refer to bar numbers, the lower row to times in seconds):

1–4	5–8	9–12	13–16	17–19	20–23
0"	10"	20"	30"	40"	48"
Introduction		Verse			Refrain
Percussion riffs	Melodic riffs	Vocal solo	+ bvox	Key change	'Straight to my heart'

(a) What is the metre of this song?

(b) A bass guitar and two synthesizers enter in bar 5. One of the synthesizers plays a riff using a marimba sound. What type of sound is used by the other synthesizer, and how does its part relate to the 'marimba' riff?

(c) Briefly describe the bass part in bars 5 to 16 and state what harmonic device this implies.

(d) How does the main vocal melody relate to this bass part?

(e) Briefly describe the bvox part in bars 13 to 16.

(f) Bar 16 ends on a chord of B minor. Which of the following chords do you hear at the start of bar 17?

A major   B major   C major   D major   E major

(g) Name the interval outlined by the vocal part in the refrain 'Straight to my heart' in the last section of the song.

(h) One of the synthesizers plays a long single note using an oboe sound during this refrain. On what note of the scale is this played?

(i) How and where does the drum part first change in this song?

The concept of the Renaissance was formulated by historians in the 19th century, and both the idea and the dates of this period are still hotly contested. For our purposes we do not need to worry too much about when the period started, since it certainly pre-dates the year 1550 when most Advanced-level music syllabuses begin to prescribe music for detailed study. The end of the period is generally taken to be 1600 and this makes good sense, for it was at about this time when a radically new musical style emerged in Italy—although many composers continued to write in the old styles well into the 17th century.

You may think that there can be few connections between the types of music we have studied in the previous chapters and the seemingly remote styles of the late Renaissance. Yet there are basic techniques which are common to the music of many different periods, styles and countries and you should make full use of what you have so far learned when studying this chapter. By doing this you are unlikely to fall into the trap of over-generalization. For instance, while it is true that many 16th-century composers wrote modal counterpoint with flowing melodic lines, it is equally true that they frequently wrote secular tonal homophony with disjunct melodies, and this style often invaded the church style. Once again we would emphasize the importance of describing not what you think you ought to be hearing, but what you actually hear.

Masses and Motets The Mass was the most important service in the Roman Catholic Church which dominated most of Europe in the late 16th century. In musical parlance the Mass (*Missa* in Latin) refers to the Ordinary, i.e., those texts which never changed and which were always sung (the Kyrie, Gloria, Credo, Sanctus and Agnus Dei).

In the middle ages the Mass was usually sung to plainsong. Follow the music below as you listen to this plainsong hymn:

 Track 1

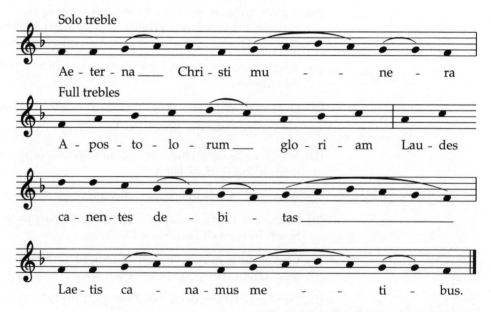

Matins hymn for the Common of Apostles

Notice that the melody has a free rhythm, is mostly conjunct and has a range of only a sixth. The whole effect is of an almost timeless flow. The same is true of the melodies which are woven together in the contrapuntal textures of such composers as Palestrina, Victoria and Lassus.

 Track 2

Listen to the Kyrie by Palestrina on Track 2, concentrating on the treble part (the first part to enter is sung by the tenors, the second by altos and the third by trebles). If you sing along with the trebles (an octave down if necessary!) you will soon discover that the melody is mostly conjunct and has a narrow range like the plainsong. You will probably feel a pulse in duple time underlying this music, but you should notice that the melody you have sung does not always have accents corresponding to this metre—it flows like plainsong.

The combination of rhythmically independent melodies is the essence of counterpoint. There are two phrases for the trebles, both with the words *Kyrie eleison, eleison*. Do you notice that they both begin with the same tune but that the second phrase has the following, different ending?

Now try singing along with the other three voices. Do you notice that each part begins with the same tune and enters before the previous part has finished? This is called **imitation**, and imitative counterpoint is very common in this period, particularly in liturgical music.

Next look at the music above as you listen to the cadence which ends Track 2. First pay particular attention to the tenor and bass. These two parts form an octave, then a seventh at the tie-over, then a sixth. The seventh is a dissonance, although this interval became so common in later music that it may not immediately strike you as forming a discord. This dissonant seventh is a **suspension** and you can hear another one between the treble and the tenor two beats later. This is the most obvious type of dissonance in this period and it always occurs on a strong beat (indeed it is the presence of suspensions at regular intervals of time which helps establish the duple metre).

By now you will probably have noticed the similarity between the first phrase of the plainsong hymn of Track 1 and the melody which Palestrina treats imitatively in the Kyrie on Track 2. This method of building contrapuntal paragraphs out of a pre-existing melody (usually plainsong) is known as **paraphrase** technique. Sometimes, as here, the connection is obvious, but in other cases the original melody may be subjected to a greater degree of variation before being used as a point of imitation. A paraphrase Mass uses this technique in all the movements and the Mass is named after the tune upon which it is based (in this case the *Missa Aeterna Christi munera*, named after the opening words of the plainsong hymn). This was one of the most common types of Mass, but even in a *Missa sine nomine* (an unnamed Mass) or a *Missa brevis* (a short Mass) of this period the vocal lines will usually be similar to plainsong.

 Tracks 1 and 3

████████████████████ *Test 73* ████████████████████

Listen to the plainsong on Track 1 and follow the music on page 98. Immediately afterwards listen to the *Christe eleison* on Track 3.

(a) Which phrase of the plainsong does Palestrina use in this music?

(b) How many voices are singing in the second extract? Identify them as accurately as you can.

(c) How does Palestrina treat the plainsong phrase in the uppermost voice?

(d) What is the relationship between all of the voice parts in Palestrina's setting?

(e) What device is used on the first chord of the final perfect cadence?

In this period the **motet** was a choral setting of sacred words in Latin which were often appropriate to a particular day of the church's year. In England, after the Reformation, similar pieces but with English words were called **anthems**. There are two types of anthem: the full anthem was essentially the same as the motet, apart from the difference in language, while the verse anthem included 'verses' for solo voice(s) alternating with passages for the full choir, all of this accompanied by an organ and/or consort of viols.

The texts of motets (e.g., the Song of Solomon or one of the Psalms) were often much more highly coloured than the Ordinary of the Mass, so composers tended to respond more to the poetic imagery by 'word painting' (e.g., the word 'rising' might be set to an ascending phrase). In the motet by Victoria on Track 4 the opening exclamation 'Oh!' is treated homophonically and in long notes to suggest the worshipper holding his breath in awe of the vision of the company of saints, while the music for *quam gloriosum* ('how glorious') opens like a magnificent flower, the trebles rising as the bass falls in contrary motion.

As is the case in most motets of this period there is a wide variety of vocal textures: imitative counterpoint contrasted with homophony, all four voices contrasted with the three lower, then the three upper voices, and so on. Each phrase of the text is given its own distinctive tune, yet the music seems to flow on effortlessly. This is achieved by the composer's technique of overlapping at the cadences. At the very point where the tunes for one phrase of music are coming to rest (e.g., the perfect cadence at the end of *In quo cum Christo*) the next phrase enters in a different voice part (e.g., *gaudent* at the same perfect cadence).

Not all Masses with titles were based on paraphrase technique. An equally popular method of construction was to take complete polyphonic passages from a motet or madrigal, change the words to those of the Ordinary and then skilfully stitch these passages together using the technique of overlapping. Each movement of the Mass then became a sort of collage of quotations from the original composition with some newly composed material added to ensure cohesion. These are known as **parody Masses** (the word 'parody' in the context having no pejorative overtones).

The advantage of both paraphrase and parody techniques is that the use of music from the same source in all movements gives the whole Mass a sense of unity: compositions which use some of the same material in all movements are said to be cyclic—this is an idea we will encounter in symphonies written 300 years later.

Tracks 4 and 5

Victoria parodied his own motet 'O quam gloriosum' in his *Missa O quam gloriosum*. Listen to the first 46 seconds of the motet on Track 4 and compare this with the first minute of the Agnus Dei from the Mass on Track 5.

The motet begins with the phrase *O quam gloriosum est regnum* which has already been discussed. Now follows the first imitative passage with the words *in quo cum Christo* where all the voices enter several times with a distinctive melody beginning with a rising fourth. The pulse is much slower in the Mass. It begins with the words *Agnus Dei* set to music which is apparently unrelated to the motet. But this overlaps with the next section, *qui tollis peccata mundi*, which has the same imitation upon the melody, beginning with the rising fourth (though the long melisma on the word *Christo* is now omitted to suit the more sombre text).

Track 4

===================== *Test 74* =====================

Victoria's four-part motet 'O quam gloriosum' divides into a number of sections corresponding to the phrases of text:

1.	*O quam gloriosum*	O how glorious
2.	*est regnum*	is the kingdom
3.	*in quo cum Christo*	where, with Christ,
4.	*gaudent*	rejoice
5.	*omnes Sancti!*	all the saints!

6.	*Amicti stolis albis*	Dressed in white robes
7.	*sequuntur Agnum*	they follow the Lamb
8.	*quocunque ierit*	wherever he goes

(a) How does the counterpoint of phrase 2 differ from that of phrase 3?

(b) *Gaudent* refers to rejoicing. How does Victoria illustrate joy in his music for phrase 4?

(c) How does the texture of phrase 6 differ from phrase 7?

(d) How does Victoria achieve contrast within his setting of phrase 6?

(e) *Sequuntur Agnum* means 'they [the Saints] follow the Lamb [Christ]'. How does Victoria illustrate this in his music?

(f) A few bars before the end of the motet you will hear a perfect cadence and, at the end, a plagal cadence.

    (i) Describe the treble part between these two cadences.

    (ii) What device does Victoria use to decorate the final plagal cadence?

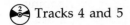 Tracks 4 and 5

Test 75

Listen again to the motet on Track 4 and immediately afterwards listen to the Agnus Dei on Track 5, the text and translation of which is:

Agnus Dei, qui tollis   Lamb of God, who takes away the
peccata mundi, miserere nobis.   sins of the world, have mercy upon us.

(a) Victoria uses the music of phrase 3 of the motet (see text in Test 74 above) for the words *qui tollis peccata mundi*. Which phrase of the motet does he use for *misere nobis*?

(b) The texts *qui tollis peccata mundi* and *miserere nobis* are both parts of the same sentence. How does Victoria achieve musical continuity between them?

(c) What is the most important modification which Victoria makes to his original material at the end of this Agnus Dei?

Madrigals

The secular equivalent of the motet was developed to a peak of perfection in the sophisticated courts of Italy. In the hands of composers such as Marenzio the madrigal became a vehicle for the most subtle expression of texts which ranged from the anguish of unrequited love, through irony to gay abandon. To achieve this, all the devices of textural contrast found in the motet were allied to a greater use of tonal contrast and freer dissonance treatment. Imitative passages were often as serious in tone as in the contemporary motet, but, if the words demanded it, imitation was used to comical effect by bringing in the entries of each voice at very close intervals of time (like the ubiquitous nymphs and shepherds chasing each other in a delightful mythical pastoral landscape).

The most frivolous type of madrigal was the dance-like *balletto*, with its syncopation (often the result of changes in metre), repeated notes and 'fa-la-la' refrain. The term is clearly related to ballet, but is distinguished by being spelt with a double 't', even in its English form, the **ballett**.

In 1588 (the year of the Armada) a collection of Italian madrigals in English translation was printed in London. This, and subsequent similar publications, helped spark a remarkably intense but brief flowering of the English madrigal. The most prolific composer in this genre was Morley. As in the work of other English madrigalists you will find many madrigals by Morley entitled 'ballett' and **canzonet** (the latter comes from the Italian *canzonetta*, a 'little song', and is in a style similar to the ballett but without the 'fa-la-la' refrain).

John Farmer was a minor composer of the period, but his humorous pastoral madrigal 'Fair Phyllis' exhibits many of the features already mentioned: listen to it on Track 6 and see how many of these features you can spot.

[101]

Here are the words of Farmer's madrigal divided into lines according to their musical treatment (lines 1–2 are repeated, as are lines 3–8):

1. Fair Phyllis I saw sitting all alone,
2. Feeding her flock near to the mountainside.
3. The shepherds knew not whither she was gone,
4. But after her lover Amyntas hied.
5. Up and down he wandered
6. Whilst she was missing;
7. When he found her,
8. O then they fell akissing.

(a) How does Farmer illustrate the loneliness of Phyllis in line 1?

(b) How does the texture of line 2 differ from that of line 3?

(c) How is the flight of Amyntas and the shepherds suggested in line 4?

(d) Describe the bass part that underpins Amyntas's wanderings in line 5.

(e) Describe the rhythms of the last line ('O then they fell akissing').

(f) Describe the tonality of the whole madrigal.

Variations

William Byrd was a supremely versatile musical genius who wrote copiously in nearly all of the contemporary genres and forms. Not least amongst his achievements was his establishment of a school of harpsichord composers now known as the **English Virginalists** (the virginal, or 'pair of virginals' was a small harpsichord which was probably not named after Elizabeth I!). Perhaps his most significant keyboard works were variations, many of them based upon popular songs and dances of the time. In these he influenced a train of composers which led from England through Holland and North Germany eventually to J. S. Bach himself.

An essential element in dance music is clearly defined metre. The subtle rhythmic complexities of sacred vocal polyphony are clearly out of place, so dances of the period tended to be more homophonic, with clear-cut phrasing, most often in four- or eight-bar groups. One factor which determines metre is **harmonic rhythm**: a change of chord tends to produce an accented beat. Listen to the first eight bars of Byrd's variations on 'Will you walk the woods so wild' as you follow the music below:

Track 7

Byrd: 'Will you walk the woods so wild' (theme)

The swinging $\frac{6}{4}$ rhythms of the tune in the treble are supported by a simple accompaniment which only briefly becomes melodically interesting in the bass of bars 5–7. The eight-bar tune divides into two four-bar phrases (AA¹), or four two-bar phrases (ABAC). This regularity is emphasized by the harmonic rhythm:

| F | F | G | G | F | B♭ F | Gm Am D | G ‖ |

Regular two- and four-bar phrasing and harmonic rhythms which begin slowly and speed up to the cadence will be encountered again in the music of the Classical era—but not with these chord progressions. Is the music in F or G? Or is it modal? In fact, Byrd was writing at a time when individual notes in the modal scales were being modified as part of a process which led to the pre-eminence of the major–minor tonal system after 1600. Here the note B is flattened when it descends to A, and the note F is sharpened as it ascends to G at the cadences. Byrd was in the happy position of being able to use whatever features he liked from both modality and the newly emergent major–minor tonality, without being restricted by the conventions of either. The best we could probably do in rational terms is to describe the music as being based upon an inflected scale (like the two forms of the 'melodic minor') consisting of the following notes:

Does that remind you of a blues scale? There's nothing new under the sun!

Now listen to the whole of Track 7. In the eight-bar variation after the music printed on page 102 the tune is repeated up an octave with just one small rhythmic change—can you spot it? The variations are mainly confined to the bass. This is now of more melodic interest, beginning with an arch-shaped figure which is treated sequentially in the first four bars, followed by a more or less continuous 'walking bass' in crotchets in the second phrase. Did you spot the rhythmic change in the tune? It occurred in the fourth bar where syncopation was caused by taking the G off the beat. Listen carefully and you will hear that Byrd immediately imitates the resulting figure at the start of the 'walking bass'.

In the third set of eight bars the almost unaltered tune appears at the original pitch, but now in the 'alto' with a new part above. In this variation the harmony is even more basic than before: a simple alternation of F and G chords with a perfect cadence in G tacked on to the end. Listen to some reggae for similar alternations of root position chords a step apart and remember that Byrd was writing variations upon the Elizabethan equivalent of a pop song. This method of leaving the original melody virtually unchanged but varying the accompanying parts is just one technique of variation. We will encounter many others.

 Tracks 7 and 8

========================== *Test 77* ==========================

Listen again to the melody and harmony of the first eight bars of 'Will you walk the woods so wild' on Track 7 and follow the music printed on page 102. Then listen to the three variations upon this tune on Track 8.

(a) In the first of the three variations on Track 8 the tune is heard almost unaltered at its original pitch. How does Byrd vary the accompaniment?

(b) In the second of these variations the tune is heard transposed up an octave. How does Byrd vary the accompaniment?

(c) In the third of these variations the tune is not heard at all. What element from the original setting, printed on page 102, is retained in this variation?

(d) What contrapuntal device does Byrd use in this third variation?

Music of the Baroque Era

At the start of the previous chapter we referred to the radically new musical style which emerged in Italy around the year 1600. Although scholars will quibble, for our purposes it is true that at this time the foundations were laid for styles and techniques which developed remarkably consistently throughout the following 150 years in a period now known as the Baroque era.

Towards the turn of the century opera was invented and, along with it, accompanied monody called recitative. This had an important bearing upon musical style in general, for the idea of a solo line accompanied by just a bass with one or more instruments providing harmonic filling (continuo instruments) implied a new approach to composition. Instead of the flexible horizontal lines of Renaissance polyphony there now emerged the idea of a progression of chords over a bass line, supporting a solo melody that was polarized from the bass and designed to be the focus of interest. Harmonies became more and more tonal during the 17th century, so that certain chords (the primary triads) predominated and helped determine the tonality of music which modulated freely between related keys with many obvious cadence points.

Homophony became the norm rather than the exception, and, where there was counterpoint, it grew out of tonal harmony rather than the harmony being a by-product of the interaction of polyphonic lines (as was so often the case in the Renaissance). Rhythms were now governed by the prevailing metre and were often dance-like, even in liturgical music.

In the Renaissance, instrumental ensemble music was often a simple transcription of vocal music, but now a process that had begun before 1600 came to fruition: music for instruments became more and more idiomatic so that defined styles for keyboard, strings and wind began to emerge. This in turn sparked off the new *concertato* style in which dissimilar groups of instruments and voices were combined and contrasted. This began with church music, where motets in the new style were often called **Sacred Concertos**, and eventually led to the emergence of the Baroque instrumental concerto.

Canzonas, Continuo and Cori Spezzati

Nearly all these new stylistic features are apparent in the great Christmas motet 'Quem vidistis pastores' by Giovanni Gabrieli (c.1555-1612), published in the second volume of his 'Sacred Symphonies' in 1615. Although **polychoral** music for two or more choirs *(cori spezzati)* was quite common in the 16th century, the technique was developed to its limits in St Mark's basilica in Venice when independent choirs of instruments were added to the vocal choirs.

In this motet there are two three-voice vocal choirs (ATBar and TTBar) and two four-voice instrumental choirs, both consisting of a cornetto (a wooden trumpet) and three trombones. A *basso per l'organo* supports these groups continually throughout the entire motet (hence the names used later in the Baroque era for a bass part with figures to indicate the improvised harmony: *basso continuo* or 'thorough bass'). In the extracts from 'Quem vidistis' on Tracks 9–11, the *basso per l'organo* is realized by a continuo group consisting of a cello, a violone, a theorbo (a large bass lute) and a chamber organ.

Canzona means a song—see the description of the canzonetta as a type of madrigal on page 101—but the term was also applied to instrumental works of the Renaissance which were transcriptions of French *chansons*. These part-songs were simpler, more homophonic and more dance-like than most true madrigals, and they proved to be as effective on instruments as on voices.

By the turn of the century the ensemble canzona had, like its counterpart for the keyboard, become an idiomatic instrumental work independent of its vocal origins. Andrea Gabrieli and his nephew Giovanni Gabrieli wrote dozens of canzonas, in Giovanni's case often scored for large ensembles in up to 22 parts.

Composers were not always consistent in their titles and the Sinfonia with which 'Quem vidistis pastores' begins (Track 9) is, despite its title, a polychoral canzona for two brass choirs and continuo. Like most canzonas it falls into several fairly well-defined sections, each with its own characteristic motif and texture. The function of the continuo as homophonic support for the melody is clearest in the purely solo sections, as you can hear in the two short extracts on Track 10. The whole motet builds to a magnificent *Alleluia* in which Gabrieli deploys all 14 parts of the four choirs of instruments and voices (Track 11).

Tracks 9–11

Test 78

(a) Listen to the Sinfonia from 'Quem vidistis pastores' on Track 9.

  (i) The music below is the opening cornetto melody (showing the double dotting and cadential ornamentation used in the recorded performance). How does the part for the other cornetto relate to this?

  (ii) Describe the rhythms of the two short sections following this melody.

  (iii) The final section of this extract differs radically from the first three sections. Describe the rhythms and the texture of this last section.

  (iv) Describe the harmonic progression at the end of all four sections.

(b) Listen to the two solo sections from 'Quem vidistis pastores' on Track 10.

  (i) Name the three continuo instruments.

  (ii) In the first short extract, the words *Mariam et Joseph* ('Mary and Joseph') are repeated. How does the second of these two phrases relate to the first and with what sort of cadence do both phrases both end?

  (iii) The second short extract is a setting of the words *stratos supplices* ('prostrate in supplication'). Describe two features of the melodic line on the twice repeated word *supplices*.

(c) Listen to the two choral sections from 'Quem vidistis pastores' on Track 11.

  (i) The first extract begins with the words *O, O magnum mysterium* ('O great mystery'). What voices or instruments are heard in the uppermost parts of the texture at the start?

  (ii) In this same extract the text is repeated. Describe two ways in which the music for the repetition of the text differs from the original setting.

  (iii) In this same extract, describe the final chords of both phrases in relation to the prevailing tonality.

  (iv) In this same extract, what pungent harmonic effect is produced by the chord at the end of the first phrase together with the first chord of the second phrase?

  (v) In the second extract (*Alleluia*) a passage in triple time is followed by a passage in duple time. Describe the textures of both of these passages.

  (vi) Which two of the following chords are used most frequently in the triple time section:
    I, II, III, IV, V, VI, VII ?

  (vii) Describe two ways in which the composer creates striking effects of dissonance in the duple-time passage.

[105]

Learned Counterpoint

It must not be thought that the invention of opera, recitative and the *basso continuo* meant the death of counterpoint. There were some reactionary composers (and revolutionary composers in reactionary mode, like Monteverdi) who continued to write a rather stiffly academic version of Palestrinian polyphony. But composers were well aware of the differences between the two styles. They called the pastiche of 16th-century style the *stile antico* (the 'antique style') and the new music the *stile moderno* (the 'modern style'). Monteverdi specifically referred to the former as the *prima prattica* ('first practice') and to the latter as the *seconda prattica* ('second practice').

The Florentine *Camerata* was a group of humanists who thought that they could re-create Greek drama. In fact, their lack of success led them to invent opera. Similarly misconceived attempts to resurrect Palestrina were unsuccessful, but the study of counterpoint helped to ensure the continued development of the **ricercar**. Just as the canzona owes it origins to the *chanson*, so the ricercar started life as a transcription of the motet. Thus, although a close relative of the canzona, it was much more serious and contrapuntal. The Italian verb *ricercare* means 'to seek out'. In the musical ricercar the composer 'seeks out' all possible ways of treating a few motifs in contrapuntal permutations. Very often the initial motif was a four-note tag which was given to students as the basis for various counterpoint exercises.

Girolamo Frescobaldi (1583–1643), organist of St. Peter's in Rome, was one of the most influential keyboard composers of the early 17th century: much can be learnt about contrapuntal techniques by listening to the extract from one of his *ricercari* which has here been arranged for oboe, horn, bassoon and trombone on Track 12. A skeleton score of this extract is printed below. Follow it as you listen to the music. The score shows only parts of the four instrumental lines at any one time, apart from bars 1–4 which are complete.

The four note tag 'A–G–B flat–A' is the subject and is marked with a solid bracket every time it occurs. It is first heard on its own in the oboe. It is then imitated by the horn, while the oboe plays a new melody against it. This is called the counter-subject and is marked with a pecked bracket.

 Track 12

Frescobaldi: Ricercar Quarto, sopra mi, re, fa, mi

The bassoon has the subject next, but when the trombone comes in it arrives two beats earlier than expected: this overlapping of entries is known as **stretto** (Italian for 'squeezed together'), and you can hear the same device being used with the counter-subject in bars 13–14. In bars 14–15 the bassoon **inverts** the subject (i.e., every interval changes direction: the *falling* second of the subject now becomes a *rising* second, the *rising* third becomes a *falling* third, etc.) The original subject enters on the trombone in stretto against this inversion (bar 15).

A new chromatic motif (marked with a wavy line) is heard on the oboe in bars 28–29 and is imitated after only two beats by its inverted form in the horn. In bar 32 a diatonic version of this motif and its inversion is heard in stretto. In bar 30 you should hear an imposing entry of the subject in the bassoon. It lasts until bar 33 with every one of the four notes now lasting a bar, a splendid example of **augmentation**. If you found it difficult to spot all of these details do not worry. If you listen often enough you will eventually hear all of the detail. In an examination it would be unlikely that you would be asked questions on an extract which packs so many features into such a short passage.

Some of Frescobaldi's ricercars are **monothematic**, i.e., there is only one theme, with all of the music derived from melodic figures in the subject and counter-subject. These are virtually fugues. By the time of Bach, fugal writing had become the most complex compositional technique of the age.

It is usual to refer to the linear parts in a **fugue** as 'voices', and to identify them with the names soprano, alto, tenor and bass, even when the fugue is

[107]

written for instruments. Fugue is not a well-defined structure like binary form—more a texture and a mode of musical thinking. However, nearly all fugues begin with an exposition in which the subject is first heard on its own, followed by an imitation in another voice (the 'answer') pitched on the dominant—either a fifth higher or a fourth lower. Despite its different name, it is important to realize that the answer is essentially the same as the subject, except for any modification or extension required by its new pitch level.

While the answer is being played, the first voice continues with the counter-subject. After this a third voice enters with the subject at the original pitch while the second voice continues with the counter-subject and the first voice takes a free contrapuntal part (although described as a 'free part', the music is often based on material from the subject or counter-subject). This process continues until all of the voices have announced the subject or answer:

Soprano						Answer
Alto	Subject	CS	Free part			
Tenor		Answer	CS	Free part		
Bass			Subject	CS	Free part	

The music below shows the subject, answer and counter-subject of an organ fugue by Bach. Follow this as you listen to Track 13 which is a recording of the whole fugal exposition.

You will hear the subject in the alto followed by the answer in the tenor as shown above. At the point where the printed music stops the subject enters in the bass. After a bar when neither subject nor answer is heard, the final voice (the soprano) enters with the answer. This pattern is shown in graphic form, above. Since this is a four-voice fugue, the end of the answer in the soprano marks the end of the fugal exposition (the extract on Track 13 continues to the first perfect cadence after the soprano entry).

What happens after the fugal exposition varies from fugue to fugue. Sometimes the subject or answer appears in almost every bar (like the fugue in C Major from Book 1 of Bach's 48 Preludes and Fugues). Sometimes there are clearly defined episodes in which, although the material derives from the exposition, neither the subject nor answer is heard (like the Fugue in C minor from the same book of the '48'). There will often be entries of the subject in related keys and the composer may use some or all of the contrapuntal devices heard in the ricercar by Frescobaldi—stretto, inversion and augmentation—as well as **diminution** (the opposite of augmentation—note durations are shortened rather than lengthened). In the Bach organ fugue a wealth of contrapuntal techniques is explored and some of them are featured on Tracks 14–16.

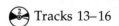 Tracks 13–16

=============================== *Test 79* ===============================

(a) Listen again to the fugal exposition on Track 13 and compare this with the extract on Track 14. How does Bach treat the subject on Track 14?

(b) We said that the organ fugue by Bach was for four voices. This was a half-truth for, after many bars and when the fugue seems to be approaching its coda, Bach brings in the pedals for the first time. Listen to the entry on Track 15: how does Bach treat the subject on the pedals in this extract?

(c) Listen to Track 16.

   (i) How does the subject in the pedals on this track differ from the subject you described in your answer to question (b)?

   (ii) There are four detached chords in this extract: which of the following terms most precisely describes them?

   dissonant   consonant   chromatic
   diatonic   diminished sevenths   dominant sevenths

   (iii) With what sort of cadence does this extract end?

Suites and Sonatas

The term 'suite' comes from the French verb *suivre* ('to follow') and refers, in musical terms, to a set of short movements intended to follow one another in performance. In the Baroque period, all of the movements were in the same key (although changes in mode between tonic major and tonic minor were used) and most, if not all, of the movements were based on dances.

The idea of linking contrasting dances dates from the late Renaissance, where the pairing of the slow pavane with the sprightly galliard is found in countless collections of keyboard and lute music. As dance fashions changed, these were replaced by the allemande and courante in the early 17th century, and were joined by the sarabande and gigue as early as 1650. These four dances, and in this order, formed the template for many solo suites until the decline of the genre at the end of the Baroque era. Each dance was most often in binary form and was characterized by it own distinctive rhythm pattern and texture:

Allemande. Moderately slow quadruple time with phrases generally beginning on an anacrusis. It often functions as a serious contrapuntal prelude to the lighter dances of the suite (see page 41, CD 1 Track 50).

Courante. A fairly fast triple time having phrases often beginning with an anacrusis. Hemiolas were common at the main cadences. The melody features rapid passage-work (the French word *courant* means 'running'), and supporting textures were often simple and functional (see page 46, CD 1 Track 55).

Sarabande. Slow triple time, without an anacrusis. The second beat of the bar is freqently emphasized by making it a dotted note. Largely homophonic texture (see page 111, CD 2 Track 17).

Gigue. A lively dance (the French title is related to the English 'jig') in compound time, although not always notated as such. Phrases often, but not invariably, begin with an anacrusis. In Italy, a simple melodic style with functional bass was used, but elsewhere two- and three-part fugal textures were preferred: in these, it became a convention to invert the opening theme at the start of the second half of the binary form.

New dances joined the suite in the 18th century, although usually without ousting the established allemande–courante–sarabande–gigue pattern. These, known as *galanterien* (light or 'stylish' pieces), were usually placed between the sarabande and gigue, and include the minuet, bourrée, gavotte and rondeau—an example of a gavotte is given on page 111 and a rondeau from an *Ordre* (a French name for suite) by Couperin appears in *Sound Matters* (No. 17). Further expansion of the suite came with the practice of providing dances with one or more variations (called *doubles*) and sometimes by prefacing the whole collection of dances with a prelude (as in Bach's 'English' suites) or other introductory movement—the opening movements of Bach's harpsichord partitas (the German word for suites) include a sinfonia, a fantasia and a toccata.

Most suites were written for the harpsichord, lute or a solo melody instrument, such as flute or violin (with or without accompaniment). Well-known examples of the orchestral suite, however, include Handel's 'Music for the Royal Fireworks' and 'Water Music', and the four orchestral suites of Bach. These tend to make more use of the *galanterien* and have fewer of the traditional dances of the suite. Many begin with an impressive introductory movement—typically, a **French overture**, with its slow, double-dotted opening and its fast, fugal sequel.

Dances were not confined to the suite: they were also used for some of the movements in another important Baroque instrumental genre—the sonata.

As we observed earlier, in the past some musical terms did not always have their precise modern meanings. Giovanni Gabrieli gave the name 'sonata' to some of his graver canzonas, and these works could involve any number of parts from three violins and continuo to massive polychoral forces. But in the middle of the 17th century Giovanni Legrenzi (1626–1690) helped crystallize a type of sonata which was distinct from the canzona and which became common throughout the rest of the Baroque era. This is known as the **trio sonata**, but the name is confusing. Although often written on three staves it requires four performers: two melody instruments (most often violins) and a continuo of cello and keyboard (or more rarely a member of the lute family such as the theorbo).

There were two types of trio sonata, the *sonata da chiesa* ('church sonata') with several serious movements and organ continuo, and the *sonata da camera* ('chamber sonata') with several lighter movements (often dances) and harpsichord continuo. After about 1700 it is less easy to distinguish between the two types and the trio sonata began to give way in popularity to the **solo sonata**. This is another confusing name, since most solo sonatas of this period require three performers—a melody instrument (such as recorder, flute, oboe or violin—composers with an eye to maximizing sales often claimed their work was suitable for any of these on the title page) and a continuo of keyboard and cello. For all practical purposes, the solo sonata can be regarded as a trio sonata with only one melody instrument: both genres share similar forms and techniques.

The most famous composer of trio sonatas in the late 17th century was Arcangelo Corelli (1653–1713), whose works were published all over Europe. He was admired for his melodic gifts, for conservative but idiomatic string writing, for a firm grasp of tonality (including unambiguous modulations to related keys, often achieved by harmonic sequences such as the 'cycle of fifths') and for balanced phrase structures. All of these features are evident in the extract from one of his chamber sonatas on Track 17. This is a sarabande and it features, in bar 19, the 'Corelli clash'—a delightful dissonance caused by aligning the late resolution of the leading note in the first violin with the anticipation of the tonic in the second violin.

The sarabande is in the **binary form** adopted for most dance movements in the Baroque era. This is a two-part structure in which the A section ends with a decisive cadence in either the tonic or a related key, and the B section modulates through one or more related keys back to the tonic: both sections could be repeated with improvised ornamentation (the repeats are omitted in our extract).

If you listen carefully you will be able to hear that the two violins interweave in the upper register while the cello plays at least an octave below them. This **polarized texture**, typical of the Baroque era, was made possible by the harmonic filling provided by the keyboard. Notice that the rhythmic motifs shown in the music below are used in various guises throughout the movement. This mono-thematicism is another hallmark of Baroque style.

Track 17

Test 80

This sarabande falls into four distinct eight-bar phrases, as shown in the skeleton score on page 111. The first of these is the A section of the binary structure, while phrases 2–4 form the B section (neither section is repeated on Track 17).

(a) Describe the disruption of the triple metre which occurs at the end of both phrase 1 and phrase 4.

(b) In what key and with what sort of cadence does phrase 1 end?

(c) What melodic device is used in both bars 9–12 and bars 21–24?

(d) In what key does phrase 2 end?

(e) In phrase 4, how do bars 29–32 relate to bars 25–28?

(f) The 'Corelli clash' in bar 19 was described above. Give the bar number of one other example of this effect.

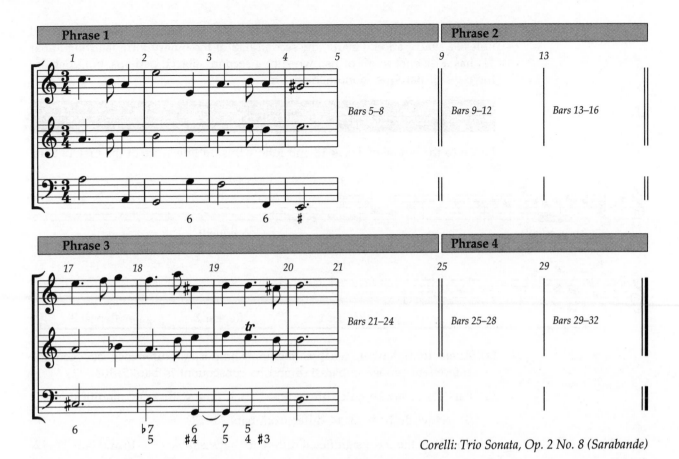

Corelli: Trio Sonata, Op. 2 No. 8 (Sarabande)

The *Style Galant*

Towards the end of the Baroque era a simpler style emerged in which melodies consisted of an antecedent (a phrase like a question, sometimes cadencing on the dominant), followed by a consequent (a phrase like an answer, often cadencing on the tonic). These were accompanied by a simple non-melodic bass part, or by chords (broken chords in the case of much keyboard music).

This style can frequently be found in the 'optional' dances of Baroque suites (the *galanterien*) and was the beginning of the *galant* style of composers such as Sammartini (c.1700–1775) and J. C. Bach (1735–1782). This transitional style was, in turn, the precursor of the true Classical style of Mozart and Haydn.

On page 109 we mentioned how the composers added a short set of variations to some of the dances of the suite, particularly the *galanterien*. These *doubles* (or 'divisions' as they were more logically known in England) retained the phrase structure, tonal scheme and harmonic progressions of the main dance, but used progressively more elaborate figuration in each variation. Sometimes the tune was retained over a busier accompaniment, sometimes the tune can be traced in a garland of passage-work, and sometimes the tune is absent altogether.

🎵 Tracks 18–21

Some of the features of the emergent *galant* style, as well as divisions, can be heard in the *Gavotta con variazione* from a sonata written in 1742 by G. B. Martini (1706–1784). Martini, although not a major composer, is famous as the teacher of such composers as J. C. Bach and Mozart.

Pointers towards the Classical style can be seen even in the short and incomplete passage on page 112. These include an opening motif whose main objective is to define the key through the use of tonic, dominant and leading note—think of the turn printed as an ornament, as was often the case in the 18th century:

The music divides into clearly perceptible, regular two-bar groups—common in the more modern dances of the *galanterien*, although rare in older Baroque dances, and another feature that presages the Classical style. The rhythm is plain and four-square: simple divisions of the pulse, with no dotted notes, tied notes or syncopation. Finally, the second half of the binary form (starting at bar 11) has a distinct motif of its own—not a second subject, perhaps, but gone are the days of Baroque monothematicism.

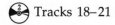 Tracks 18–21

Listen to the whole of Track 18 and follow this outline score of the first 18 bars.

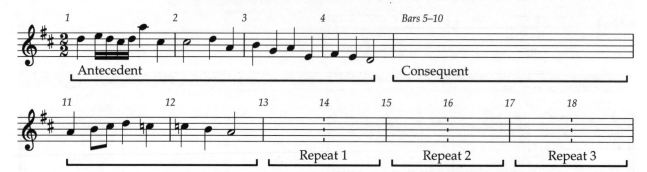

(a) Apart from length, what is the most important difference between the antecedent phrase in bars 1–4 and its consequent in bars 5–10?

(b) Bars 11–12 are repeated three times, each time with some modifications.

    (i) How do bars 13–14 differ from bars 11–12?

    (ii) State the most significant difference between bars 15–16 and bars 11–12.

    (iii) What melodic ornament can you hear at the start of bar 18?

(c) How does the texture of the music in bars 19–28 (not printed) differ from the rest of the music on Track 18?

(d) Describe the three cadence chords implied by the two-part writing at the end of this track. What ornament is played on the penultimate beat?

(e) Listen to the music on Track 19. Describe the way in which Martini has varied the melody of bars 1–10, some of which is printed above.

(f) Listen to the music on Track 20. Describe the way in which Martini has varied the original accompaniment of bars 1–10.

(g) Listen to the music on Track 21. In this variation, what has been retained from the original theme in bars 1–10 and what has been omitted?

Baroque Concertos   It has already been observed that the *stile concertato* of composers like Giovanni Gabrieli led to the purely instrumental concerto. Corelli wrote a set of concertos in which a trio sonata combination of two violins, cello and keyboard (the *concertino*) is contrasted and combined with a larger string orchestra (the *ripieno* or *concerto grosso*) which includes violas and double bass. The term **concerto grosso** was also applied to the work as a whole, and as good a translation as any is the title which Handel gave to his Op. 6—the 'Grand Concertos'.

In Corelli's concerti grossi there is no contrasting material for the two groups, the concertino play throughout all of the movements while the ripieno simply double or reinforce them intermittently, producing the **terraced dynamics** which are such a feature of Baroque style. In some movements the ripieno double the concertino throughout, so that the concertato principle only emerges as a contrast between movements. Handel's Op. 6 have many of the same features.

Antonio Vivaldi (1678–1741) assimilated Corelli's secure handling of tonality and textural contrast, but in some of his concertos he sought to differentiate the music for the ripieno from that for the soloist or concertino, thus increasing the element of contrast. Well-known and extreme examples are the four programmatic solo violin concertos known as 'The Four Seasons'. In these the soloist indulges in virtuoso passage-work which contrasts vividly with the lively but relatively simple music assigned to the ripieno.

In many of his allegro movements Vivaldi brought to perfection the **ritornello** principle. The term *ritornello* ('little return') was applied to the instrumental sections in 17th- and 18th-century vocal works, but Vivaldi, in his concertos, raised it to a structural principle similar to rondo form. In ritornello form, a tutti section is first heard at the start of the movement, in the tonic key. It then recurs, in full or in part, at intervals throughout the rest of the movement. These 'little returns' are often in related keys (although the last is invariably in the tonic) and are separated by solo episodes, the material of which may or may not derive from motifs in the ritornello. Bach's concertos tend to follow Vivaldi's style and structure: indeed, he transcribed several of them for organ and one for four harpsichords with strings.

The music below is the ripieno violin part of the first ritornello of an allegro from a concerto grosso by Vivaldi: the first 41 bars of this movement are recorded on Track 22. Like Corelli (but unusually for Vivaldi) the concertino is scored for trio sonata forces, but the ripieno has, in addition to the normal Baroque string forces, a part for second violas.

Vivaldi: Concerto Grosso Op. 3 No. 2 (first Allegro)

 Track 22

Test 82

Listen to the extract on Track 22 and follow the violin part from it printed above. The extract consists of five clearly defined sections:

| (a) **Tutti** | (b) **Soli** | (c) **Tutti** | (d) **Soli** | (e) **Tutti** |

There is a question on each of these five sections, (a) to (e), below:

(a) In the first tutti, compare the outer parts of bars 4–6 with the outer parts of bars 7–9.

(b) In the first solo episode:

    (i) Which instruments are playing?

    (ii) How do their parts relate to each other?

    (iii) What melodic device used in the ritornello is also used here?

(c) In the second tutti, what from the first tutti has been omitted?

(d) In the second solo episode:

    (i) What elements are similar to the first episode?

    (ii) How does the beginning of the cello melody relate to the violin melody?

    (iii) Describe two features of the harmonic progression in the continuo.

(e) How does the third tutti differ from the first?

Variations

In 'Will you walk the woods so wild' (page 102, Tracks 7–8) all but one of the variations left the tune almost unchanged against varying accompaniments. In contrast, Byrd wrote other keyboard works with the title 'A Grownde' in which he left the bass almost unchanged against varying tunes. This variation technique, **ground bass**, became one of the most popular forms of the 17th century, particularly in England.

Henry Purcell (1659–1695) is particularly noted for his grounds. In some cases, most famously Dido's Lament (from his opera *Dido and Aeneas*), a clearly defined bass is repeated unchanged throughout an entire song. The melody is specially designed to overlap the regular cadences of the bass so that there is a subtle tension between the two, often leading to a carefully prepared climax. In other grounds the bass was sometimes modified to reflect particular imagery in the text or, more radically, to lead to a contrasting key in which the ground was resumed at a different pitch (such as Dido's earlier song in *Dido and Aeneas*, 'Ah! Belinda'). Although Purcell admitted his indebtedness to contemporary continental composers such as Corelli, his fusion of Italian tonal harmony, the dotted rhythms of French dance music and a freedom of dissonance treatment which harks back to earlier English composers led to a style which is unmistakably his alone.

The extract from 'The Plaint' on Track 23 is taken from Purcell's semi-opera, *The Fairy Queen*. In this, the ground bass printed below is heard five times, but in only two of the repetitions do the melodic phrases end at the same point as the bass cadences. Characteristic features of Purcell's style include the melodic chromaticism of the bass, the use of rests to suggest sighs, frequent telling appoggiaturas, suspensions and accented passing-notes, diminished intervals in the melody, instrumental echoes of vocal phrases, modification of the ground and 'French' dotted rhythms. Notice how the rhythmic variety of the vocal part typifies Purcell's justly famous expressive treatment of the English language.

Track 23

═══════════════════ *Test 83* ═══════════════════

The ground bass of 'The Plaint' is printed below at the pitch at which it is performed on Track 23. It is heard five times in this extract. Each of the questions below is related to one of these repetitions.

The text (with many a repetition) reads: 'O let me weep, for ever weep!'.

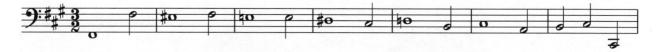

(a) What type of voice is singing in this extract?

(b) In the vocal melody above the first playing of the ground:

    (i)   on which two words can you hear a suspension and its resolution,

    (ii) between which two words can you hear a diminished interval?

(c) How does Purcell avoid a break in the musical flow at the cadence which marks the end of the first playing of the ground and the beginning of the second?

(d) How does the third playing of the ground differ from the first playing:

    (i)   in the bass?

    (ii) in the vocal melody?

(e) Describe the relationship between the singer's melodies and those of the obbligato violinist above the fourth playing of the ground.

(f) How does the violin melody above the final playing of the ground differ from any other melodies in this extract?

Johann Sebastian Bach (1685–1750) brought Baroque variation techniques to a peak of perfection, as he did with most other forms and genres except opera. Perhaps his best-known set is the 'Goldberg' Variations in which the harmonic framework and phrase structure of the initial aria is maintained in each of the 30 free and canonic variations. But variation techniques were also used in a genre which was central to Bach's life as a church musician: the organ chorale or **chorale prelude**. Just as Catholic composers of the 16th century made use of plainsong melodies in their Masses, so Protestant composers in the 17th and early 18th centuries made use of Lutheran hymn tunes (many of which were, in fact, metrical versions of plainsong with new German words to replace the Latin texts). These composers developed a wealth of variation techniques: in some preludes the opening phrase of the chorale was fashioned into the subject of a fugato which preceded the entry of the chorale melody; in others the melody was elaborately ornamented above a freely contrapuntal accompaniment, and in yet another type the chorale was treated in canon.

On Track 24 you can hear an extract from one of Bach's organ preludes. First, a melody in the alto register occurs, accompanied by a simple walking bass played on the pedals. The chorale melody ('Wachet auf') then enters, in a version with only slight ornamentation, played on a reed stop in the tenor register. This is the **cantus firmus** and the opening melody and bass are adapted to fit against it, making a three-part texture similar to that of a trio sonata, but without the harmonic filling of a continuo part: as in his trio sonatas for organ (CD 1, Track 51), Bach ensures that his harmonies are clear and complete as they stand.

🔊 Track 24

====================== *Test 84* ======================

Listen to Track 24 as you follow the walking bass of the first 12 bars printed below. The melody above this bass falls into four two-bar phrases and one four-bar phrase: these are indicated as phrases 1–5 by the brackets under the bass part.

Bach, Organ Prelude 'Wachet auf', bass of bars 1–12

(a) In which phrase of the melody can you hear a one-bar sequence?

(b) Which phrase is repeated?

(c) (i) What sort of melodic ornament can you hear at the end of each of the first three phrases?

    (ii) What is the difference between the form of this ornament at the end of the second phrase and the form it takes at the end of the third phrase?

(d) How is the opening alto melody altered to fit the cantus firmus when it enters in bar 13?

[115]

Recitatives, Arias, Chorales and Choruses

The recitative of early opera grew out of a desire to grant supremacy to the text, with music as its handmaid. A single vocal melody followed the rhythms of the words and illustrated the emotional significance of them by appropriate contours, e.g., smooth, conjunct lines for peaceful sentiments and jagged disjunct lines for warlike sentiments. Harmony was relegated to a supporting rôle, and was provided by a simple bass line, played on an instrument such as a cello, with improvised harmonic filling played on the lute, harpsichord or organ.

By the beginning of the 18th century these ideals still applied, but there was much more systematic tonal planning. Innocence could be expressed by consonant diatonic harmonies moving to related keys, while, at the other extreme, anguish could be suggested by strong dissonance, chromaticism, diminished intervals in the melody and unexpected modulations to unrelated keys.

In opera, and related genres such as oratorio and cantata, the dramatic action was conveyed by the fast-moving *recitativo secco* ('dry recitative') in which the voice was accompanied by continuo instruments only. Where the composer wished particularly to highlight the drama he might resort to the *recitativo accompagnato* ('accompanied recitative') in which strings or other orchestral instruments formed the background. Thus, in Bach's St Matthew Passion, the narrative is carried swiftly in *secco* recitative while Christ's own words are surrounded by a halo of string chords. Extracts from both *secco* and accompanied recitative by Bach can be heard on Track 25.

The solo **aria** developed later than the recitative, and, by the beginning of the 18th century, they had become the antithesis of one another. Where the recitative was non-metrical, the aria was metrical; where the recitative swiftly conveyed the drama, the aria was a reflection upon that drama by one of the characters; where moods could change rapidly in the recitative, the aria often represented just one unified 'affection' (mood) expressed through a mono-thematic structure relying upon a limited number of stereotyped melodic motifs.

In the hands of late Baroque composers the aria had become a highly formal structure known as the *da capo* **aria**. This ternary form song consists of a 'closed' A section which begins and ends in the same key (unlike the 'open' A section of binary form, which modulates to a new key). This is followed by a B section in a contrasting key or keys (in which the main affection was viewed in a different light, although often using the same motifs in a modified form). The A section was then repeated from the beginning (*da capo* = from the head or the top), but usually with improvised and often spectacular vocal ornamentation.

More elaborate *da capo* arias in the late Baroque period were sometimes cast in ritornello form, the singer taking a similar rôle to the soloist in a concerto movement and being accompanied by a concertino section of reduced orchestration while the tutti ensemble provides the usual ripieno sections. The repeat of the A section in these arias is often shown as *dal segno* ('from the sign'), with the 'sign' being placed at or near the initial vocal entry in order to remove or shorten the opening ritornello on its return.

There are three types of *da capo* aria, differentiated by the accompaniment used. A **continuo aria** is, not surprisingly, accompanied by just the continuo instruments. An **obbligato aria** has, in addition, one (or occasionally two) solo instruments that interact with the voice, providing echos, counterpoints and intervening ritornelli. The **concerted aria** has full orchestral accompaniment (at least strings and continuo, and sometimes wind instruments as well) and almost always uses ritornello form.

Composers were thus clearly aware of the need to vary the basic plan of the *da capo* aria in order to prevent it becoming too much of a predictable formula. In the hands of composers such as Handel (in his Italian operas and English oratorios) and Bach (in his cantatas and passions) the basic scheme was often modified still further to accommodate features such as interjections from the chorus or other singers, or passionate accompanied recitative where the emotional message of the text demanded it. An extract from a straightforward example of a *da capo* aria by Handel that uses ritornello form can be heard on Track 26.

The chorus virtually disappeared from Italian opera in the late Baroque: Handel's few operatic choruses are simply ensembles for the assembled soloists. However, as the chorus declined in opera, so it rose to central importance in **oratorio**, helping to compensate for the lack of visual attraction. In Handel's oratorios and Bach's passions, the chorus both comments on the drama and participates in it, using a variety of musical techniques and forms that have previously been mentioned. Handel's greatest oratorio, *Messiah*, has examples of many of these—simple homophonic writing ('Since By Man Came Death'), homophonic choral writing with an elaborated accompaniment ('Worthy Is The Lamb'), antiphony ('Lift Up Your Heads'), fugue ('And With His Stripes We Are Healed'), fugue with independent accompaniment ('And He Shall Purify') and ritornello form ('And The Glory Of The Lord'). The choruses in elaborate orchestral settings of the Mass in the 18th century also draw on this wide range of compositional techniques, even though the liturgical texts do not offer the more dramatic possibilities of oratorio and passion settings.

In many cases, two or more of these techniques or forms are combined in the same chorus. Bach, in particular, excelled in building up complex and exciting textures which layer a number of elements on top of one another, crowning the whole edifice with a cantus firmus chorale melody, as shown below.

The importance of the Lutheran **chorale** in the liturgical music of Protestant Germany has already been mentioned. On Track 27 you can hear an extract from a relatively simple harmonization by Bach of a chorale melody by Philipp Nicolai (1556–1608). This same tune is the cantus firmus of the Chorale Prelude on 'Wachet auf' studied earlier. But Bach (with Handel) sums up the achievements of the whole Baroque era. So on Track 28 you can hear how Bach masterfully combines concerto style (the orchestral ritornellos and accompaniment to the chorale), the cantus firmus (the trebles doubled by horn) and fugal style (the lower three voices of the chorus) in one magnificent movement.

Track 25

Test 85

(a) What are the main differences between the two extracts on this track?

(b) The text of the first extract reads:

Er kommt, er kommt,	He comes, he comes,
der Bräutgam kommt!	the bridegroom comes!
Ihr Töchter Zions, kommt heraus,	You daughters of Zion, come out,
sein Ausgang eilet aus der Höhe	he hurries from on high
in euer Mutter Haus.	to your mother's house.

   (i)   How does Bach illustrate the meaning of the word 'high' *(Höhe)*?

   (ii) Upon what ornament does the tenor end (on the word *Haus*)?

   (iii) Name the cadence that follows this word *Haus*.

(c) The text of the second extract reads:

So geh herein zu mir	So come in with me,
du mir erwählte Braut!	you, my chosen bride!
Ich habe mich mit dir	I have long placed
von Ewigkeit vertraut.	my trust in you.
Dich will ich auf mein Herz,	I will set you upon my heart,
auf meinen Arm	upon my arm
gleich wie ein Siegel setzen	as a seal
und dein betrübtes Aug ergötzen.	and restore delight to you saddened eyes.

   (i)   With what type of ornament does each of the first two phrases end?

   (ii) Describe two ways in which Bach highlights the important word *Herz* ('heart').

   (iii) How is anguish suggested on the words *Betrübtes Aug* ('saddened eyes')?

Test 86

In this aria from the opera *Orlando*, by Handel, an orchestral introduction is followed by a contralto solo, the text of which refers to deeds of daring.

(a) What is the relationship between the orchestral introduction and the contralto part?

(b) (i) Describe the texture and tonality of the orchestral introduction.

    (ii) How does this introduction illustrate the warlike mood of the text?

(c) In the first section of the vocal melody (*Fammi combattere mostri e tifei*, etc.), how does Handel highlight the key words *combattere* (fight) and *valor* (courage) when these words are sung for the second time?

(d) How does the tonality of the second section of the vocal melody (*Muraglie abbattere disfare incanti*) differ from the first section?

(e) The first section returns at the end of this middle section. How do the first few bars of the repeated vocal solo differ from the same bars when the voice first entered at the beginning of the aria?

(f) Describe the orchestral interludes between the vocal solos.

(g) What is the form of the whole aria from which this extract has been taken?

Test 87

Listen again to Track 27 and compare the treble part of this chorale with the cantus firmus of the chorale prelude on Track 25.

(a) In phrase 1, *Gloria sei dir gesungen* ('Glory to you be sung'), in what voice and on which word can you hear the opening triadic melody sung in diminution?

(b) In phrase 2, *mit Menschen und englischen Zungen* ('with men's and angel's tongues'), in what voice and on which word can you hear two suspensions?

(c) In phrase 3, *mit Harfen und mit Zimpeln schon* ('with harps and even with cymbals'), in what voice and on which word(s) can you hear the flattened seventh of the scale immediately followed by the sharpened seventh?

Test 88

(a) This extract from a chorus by Bach begins with an orchestral introduction. It consist of three ideas: (i) a dotted rhythm figure, (ii) a melodic figure and (iii) a figure built upon rising scales.

    (i) Describe the scoring in the section based on a dotted noted figure.

    (ii) Describe the rhythms of the second section (violin and oboe solos).

    (iii) Describe the sustained, descending oboe melody above the ascending scales of the third section.

(b) How does the orchestral accompaniment around the cantus firmus of the chorale melody in the soprano part relate to other music in this extract?

(c) Describe the texture of the music for the lower voices under:

    (i) phrase 1 of the cantus firmus (*Wachet auf, ruft uns die Stimme*).

    (ii) phrase 2 of the cantus firmus (*der Wächter sehr hoch auf der Zinne*).

    (iii) the opening of phrase 3 of the cantus firmus (*wach auf*).

(d) Describe the structure of the whole extract.

Classical Music

You may have noticed that the later extracts in the last chapter, particularly the Handel and Martini, included much more memorable melodic material than the ricercar by Frescobaldi or the organ fugue by Bach. This is because the latter rely for their effect upon exhaustive explorations of the contrapuntal potential of very short motifs, while Handel and Martini are more concerned to express a particular mood as simply as possible by means of a melody-dominated texture with an unobtrusive, supporting accompaniment. This new approach heralds the dawn of the Classical style which, in its earliest phase, is variously labelled the 'pre-Classical', Rococo or *galant* style. It first emerged in opera (the Handel on Track 26 dates from 1733), but soon found expression in instrumental music. Giovanni Battista Sammartini (1700–1775), from whom Mozart learned much, was writing *galant* symphonies at about the same time as Handel was writing *Orlando*, and the Martini sonata on Tracks 18–21 was written in 1742. Compared to much Baroque music the chief features of the early Classical style are:

❑ simpler, more memorable melodies, often developed from short motifs by the use of obvious sequences and repetition,

❑ balanced two-, four- and eight-bar phrases, particularly of the antecedent–consequent variety, with regularly spaced cadences (**periodic phrasing**),

❑ elegant melodic decoration including frequent appoggiaturas on strong beats, chromatic passing-notes and conventional ornaments such as mordents, turns and cadential trills (it was the proliferation of ornamention that gave rise to the term Rococo, derived from *rocaille*—'rocky' or 'craggy'),

❑ simpler, diatonic structural harmony, with a slower rate of change which usually accelerated towards the Ic–V^7–I cadences (often 'feminine'),

❑ light, clear, homophonic textures (in keyboard music often consisting of just a melody plus a broken-chord accompaniment).

In the Baroque era, wind instruments had only occasionally been used in the orchestra. Oboes and bassoons sometimes doubled the strings or had long, linear solo parts, while other instruments were used mostly for special effects, such as trumpets and timpani in ceremonial music. By 1800, two each of flutes, oboes, clarinets, bassoons, horns, trumpets and timpani, with an enlarged string section to balance, was regarded as the optimum for a full orchestra. Opera and oratorio sometimes called for still more—piccolo, contra-bassoon, extra brass (especially trombones) and 'Turkish' percussion, all eventually finding their way into the choral works and symphonies of Beethoven. Such ensembles had no need for the harmonic support of a continuo, which dropped from fashion at the time the piano succeeded the harpsichord as the main keyboard instrument, around the 1770s. In chamber music, it was found that replacing the harpsichord in the trio sonata by a viola led to the much more homogeneous timbre of the string quartet—perhaps one of the most characteristic sounds of Classical music.

Opera

Many of the features of Classical style are apparent in the aria 'Dove sono' from the comic opera *Le nozze di Figaro*, by Wolfgang Amadeus Mozart (1756–1791), on Track 29. But great genius transcends convention. The two-bar sequential phrases of *Dove sono* and *i bei momenti* are linked by an oboe **obbligato** which also joins this opening to the second line of the text, to form an eight-bar antecedent. The consequent (*dove andaro i giuramenti*) begins with the same four bars as the antecedent, but its second half is lengthened by short sequences to form a six-bar phrase, making the consequent ten bars long. In the aria the Countess fondly remembers the sweetness of her life with the Count. But he is now unfaithful and deceitful. Those short sequences wonderfully suggest her pain as she thinks of his 'lying lips' (*quel labbro menzogner*). Mozart is famous for his ability to delineate characters and to awaken our sympathy for them by such subtle touches without disturbing the Classical sense of poise. His music keeps form and content in perfect balance. If this is true on the microscopic level of phrasing, it is equally true on the macroscopic level of the overall structure of the aria. Listen to all of Track 29 and you will discover that, like Handel's aria, it seems to be in ternary form (the sections are indicated against the text below), although the music more closely mirrors and enhances details of the text: but, when the A section returns, it is cut short by a heart-stopping pause on the dominant leading to a complete change of mood (section C below).

A	*Dove sono i bei momenti,*	Where are the blessed moments
	Di dolcezza e di piacer?	Of sweetness and pleasure?
	Dove andaro i giuramenti,	Where are the promises
	Di quel labbro menzogner?	Of those lying lips?
B	*Perchè mai, se in pianti e in pene*	Why, if in weeping and in pain,
	Per me tutto si cangiò	If for me everything has changed,
	La memoria di quel bene	Can I not banish the memory of that
	Dal mio sen non trapassò?	happiness from my breast?
A	*Dove sono i bei momenti,*	Where are the blessed moments
	Di dolcezza e di piacer?	Of sweetness and pleasure?
	Dove andaro i giuramenti,	Where are the promises
	Di quel labbro menzogner?	Of those lying lips?
C	*Ah, se almen la mia costanza*	Ah! if at least my constancy
	Nel languire amando ognor,	In everlasting longing and love
	Mi portasse una speranza.	Might give me hope
	Di cangiar l'ingrato cor!	Of changing that ungrateful heart!

 Track 29

Test 89

(a) The first section of Mozart's aria (A in the text above) is in C major. The second section (B in the text above) is preceded by an oboe solo in G major.

   (i)   In what key is the next oboe solo?

   (ii) Why does the key change in the first line of section B (*Perchè mai...*)?

(b) In section B there is a varied repeat of the setting of *La memoria di quel bene Dal mio sen non trapassò*.

   (i)   State three ways in which the melody of the repeat differs from the original phrase.

   (ii) Describe the cadence, and its approach chord, at the end of this phrase.

(c) Like the repeat of section A, section C is in the tonic key of C major. For which line of the text in stanza C does the key briefly change? Describe this change and give a reason for it.

String Quartets

Just as the trio sonata was one of the most typical genres of chamber music in the Baroque era, so the string quartet was typical of Classical chamber music. Like early symphonies, the first quartets of Joseph Haydn (1732–1809), which he called divertimentos, were in a light, melody-dominated *galant* style. By the late 18th century however, in the hands of Mozart and Haydn, the string quartet was capable of expressing the most profound and intimate musical thinking. This was partly due to the development of dialogue technique whereby every instrument has some say in the melodic argument. Instead of just a violin tune with simple homophonic accompaniment, a range of textures was now possible: all four instruments in unison or octaves, two-, three- and four-part counterpoint, antiphonal exchanges between upper and lower instruments and so on.

Towards the end of the Baroque era there was a tendency for the second 'half' of binary movements to become much longer than the first, due to the practice of 'rounding off' the movement by ending with material from the first section, transposed to the tonic key if necessary. At first this was just a case of adapting the cadence from the A section, but by the time of Bach and Domenico Scarlatti whole passages were being recapitulated in this way. This inevitably blurs the distinction between binary and ternary forms, although it is important to realize that the middle section of this **rounded binary** form is not contrasted in content, like the central portion of ternary form. It also usually merges straight back into the reprise of the opening material, rather than ending with a conclusive cadence in a related key as is found in ternary form.

The **minuet** was the only one of the Baroque dances to survive into the Classical period. Rounded binary form was now well established and composers also retained the Baroque practice of pairing two dances of the same type, e.g., minuet I and minuet II. The second of these was often in a different, but related, key with a lighter texture. Originally this was a three-part texture, giving rise to the term **trio**, a name that stuck even when the number of parts increased.

The two minuets were intended to be performed as a ternary form sandwich, minuet–trio–minuet, rather like the *da capo* aria. Conventionally, both the A and the B sections are repeated in the first playing of the minuet, and in the trio, but are omitted in the *da capo* of the minuet. Since each of the rounded binary minuets is already cast in an ABA[1] pattern, the overall composite structure looks complex on paper, although it is usually very clear when heard:

I Minuet: AA BA¹BA¹   **II** Trio: CC DC¹DC¹   **I** Minuet *da capo*: A BA¹

Remember that the binary form origins of the minuet dictate that the middle sections of each dance (B in minuet I and D in the trio) are unlikely to be greatly contrasted with their outer sections, except in key.

 Track 30

===================================== *Test 90* =====================================

The music below is the first four bars of the first violin part of a binary form minuet from a string quartet by Haydn. This phrase is answered by another four-bar phrase to complete section A. Section B, together with a modified repeat of section A, follows immediately forming a further 24 bars.

(a) Describe the texture of the accompaniment to these four bars.

(b) In which of the following keys does section A end?
     D major   D minor   A major   B minor

(c) From which two bars printed above is the melody of bars 5–8 derived and how are these two bars treated when they are used in bars 5–8?

(d) (i) Which three-note motif from the music printed above is used at the beginning of section B?

     (ii) Describe the rhythm and texture at this point.

(e) Just before section A returns you will hear all the instruments playing a descending figure in octaves. From which two notes of the music printed above is this figure derived?

(f) After the modified repeat of section A another section is repeated in a modified form. State where you first hear this music and describe the ways in which it is now modified.

(g) From which part of the whole movement has this extract been taken?

The Sonata Principle

You will have noticed the variety of textures in just half a minute of music taken from the Haydn string quartet. You will also have noticed the way the whole movement is derived from motifs in the first four bars. This mono-thematicism is, of course, a legacy of the Baroque era. It works well within the structure of this short minuet, but longer movements require contrasting themes and tonal centres in order to sustain interest. In the Classical period composers became absorbed by the desire to balance unity and variety over a longer time span, and one of their greatest achievements was the development of the sonata principle. This involved the concepts of:

❑ two tonal centres, most often tonic and dominant (or, in the case of minor key movements, tonic and relative major); these tonal centres are usually associated with contrasting thematic material. This is followed by

❑ a section of conflicting and rapidly changing tonality (most often associated with explorations of the potential of motifs from the first two tonal centres); then, to balance all this unrest,

❑ a concluding section in which thematic material from the first section is repeated, but now entirely in the tonic key.

This grew directly from rounded binary forms such as the minuet on Track 30:

Rounded Binary Form

The Sonata Principle

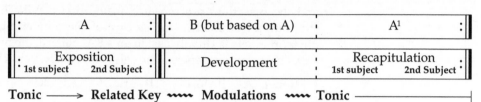

The first section (**exposition**) derives from the A section of the binary form, but instead of just modulating to the dominant (or relative major) there is now a whole contrasting section in this key (the 'second subject'). The second section (**development**) corresponds to the opening of the B section in binary form, but it is likely to be longer with a wider range of keys and a more thorough exploration of themes and motifs from the exposition. The term 'development' is, incidentally, a bit misleading—themes are as likely to be dismembered and fragmented as they are to grow and develop. The third section (**recapitulation**) is similar to the modified repeat of the A section at the end of binary form but, to balance the whole movement, it is likely to be longer.

These are the general principles of sonata form, but, within this general scheme, composers' structures varied widely. Haydn sometimes wrote mono-thematic movements in sonata form which rely more on contrasts of keys rather than contrasts of keys *and* themes. Mozart sometimes wrote new melodies in his development sections, and Beethoven, particularly in his later works, often expanded the perfunctory series of perfect cadences which end the recapitulation (the **coda**) to become a section which, in style and length, began to rival the development in importance.

The sonata principle's origins in binary form are often revealed by the repeat signs (shown as merely a double bar in the sonata movement on page 124, since no repeats are observed). These divide the movement into two, not three sections. The practice of repeating the long second section (development and recapitulation combined) makes little sense and quickly dropped out of favour although the exposition is still often repeated in earlier Classical works.

The idea of form based on key seems strange to our ears, accustomed as they are to a myriad of key relationships and, indeed, to the idea of music that is in no key at all or even several keys at once. But to the ears of the 18th-century musician, this was the great strength of the sonata principle and the means by which it offered the greatest flexibility. Composers found that such a basic foundation could contract or expand as required, sustaining movements of considerable length by the time of Beethoven. The double return, of the home key *and* the opening theme, was so definitive that it allowed increasingly complex and lengthy explorations in the development, the addition of new sections such as the coda and the introduction, the idea of separating the first and second subjects by new transitional sections, and the possibility of expanding the single second subject into a whole group of melodic ideas.

Furthermore, the sonata principle offered scope for new types of thematic relationships, particularly facilitating the idea of 'organic growth' in which a motif consisting of just the bare outline of an interval or two can sustain, and develop into, a complete movement or even an entire multi-movement work—perhaps no better or more famous example of this is Beethoven's Fifth Symphony.

All of this conspired to make the sonata principle an irresistible force in Classical composition. It was used almost invariably for the first movements (and sometimes other movements) of symphonies, sonatas, string quartets and other types of chamber music.

Various related forms are also frequently found: sonata form with an abridged or omitted development was preferred for overtures and for the slow movements of multi-movement works, while the hybrid sonata-rondo (see page 125) was an alternative to the plain rondo in finales. A synthesis of Baroque ritornello form and the sonata principle was developed in the Classical concerto. In these works, the soloist's material corresponds quite closely to the sonata principle, but it is preceded by an introductory orchestral ritornello in the tonic, often anticipating much of the exposition proper, and the exposition is rounded off by a similar ritornello in the dominant. The recapitulation is conventionally halted by a cadential second inversion—the cue for an elaborate **cadenza** from the soloist—after which the orchestra completes the anticipated perfect cadence with a final short ritornello in the tonic.

The sonata principle is indissolubly linked with the rise of new instrumental genres in the Classical period, particularly the symphony and string quartet. However, it permeated even vocal music—from individual movements in Haydn's late Masses to the sextet from Act III of Mozart's *Le nozze di Figaro*, the opera mentioned at the start of this chapter.

Such was the strength of 'sonata form' (as it is often called) that its use can be traced, albeit with increasing self-consciousness, through to 'late Romantic' composers in the early 20th century. However Schubert, frequently described as the last of the Classical composers and the first of the Romantics, demonstrates how form based on key was ultimately, in the 19th century, an unsustainable idea. Schubert was not only the acknowledged master of melody—he also realized that audiences recognized melodic signposts much more easily than tonal ones. This was not least, perhaps, because of the tendency to explore an ever wider palette of keys, in which it became increasingly difficult to perceive the hierarchical logic of Classical modulations.

Thus Schubert has no qualms about transposing an entire exposition down a fifth to form the recapitulation in several of his major works: so what if the first subject returns in the subdominant?—at least the movement ends in the right key! The important thing for Schubert was the return of the *themes* of the exposition. For precisely the same reason, musical theorists of the 19th century gave up the 18th-century practice of explaining the sonata principle in terms of binary form, and instead wrote of 'sonata form' as an extended ternary form, based on its thematic material rather than its key structure.

An example of a slow movement in sonata form by Beethoven is given in *Sound Matters* (No. 24). Most sonata form movements are too long to be used complete in aural questions, but the movement by Mozart on Track 31 (played here without repeats) gives some idea of the sonata principle at work on a small scale. As you listen, follow the form outlined in the skeleton score on page 124.

Track 31

When following a score like this, read the tempo direction and look for any notes about the instrumentation before you read through it. During this reading time try to form an idea of the sound of the printed parts and imagine them at the speed indicated. It is a good idea to follow the score with your finger as the music is played: it is very easy to get lost, especially when there are blank bars. As you do this, jot down your answers on the score: in an examination you could then transfer these to any spaces provided next to the questions during the pauses between playings, or at the end of the whole question.

Mozart: Divertimento No. 4, KA 229 (Allegro), arranged for oboe, clarinet and bassoon

Listen again to the Allegro by Mozart as you follow the skeleton score on page 124. The main sections of this movement in sonata form are shown on the score together with the first and second subjects (marked I and II respectively).

(a) In the exposition (bars 1–28):

    (i) Describe the texture in bars 1–4 and give the bar numbers where a similar texture occurs again in the exposition.

    (ii) Describe the melodic line played by the bassoon in bars 5–6.

    (iii) Give the bar numbers in which the clarinet motif in bars 9–10 first occurs.

    (iv) What compositional device is heard in bars 12–13?

    (v) Describe the texture of bars 16–25 (the second subject).

    (vi) What compositional device is used in the codetta to reinforce the key of the second subject?

(b) In the development (bars 29–44):

    (i) To which bars in the exposition does the figure in bars 29–30 relate? How does this figure differ from its original version?

    (ii) How are the tonalities of bars 29–32 and bars 33–38 related?

    (iii) From which bars in the exposition do bars 40–44 derive?

(c) In the recapitulation (bars 45–63):

    (i) In what key does the second subject occur (bar 60)?

    (ii) Compare the melody of the second subject here with the original version in the exposition (printed at bars 16–25). Apart from the keys used, describe one important difference between the two melodies.

(d) In the coda (bars 70–78):

    (i) Which bars of the exposition are referred to by the oboe in bars 70–73?

    (ii) How do the clarinet and bassoon parts relate to the oboe in bars 70–74?

    (iii) To which other bars of the exposition does this coda make reference?

Rondos

Some of the elegant and highly decorated dances (which are often harbingers of the *galant* style) by French Baroque composers were written *en rondeau*. This was a simple form in which a refrain alternated with contrasting episodes (e.g., ABACADA). The number of *couplets* (episodes) could vary, but the repeating theme (*grand couplet* or *rondeau*) was always a closed section ending in the tonic and invariably appeared complete (unlike the ritornellos of the concerto grosso).

The rondo, to use the Italian term, was sometimes adopted by Viennese Classical composers for the finale of symphonies, concertos, quartets and sonatas. The style, derived from light-hearted *opera buffa* (comic opera), provided relief from the serious business of sonata form used in earlier movements.

More often a hybrid **sonata-rondo** form was used for finales. It has the symmetrical structure, ABACAB^{1}A, in which A and B correspond to the first and second subjects of sonata form and C to the development (B^1 is in the tonic). The distinctive feature is the two reappearances of the rondo theme-cum-first subject (A) at those points where, in conventional sonata form, there would have been a codetta and coda.

The following extract is taken from the rondo finale of the Sonata Op. 79 by Ludwig van Beethoven (1770–1827). Although this was written as late as 1809 (by which time the composer had written six of his symphonies), in style and form it harks back to the cheerful rondos of the 18th century.

(a) Listen to the first 29 seconds of this extract. It begins with these four bars:

    (i)   Describe the melody and modulation in the next four bars (bars 5–8).

   (ii) What happens in the following eight bars (bars 9–16)?

The next section starts with the following four bars:

  (iii) Describe the melody and modulation in the next four bars (bars 21–24).

  (iv) Describe the form of the music in this whole 32-bar section.

(b) The music you have just heard constitutes the refrain or rondo theme (section A). Now listen to the whole extract and identify all of these sections:

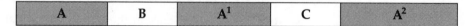

A	B	A¹	C	A²

    (i)   How is the key of the first episode (section B) related to the key of the rondo theme (section A)?

   (ii) Describe two ways in which A^1 differs from A.

  (iii) The loud second episode (C) begins as follows:

        What happens in the next four bars?

  (iv) What do the remaining eight bars of episode C consist of?

   (v) Describe two ways in which A^2 differs from A.

Symphonies

Some of the finest examples of the sonata principle are to be found amongst the various movements of the 12 symphonies Haydn wrote for the London impressario Salomon. Haydn's earliest symphonies are most often scored for pairs of oboes and horns together with strings and continuo—apart from the horns, an ensemble more typical of Baroque music. But in the 'Drumroll' Symphony (No. 103 in E flat) he uses the full Classical 'double wind' orchestra listed on page 119.

🅒 Track 33

Most of the 'London' Symphonies begin with a **slow introduction** followed by a lively sonata form Allegro. The music below shows the opening of the slow introduction to the 'Drumroll' Symphony, the solo in the first bar being the cause of the work's nickname:

In the 18th century introductions, when used at all, were seldom related to the ensuing sonata movement, but here is an exception. The unharmonized and gloomy semitone of the Adagio's final phrase, is suddenly transformed into the start of a preposterously happy first subject—follow the outline score below as you listen to the whole of the exposition and notice how much larger the form is compared to the little sonata movement by Mozart on page 124:

Track 34

Violas, cellos and basses

Repeat of two previous bars

Violins

Haydn: from Symphony No. 103 in E flat (first movement)

Haydn has several melodic ideas (marked a, b and c) in his **first subject**. Notice some typical Classical features here. In phrase (a) the harmonic pace begins slowly but speeds up to the conventional Ic–V^7–I cadence (tonic and dominant harmony predominate throughout the piece). In phrase (b) the one-bar scale figure is repeated twice. In phrase (c) another one-bar figure is repeated twice in sequence shown by the wavy lines. Similar wavy lines indicate a number of other sequential passages in the extract. In bars 56–59 motif *(x)* from the beginning of the first subject is progressively reduced to just a single pitch above the repeated imperfect cadences which mark the end of this section.

Haydn delays the **second subject** with a long **transition**, prominently featuring motif *(x)* and leading the music through various keys to culminate in a dramatic diminished seventh and a riotous syncopated diminution of the adagio melody. This all amounts to a development of previously stated ideas—in later Classical works developmental procedures could crop up in any section of the movement.

The second subject is in real country dance style, with a melody floating over a simple accompaniment ('oom-cha-cha' in the lower strings). The final figure *(y)* is transferred to the lower instruments to make a brief **codetta**, where Haydn takes the motif twice through the progression I–VI–II^{7}b–V^7 (one of the great harmonic clichés of the Classical style) to whip up excitement for the rousing perfect cadences which conclusively establish the dominant key of B flat major.

Tracks 34 and 35

Test 93

Listen to the recapitulation (Track 35) from the first movement of the 'Drumroll' Symphony. As you listen, follow the music of the exposition printed above and note how Track 35 differs from this. These are longer extracts than you might expect in an examination: you will probably need to play Track 34 (the exposition) and Track 35 (the recapitulation) many times to answer the following questions.

(a) Which section of the exposition is omitted in the recapitulation?

(b) What is the single most important difference between the second subject in the exposition and the second subject in the recapitulation?

(c) In the exposition an oboe doubles the violins in the second subject. What does the oboe do at the corresponding point in the recapitulation?

(d) At the end of the second subject in the recapitulation new material is introduced leading up to an appoggiatura on the long-held diminished seventh chord. Describe this new material.

(e) After this chord, the music of the slow introduction surprisingly returns. Describe the second phrase of this slow section in relation to the first phrase.

(f) After the slow section the Allegro is resumed. With what does it begin?

(g) The movement ends with a phrase treated antiphonally between the horns, woodwind and tutti, followed by a figure descending in the bass.

   (i) From which bars in the exposition is the antiphonal figure derived?

   (ii) From which bar in the exposition is the bass figure derived?

Romantic Music

Programme Music

Tracks 36–39

What was the first movement of Haydn's 'Drumroll' Symphony about? Gloom in the Adagio transformed to joy in the Allegro? Maybe, but what picture is it trying to paint, or what story is it trying to tell? We are, of course, asking the wrong questions and certainly cannot expect an answer. Some might feel that the work exists in a more abstract intellectual domain, being concerned with the balance and interplay of musical patterns, textures and structures. The splendid assertion of motif (x) at the end of the first movement could almost have Q.E.D. written after it, so convincingly does it seem to cap the rational edifice of this musical structure. But note that, even if this is a legitimate interpretation, the logic is *musical* logic which can be only hinted at in mere words—besides, Haydn might just as well have thought that motif (x) provided a splendid opportunity for the horns to let fly!

Now listen to the extract from a symphony by Hector Berlioz (1803–1869) on Track 36. We are in a new sound world. Rustling strings lead to a dramatic call to attention from the full wind band, then the actor steps on to the stage in the shape of a solo viola who delivers a meditative soliloquy against the lightest of accompaniments. Listen to Track 37. Our viola-hero now introduces himself with a good deal more passion and goes on to conduct a dialogue with a somewhat amorous cornet. On Track 38 he is obviously an observer, for his melody is set against a prominent processional tune.

This sort of literary interpretation of the meaning of the symphony would be impertinent if it were not for the fact that Berlioz himself invites it. The work is entitled *Harold en Italie* ('Harold in Italy, Symphony in Four Movements with a Viola Solo'). Harold is the eponymous hero of a gigantic (and almost unreadable) poem by that most Romantic of figures, Byron. Berlioz wrote that it was his intention 'to put the viola in the midst of poetic recollections … and make it a sort of melancholy dreamer after the manner of Byron's *Child Harold*'. Each movement bears a suggestive title: Tracks 36 and 37 come from the first movement, 'Harold in the Mountains' and Track 38 from the second movement, 'Pilgrims' March'.

In their desire to illustrate a definite programme, or at least paint a specific scene, Romantic composers devised new techniques and structures. *Harold In Italy* is not a concerto, it is a symphony 'with a viola solo'. Harold's theme (printed below) is an *idée fixe*, Berlioz's own term for a motto theme—a recurring idea used for some special dramatic purpose throughout a work. It appears in different contexts in all four movements, imparting a sort of unity to what would otherwise be a mere series of picturesque evocations.

Music in which thematic material is re-used in later movements is said to be **cyclic**. Themes are often transformed in some way for these later appearances (something Berlioz did with the *idée fixe* in his *Symphonie fantastique*, although not in *Harold In Italy*, where it remains largely unchanged on each appearance). Thematic transformation is not just a question of simple variation. Often rhythm, harmony, orchestration and melodic detail are all changed, leaving only the outline of a few intervals to make the link between a transformed theme and its original context. **Thematic metamorphosis** is particularly associated with the composer Franz Liszt (1811–1886) who used it as a prime means of development in a number of his major works, especially those in a genre he virtually invented—the **symphonic poem**. In this book there is no example of a symphonic poem, but you will find an excerpt from the tone poem (as Strauss preferred to call it), *Till Eulenspiegels lustige Streiche*, in *Sound Matters* (No. 36).

A similar quest for pictoral colour had led to the use of unusual instruments in Classical opera—harp, trombone, 'Turkish' percussion (bass drum, cymbals and triangle) and glockenspiel were used by Gluck, Haydn and Mozart. The 'double wind' orchestra of the late 18th century was augmented in the Romantic era by piccolo, cor anglais, bass clarinet and double bassoon—instruments which also first appeared in opera. The introduction of valve horns and trumpets in the 1820s made the brass section more versatile and its regular complement soon became four horns, two trumpets (plus two cornets in France) three trombones and tuba. A range of percussion instruments was used for further colour and, inevitably, the size of the string department was increased again to balance. Such large ensembles were well suited to the newly fashionable public concert halls: the hall in the Paris Conservatoire (1811) had a seating capacity of over 1,000 while the Royal Albert Hall (1871) was built for 6,500.

Berlioz was one of the most skilled and (through his book on the subject) influential orchestrators of the early 19th century. The delicacy of the passage on Track 36, where the *idée fixe* is accompanied by just one harp and the simplest of bass parts on the violas, is just as significant as the devastating combination of full symphony orchestra (replete with four gongs, ten pairs of cymbals and sixteen timpani), four brass bands and huge chorus in his *Grande Messe des Morts*. The length, size and operatic drama of such works continues the trend, already apparent in the 18th century, for church music to become less devotional and more spectacular—more at home in the concert hall than the church.

Romantic composers also made increasing technical demands on their players. This is clearly seen in such virtuosic works as Liszt's 12 *Transcendental Studies* (*Sound Matters*, No. 30). It was the virtuoso Paganini who requested Berlioz to write *Harold In Italy*, and who subsequently refused to play the work because the modest solo viola part was insufficiently flamboyant.

Although the 19th century saw an increasing use of complex chromatic harmony, you should not presume that it is invariably to be found. In the extract on Track 36 the harmony is as simple and diatonic as Handel but, when the music demanded it, Berlioz could use extreme chromaticism or even modality (both of these becoming increasingly important during the next 100 years).

Berlioz: idée fixe *from* Harold in Italy

Tracks 36–39

Test 94

(a) Listen to Track 36.

    (i) What technique do the string players use to achieve the rustling effect at the beginning of this passage?

    (ii) Before the viola enters you will hear two rising arpeggios on the harp. How do these two chords differ?

    (iii) At the end of the track the violins play a three-note figure. Describe this in relation to the *idée fixe*.

(b) Listen to Track 37.

    (i) What technique does the viola employ in the passage before the entry of the *idée fixe*?

    (ii) Describe the relationship between the melodies played by the cornet and the viola (the latter doubled by upper woodwind instruments).

    (iii) What percussion instrument can you hear in this passage?

(c) Listen to Track 38.

    (i)   The *idée fixe* is played on the solo viola. List, in the order in which they occur, the instruments that play counter-melodies against this *idée fixe*.

    (ii)   How do the phrase lengths of these counter-melodies compare with the two phrases of the *idée fixe*?

    (iii)   Which of the following best describes the relationship between the *idée fixe* and the counter-melodies: periodic phrasing, overlapped phrasing, cross-phrasing, asymetric phrasing?

(d) Listen to Track 39.

    (i)   Before the *idée fixe* enters an oboe and piccolo play a melody in $\frac{6}{8}$ time over an accompaniment provided by low woodwind and divisi violas. Describe this accompaniment.

    (ii)   What two instruments play the *idée fixe*? What special instrumental technique is used by one of these two instruments?

    (iii)   What connection is there between the viola solo and the *idée fixe*?

Lieder

The Romantic era was an age of extremes. While Berlioz, Bruckner and Wagner developed large forms using large resources, Schubert, Schumann and Brahms explored that most intimate of genres, German Romantic song (*Lied* singular, *Lieder* plural). Such songs with piano accompaniment were known in the 18th century and both Haydn and Mozart wrote a few folky examples. Beethoven composed his famous song cycle *An die ferne Geliebte* ('To the Distant Beloved') in 1815–16, but by then the teenage Schubert had already written two settings of poems by Goethe (the leading German poet of the age) which were to establish the genre as one of the most important expressions of Romanticism in music.

Schubert frequently selected one feature of the poem to illustrate in the music throughout the song. This motif, usually in the accompaniment, acts as a unifying force. In *Gretchen am Spinnrade* ('Gretchen at the Spinning Wheel', 1814), it is the spinning wheel, suggested by a rippling semiquaver accompaniment. In *Erlkönig* ('The Erl-King', 1815), it is the wild flight of a horse portrayed in driving triplets. Such pictorial allusions are easy to spot. Less obvious, but psychologically more powerful, is the way Schubert communicates and enhances the restless agony of Gretchen's spinning. The accompaniment figure becomes the outward symbol of her emotional state, turning faster and faster through unresolved augmented sixth chords as her memories blur into fantasy, and suddenly stopping on the longest and highest note of the song (supported by a diminished seventh chord) as she recalls Faust's kiss. Then, as the false vision fades, the accompaniment figure—like the spinning wheel—is falteringly kicked back to life and the relentless spinning of fate returns once more.

Many of Schubert's Lieder are strophic, that is they use the same music for each verse of the poem. *Erlkönig*, though, is a **ballad** (a song with a narrative lyric) providing opportunity for a vivid dramatic treatment as the poem unfolds. Here, too, the materials which unify the song are also modified to provide its variety and to enhance the drama of the text. The key, at first intensely minor, changes to major and the triplets fade to *pianissimo*—but, like the wildly galloping horse, they do not stop—for sections in which the child of the rider, delirious with marsh fever, loses touch with reality and imagines approaching death in terms of the Erl-King's seductive promises. The minor key returns, along with a higher tessitura and a searing dissonance of C, D and E flat, to accompany the child's screams of 'My father, my father'. And this happens three times, each a tone higher, as the night-ride becomes increasingly desperate. Only in the final bars, as the singer breaks down into recitative, do the triplets finally stop when the father realizes that the child in his arms lies dead.

All the devices of figuration, texture, harmony and tonality were at Schubert's service: his combination of ravishing melody and profound psychological insight has ensured his reputation as the first and greatest of Romantic song composers.

Listen to the Lied, *Ihr Bild* ('Her Portrait'), set to music by Schubert in 1828:

1	*Ich stand in dunkeln Träumen*	I stood in dark dreams
2	*Und starrt ihr Bildnis an.*	And gazed at her portrait,
3	*Und das geliebte Antlitz*	And the beloved countenance
4	*Heimlich zu leben begann.*	Secretly began to live.
5	*Um ihre Lippen zog sich*	Around her lips there played
6	*Ein Lächeln wunderbar.*	A wondrous smile.
7	*Und wie von Wehmutstränen*	And as though with tears of sadness
8	*Erglänzte ihr Augenpaar.*	Her two eyes shone.
9	*Auch meine Tränen flossen*	My tears also flowed
10	*Mir von den Wangen herab.*	Down my cheeks.
11	*Und ach! ich kann es nicht glauben,*	And O! I cannot believe,
12	*Daß ich dich verloren hab!*	That I have lost you!

(a) What texture is used to suggest the emptiness of the poet in lines 1–2?

(b) Describe the rhythm used for the words *starrt ihr Bildnis* in line 2.

(c) Describe the piano interlude between lines 2 and 3.

(d) How do the texture and tonality of lines 3–4 differ from the texture and tonality of lines 1–2? Why is there such a difference?

(e) Dissonances highlight the word *Lächeln* ('smile') in line 6 and the syllables *-tränen* ('tears') in line 7. Why do these dissonances have opposite effects?

(f) Although the music of lines 1–4 and lines 9–12 is the same, the first verse ended with a ray of hope, whereas the last verse ends in despair. What change does Schubert make to the piano postlude to reflect this despair?

Opera

In Italy in the 19th century opera became almost a national sport, with the composer Giuseppe Verdi (1813–1901) as its hero. His early operas dealt with subjects which could be interpreted as assertions of patriotism in a period when Italy was trying to throw off the yoke of Austrian domination. Their vigorous vocal melodies (often doubled in the orchestra to add strength), crude 'um-pah' and 'um-pah-pah' accompaniments (using mainly primary triads) and unsubtle but effective orchestration ensured popularity. In his later operas Verdi, having achieved success, moved away from heroic themes to write music which, in its ability to characterize the protagonists, rivals even Mozart. This is especially true of the great ensembles such as the Quartet from Act III of *Rigoletto*, where the differing emotional states of the soloists are captured in four melodic lines (lyrically boastful, flirtatiously staccato, despairingly sobbing and menacingly chromatic), brought together in a web of counterpoint in which the characters nevertheless retain their separate identity. No wonder the author of the original story of *Rigoletto*, Victor Hugo, regretted that it was 'beyond the power of poetry to achieve this simultaneous representation of four different moods'.

During a period of composition that spanned more than 50 years, Verdi moved away from the coloratura style, set arias and simple accompanimental rôle for the orchestra, and allowed complete acts to unfold with a real sense of dramatic and musical continuity. In old age he penned two of the greatest operas of all time. Both were adaptations of Shakespeare, one a comic opera *Falstaff*, and the other the great tragedy of jealousy, *Otello*. Although closed numbers are still present, giving the listener an aesthetic satisfaction over and above the immediate interest of the drama, they are wonderfully concealed by a continuous flow of melody in these late masterpieces. To achieve this Verdi used flexible vocal lines which vary between cantabile melody and **parlante** (a style of singing half way between aria and recitative) with the orchestra ensuring musical continuity by maintaining the melody even when, in the interests of characterization and drama, the voices drop out or sing non-melodic material.

All of these features are apparent in the extract from Act III of *Otello*. Othello, whose mind has been poisoned by the evil Iago, is in the Great Hall of his castle in Cyprus when his innocent wife, Desdemona, (whom he suspects of adultery) enters. After a very short orchestral introduction she greets him with the musical phrase quoted below and Othello responds in a courtly fashion.

Verdi: Otello, *Act III, scene 2*

These exchanges are conducted in music which, in its regular phrasing and largely diatonic style, could almost be by Mozart. But, when Othello insinuates that his wife may not be as pure as her virginal appearance suggests, the music reflects this. The phrase quoted above is constantly modified to express the subtleties of the dialogue, yet, like Classical music it eventually cadences in the key in which it began and the orchestral introduction returns like a ritornello. Familiarize yourself with all these features before you attempt the questions.

 Track 41

Test 96

Here is the text of the opening of Act III, scene 2 of Verdi's *Otello*:

Desdemona:	*Dio ti giocondi, o sposo dell'alma mia sovrano.*	God make you joyful, husband, sovereign master of my soul.
Otello:	*Grazie, madonna, datemi la vostra eburnea mano.*	Thanks, my lady, give me your ivory-white hand.
	Caldo mador ne irrora la morbida beltà	Heat and moisture do not spoil its tender beauty.
Desdemona:	*Essa ancor l'orme ignora del duolo e dell'età.*	It has not yet felt sorrow or age.
Otello:	*Eppur qui annida il demone gentil del mal consiglio,*	and yet the courteous evil devil nestles here, who illuminates
	che il vago avorio allumina del piccioletto artiglio.	the pretty whiteness of this talon.
	Mollemente alla prece s'atteggia e al pio fervore.	Softly it assumes the pose of prayer and pious fervour.
Desdemona:	*Eppur con questa mano io v'ho donato il core...*	And yet, with this hand I give you my heart...

(a) What from the instrumental introduction is retained in the vocal phrases of both Desdemona and Othello?

(b) Desdamona's first line is a four-bar phrase cadencing in the tonic. How does Othello's answering phrase (*Grazie, madonna, ... eburnea mano*) differ?

(c) In this same answering phrase, which instrument maintains the melodic line when Othello rests between *Grazie, madonna* and *datemi la vostra ...*?

(d) Which instrument maintains the melodic line between Othello's first and second sentences (*Grazie ... mano* and *Caldo mador ... beltà*)?

(e) Describe two ways in which Verdi suggests Othello's perturbation in his sentence *Caldo mador ne irrora la morbida beltà*.

(f) What in the music suggests the logical end of the musical sentence at the end of Desdemona's phrase *Essa ancor l'orme ignora del duolo e dell'età*?

(g) How do Verdi's harmonies for *Eppur qui annida il demone gentil del mal consiglio* suggest Othello's jealousy?

(h) With which cadence does the phrase *che il vago ... artiglio* end?

(i) Which instruments maintain the melodic thread as Othello sings *Mollemente alla prece ... fervore*? What melodic device is used here?

(j) How does Verdi highlight the importance of the word *mano* ('hand') in Desdemona's last sentence?

Opera in Germany, far from being a sport, was almost a religion in the hands of Richard Wagner (1813–1883). Wagner created what he called the 'complete art work', a fusion of literature, music, art, architecture and philosophy, which he masterminded himself in *Der Ring des Nibelungen* ('The Ring of the Nibelung'): three vast operas and a prologue based on Norse mythology. His music has an epic quality that reflects the profound symbolism of his subjects. Wagner found the musical equivalent of verbal symbolism in his famous *leitmotiv* technique whereby an object (like a sword), or a concept (like fate) can be represented by a short, telling musical motif which can be woven into the texture of the music wherever that object or idea emerges in the drama. These motifs (there are more than 100 that unify the four operas of *The Ring*) are transformed to reflect new situations or changes in perspective, modified to suggest changes in personality, and manipulated and developed in the orchestra to present a whole new plane of drama, heard but not seen. Thus, the audience, through hearing, say, a leitmotiv associated with greed, can participate in the drama, realizing the true intentions of a character before any words are exchanged on stage. The leitmotiv can be seen as a relative of Berlioz's *idée fixe*, but the technique is pursued with ruthless logic over periods of hours (or, in the case of *The Ring*, days).

Like Verdi, Wagner gradually moved towards through-composed opera, but his approach was much more symphonic than that of Verdi. In other words, there is an ongoing musical logic, running parallel with the drama, in which musical ideas constantly evolve into new ones without a break in the thread of sound. This involved an increasingly important rôle for the orchestra where, in Wagner's later operas, the drama unfolds almost as much as it does on stage.

Wagner's style is often intensely chromatic, using counterpoint to disguise cadences or even to obliterate them by delayed or elliptical resolutions of dissonant chromatic chords onto further dissonant chromatic chords. The avoidance or disguise of cadential formulas (and of any sort of musical cliché) was of great importance: Wagner sought unbroken continuity and significance in every detail, describing his aim as **unending melody**. This was often achieved by allowing one voice to dominate in the chromatic polyphony, threading its way though the most complex of orchestral textures, passing from one instrument (or group of instruments) to another so that the tone colours constantly changed. Over this the voice rides upon the orchestra's swell like an expert surf-boarder, sometimes coinciding with the instrumental waves, sometimes cutting across them—but it is the orchestra which carries the complete symphonic argument.

⊙ Track 42

=== *Test 97* ===

The music below shows the 'unending melody' in the orchestra at the beginning of the *Liebestod* ('Love-death') from the end of Wagner's *Tristan und Isolde* (first performed in 1865). From bar 12 the music gives Isolde's vocal part.

mu - tig schwillt ___ voll und hehr im ___ Bu - sen ihm quillt! ___

Wagner: opening of the Liebestod *('Love-death') from* Tristan und Isolde

Here are the words Isolde sings about her dying hero:

Mild und leise wie er lächelt	Softly and gently how he smiles,
wie das Auge hold er öffnet –	how his eyes sweetly open –
seht ihr's Freunde? seht ihr's nicht?	can you see it, friends? can you not see it?
Immer lichter wie er leuchtet	How he shines, ever more radiant
Stern-umstrahlet hoch sich hebt?	bathed in stars as he rises?
Seht ihr's nicht?	Can you not see it?
Wie das Herz ihm mutig schwillt	How his heart swells courageously,
voll und hehr im Busen ihm quillt!	Full and sublime it beats within his breast!

(a) Which brass instruments play two chords in bar 2?

(b) (i) Identify the interval sung by Isolde at the places marked with a pecked bracket in bars 2, 4 and 5 (the interval is the same each time, though it is transposed at each repeat).

   (ii) How does this interval relate to the notated instrumental melody?

(c) The main melodic line begins in the orchestra on the bass clarinet (bars 1–2). Which instruments have the melody notated in:
   (i) Bars 3–4,   (ii) Bar 5,   (iii) Bars 9–11?

(d) What instrument enters in bar 9 and is only heard in bars 9–12?

(e) Which instruments play the fast figuration around the main melodic lines in bars 12–15?

The Sonata Principle

The Classical genres of sonata, symphony, concerto and chamber music continued in use during the 19th century, although after Beethoven it was perhaps inevitable that composers should see such works more as great public statements of their competence in traditional forms than as part of a day-to-day mode of expression. The Classical ideal of sonata form structured by related keys was irrevocably disturbed by the long, lyrical themes, wide modulation and chromatic harmony of most of the Romantic composers. This is seen before the death of Beethoven, in the sonata form movements of Schubert. Beethoven often built whole sections out of tiny motifs, like the three-note motif in the Rondo from his Piano Sonata Op. 79 in the last chapter. Schubert, on the other hand, preferred complete melodies, often extended in long sequences and repeated in remote keys for greater emotional impact, giving many of his movements in sonata form a decidedly Romantic cast. In this he was followed by the prodigiously talented young Mendelssohn in such works as his Violin Concerto.

 Track 43

The composer who, more than any other, kept the sonata principle alive in the later 19th century was Johannes Brahms (1833–1897). In the extract from his Violin Sonata in G (1879) you can hear how he combined Beethovenian motivic development with Romantic lyricism and rich textures. Although he employed the full palette of Romantic harmonies, these are almost always used functionally, as cadence preparation or for passing modulation rather than just for colour. This is very much a Classical trait, as is his preference for triad-based melodies—the interval of a falling third is a most characteristic fingerprint.

A particular speciality of Brahms was **cross-rhythm**. We have come across this on a small scale in the hemiola, in which a bar of $\frac{3}{2}$ temporarily displaces two bars of $\frac{3}{4}$ metre. Brahms's cross-rhythms are often longer and more complex. Not only can whole sections run against the prevailing metre, but two or more parts can conflict with each other to produce polyrhythms. This may be obvious in the notation, such as a piano right hand in $\frac{6}{8}$ while the left has three crotchets per bar (effectively $\frac{3}{4}$ time) or long passages of quaver duplets against triplets. Equally, the effect may be achieved by **cross-phrasing**, such as slurring every three crotchets in quadruple time, continuing over bar-lines as necessary. These are not intellectual devices apparent only on paper: they are, in fact, often more obvious to the ear than to the eye. Listen out for some of the characteristics of Brahms's style (motivic development, melodic lyricism, rich textures and cross-rhythms) in this extract from the beginning of the G major Violin Sonata.

 Track 43

=========================== *Test 98* ===========================

Follow this skeleton score of the violin part as you listen to the extract:

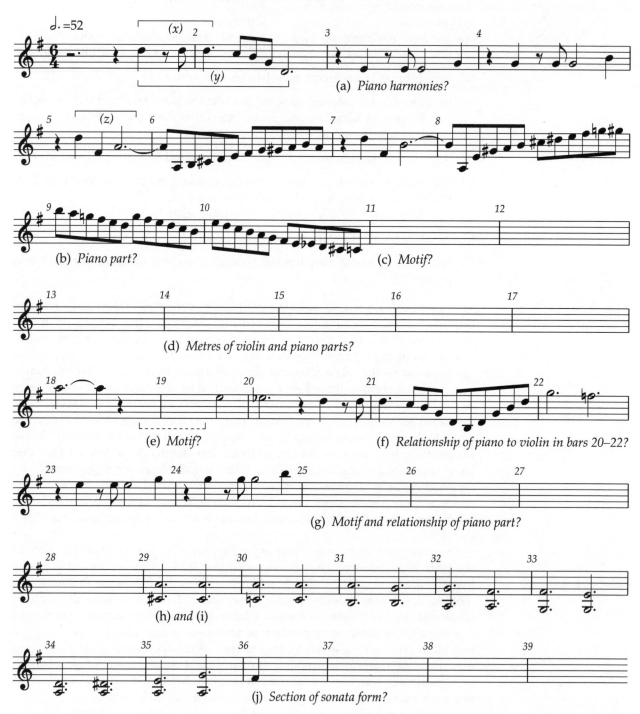

(a) *Piano harmonies?*

(b) *Piano part?* (c) *Motif?*

(d) *Metres of violin and piano parts?*

(e) *Motif?* (f) *Relationship of piano to violin in bars 20–22?*

(g) *Motif and relationship of piano part?*

(h) *and* (i)

(j) *Section of sonata form?*

Brahms: Violin Sonata in G, Op. 78 (first movement)

The main motifs deployed in bars 1–10 are labelled (x), (y) and (z) in the score above. Most of the following questions relate to these and to the scale figures in the violin part in these bars. In answering the questions on rhythm and metre note that the beat (as indicated by the metronome mark) is a dotted minim.

(a) Describe the piano harmonies in bars 3 and 4.

(b) How does the piano part from the end of bar 9 to the end of bar 10 relate to the violin part in these bars?

(c) Listen to the violin part in bar 11. From which motif, (x), (y) or (z) is this phrase derived?

(d) (i) Listen to the violin part in 14–17. How does this differ from the metre indicated by the $\frac{6}{4}$ time signature?

(ii) Listen to the piano part in the same bars. Describe how this differs from both the metre indicated by the $\frac{6}{4}$ time signature and the metre you have noticed in the violin part.

(e) To which motif, (x), (y) or (z), does the violin part indicated by the pecked bracket in bars 18–19 refer? How has the motif been treated here?

(f) What is the relationship between the right-hand piano part in bars 21–23 and the given violin part in bars 20–22?

(g) (i) Which of the motifs, (x), (y) or (z), is used in the violin part of bars 25–27?

(ii) Describe two ways in which Brahms treats this motif in the violin part in these bars.

(iii) How does the piano part relate to the violin part in these bars?

(h) In bars 29–33 you can see that the double-stopping in the violin forms a series of suspensions. To which earlier bars in the piano part do these suspensions refer?

(i) To which of the motifs, (x), (y) or (z), does the piano refer in those same bars (29–33)? Describe how these motifs are treated in these bars.

(j) Which section of the sonata form movement begins at bar 36?

Characteristic Dances

Just as the minuet was one of the most popular dances of the 18th century, so the **waltz** became the most popular dance of the 19th century. Although both are in $\frac{3}{4}$ time, they are as different from each other as Baroque style is from Romantic style. The Baroque minuet was elegant and stately with no variations in tempo. The Viennese waltz, on the other hand, reflected Romantic sensibility in its more fluid rhythms, slight anticipations of the second beat and general use of rubato (especially *ritardandi* leading to expressive appoggiaturas). Any of the waltzes by the elder or younger Johann Struass will give you a good idea of the dance style which swept across Europe in the 19th century.

Like the minuet before it, the waltz was adapted for use in the concert hall in such works as Berlioz's *Symphonie fantastique*. In the second movement (see *Sound Matters*, No. 27) a vivid impression is given of a glittering ball in which the appearance of the hero of this programme symphony is signalled by the *idée fixe*. So common was the use of rubato, even when it was not indicated by the composer, that Berlioz felt obliged to write *sans retenir* ('without slowing') at a point where some conductors might otherwise have indulged themselves.

Without the blessing and bane of television, amateur music making was prevalent in polite society throughout the 18th and 19th centuries. In the Romantic era no drawing-room was complete without a piano, and no young lady could be considered properly educated unless she were at least modestly accomplished as a pianist. Late Beethoven was clearly *de trop* in such a context, and it was with this in mind that composers churned out a vast repertoire of short lyric piano pieces in simple binary and ternary forms which, like the larger scale symphonic programme music, were intended to invoke particular scenes or moods. Mendelssohn's *Songs without Words* consist of six books of these **characteristic pieces**, with helpful titles such as 'Hunting Song' and 'Gondola Song'. Schumann's *Kinderszenen* is a collection of character pieces meant to evoke life viewed through the eyes of a child. The second edition of his *Davidsbündlertänze* ('Dances of the League of David') was subtitled 'Characteristic Pieces'. This collection (perhaps a little demanding for accomplished young ladies of fashion) was one of several by Schumann intended to be performed as a complete cycle just as Lieder, a related salon music genre, were sometimes composed as song cycles. The *Davidsbündlertänze* represent Schumann's fight against the reactionary musical Philistines of his time, and wonderfully evoke the two sides of his own character: those signed by his imaginary Eusebius being introverted, and those signed by Florestan being extrovert in mood. Here Schumann combines the idea of the character piece with shadowy evocations of the dance in his favourite and recurring theme of the masked ball. Literary allusions, enigmatic references and secret cyphers permeate the work of Schumann, one of the most 'romantic' of 19th-century composers.

An important political development in the 19th century was the disintegration of old imperial orders and the emergence of nation states. A consequence of this was an awakening of artistic awareness in countries that had been peripheral to the dominance of musical developments in Italy, France and Germany/Austria. First and foremost in Russia, but also in other parts of Eastern Europe as well as in Norway and Spain, composers turned to the folk- tales and traditions of their own countries to assert their roots and independence. These found expression most easily in opera (Glinka's *A Life For The Czar*, of 1836 was one of the first) and in symphonic poems such as the Czech composer Smetana's *Vltava*.

Nationalist music was at first dominated by contemporary styles in Austro-German music, although composers often attempted to give their work a degree of local colour by the inclusion of folk tunes or (more commonly) features of folk music such as characteristic dance rhythms or modal inflections. However, it was not until the nationalist composers of the 20th century, and particularly with those who made a real study of folk music (such as Vaughan Williams in England, and Bartók and Kodály in Hungary) that a less superficial marriage of folk and art traditions was achieved. Some would argue that the very different social purpose of the two types of music makes real integration impossible. The whole question of nationalism in music is, in any case, open to dispute, but it is a useful way of distinguishing those composers who deliberately tried to cast off the yoke of Austro-German hegemony in the 19th and 20th centuries.

All of these strands of Romanticism (the dance, the character piece and national styles) combine in the many 'characteristic dances' of the period (the term has been borrowed from Tchaikovsky's title for his collection of national dances in his ballet *The Nutcracker*).

As a boy Fryderyk Chopin (1810–1849) became familiar with the Polish **mazurka**, a song and dance of the countryside around Warsaw (where he was born and brought up before the family moved to the city). There are three types of mazurka ranging from slow to fast, but all have characteristic rhythms such as the two types of 'dotted' rhythm in the music example below. These are the first four bars of his Mazurka in B flat, Op. 17 No. 1, which he wrote in 1832 shortly after settling in Paris. Chopin rarely used actual folk melodies which, in their original form, would often have been accompanied by a one- or two-note drone on the bagpipes. He sometimes imitates the effect by a pedal point in his piano music, but more often he transforms this simple style by adding sophisticated chromatic harmonies. However, in the example below the harmony could not be simpler: just the three primary triads are used and the only melodic chromaticism is the pair of chromatic lower auxiliary notes in bar 1. In folk music, the phrases of a mazurka are often repeated many times (the exact number of repeats being determined on the spot according to the wishes of the dancers). These repeats are reflected in Chopin's evocations of the dance, but again are often transformed by Chopin's subtle variations of each phrase.

Track 44

The diagram represents the first 24 bars of the mazurka. The first phrase is represented by the letter A and its music is printed below, while phrase B is a contrasting four-bar phrase. All phrases are four bars long but, as in much Romantic music, this is disguised to some extent by the liberal use of rubato.

| A | A¹ | B | B¹ | A² | A³ |

Chopin: Mazurka, Op. 17 No. 1, bars 1–4 (phrase A)

(a) In the repeat of the first phrase (A¹), which bar is rhythmically altered?

(b) (i) How does the tessitura of the melody of phrase B differ from that of phrase A?

    (ii) How does phrase B¹ differ from phrase B?

(c) (i) What is the most important difference between the last two phrases (A² and A³) and the first phrase (A)?

    (ii) Which beat of the bar is most strongly accented at the end of the extract?

The following diagram represents the middle section of the ternary structure of this mazurka. Each section is again four bars long.

| Left-hand chords only | C | C¹ | C | C² |

(d) How does the rhythm of the section for left hand alone conflict with the overall metre of the mazurka?

(e) With what type of melodic decoration does phrase C end?

(f) (i) Describe the modification to phrase C which you can hear in the second half of phrase C¹.

    (ii) Describe the modification to phrase C which you can hear after the two very high notes in phrase C².

(g) What harmonic device is used throughout the extract on this track, and what is this device meant to suggest?

Antonín Dvořák (1841–1904), following in the footsteps of his friend Brahms (whose Hungarian dances based on gypsy themes had been such a success) produced two sets of Slavonic Dances which, although mostly composed from entirely original thematic materials, closely followed the idioms of Czech, Slovak, Balkan and Ukrainian folk dances. These idioms include the repetitive use of fragmentary melodies based round the interval of a third and a fifth, the use of modes often approximating to the descending melodic minor, pentatonic melodies and alternating fast and slow sections. Dvořák's harmonies often reflect the nature of his melodies in their modality and use of parallel root position chords. Many of these features are evident in the extract from his Slavonic Dance No. 7 (1878) on Track 46.

[139]

The extract falls into three short and clearly defined sections. The questions are related to these sections.

Section 1

(a) Bars 1–2 of the oboe part are given below. What happens in bars 3–4?

Oboe

(b) The two-bar oboe phrase heard in bars 5–6 is also given above. Describe three ways in which this phrase is treated by the oboe in the next ten bars.

(c) Listen to the pizzicato bass part in these first 16 bars.

    (i) What sort of scale does the bass play?

    (ii) What sort of chords are played above this bass part?

(d) What is the relationship between the oboe and bassoon parts in the first 12 bars of this section?

Section 2

(e) The first bar of the flute part (doubled by the oboe) at the start of this second section is given below. What happens in the next bar?

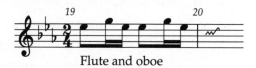

Flute and oboe

(f) The first four bars begin in C minor. To which key does the music modulate at the end of this phrase?

(g) The first four-bar phrase is followed by three more four-bar phrases. Compare each of these three four-bar phrases with the first four-bar phrase.

Section 3

(h) The third section repeats most of the music of the first section. How does the orchestration of this repeat differ from the original scoring?

Pyotr Il'yich Tchaikovsky (1840–1893) was the most Westernized of the major 19th-century Russian composers and is sometimes dismissed as a confectioner of lyrical melodies set in lush orchestral textures. Yet in many of his compositions the influence of folk music is glaringly obvious. In his first great success, the Fantasy-Overture *Romeo and Juliet* (1869), he wedded the Shakespearian subject matter of his orchestral programme music to sonata form and, in the love theme of the second subject, he used Western European chromatic harmony with weeping appoggiaturas. But the work opens with a modal theme reminiscent of Russian Orthodox chant (to represent Friar Lawrence) and the first subject of the sonata-allegro (representing the conflict between the Capulets and the Montagues) begins with a striking phrase which emphasizes the first three degrees of the minor scale together with a prominent fourth. Compare this with 'The Song of the Volga Boatmen' and note that, like this and many other Russian folk melodies, short motifs of a narrow range are often repeated. You can hear examples of themes that circle nostalgically round the same few notes of a minor or modal scale in the work of many Russian composers, right up to the 20th-century works of Rachmaninov and Stravinsky. Tchaikovsky, like Dvořák, sucessfully combined Western European forms and techniques with idioms derived from the folk music of his home land. The trepak from his ballet *The*

Nutcracker (1892) on Track 47 may not have balalaikas (Russian guitars), but in most other respects it is as typical of this wild Cossack dance as many of the modern offerings presented by Russian dance ensembles.

Test 101

This trepak by Tchaikovsky is in ternary form. The questions relate to the three obvious sections of this structure.

Section 1

Tempo di trepak, molto vivace

Violin

Tchaikovsky, Trepak from The Nutcracker, *bars 1–4*

(a) The music above shows the first violin part of the first four bars. In which bar and upon which beat can you hear an off-beat accent in this phrase?

(b) The next four bars are derived from the four bars printed above.

    (i) Which three-note rhythmic motif is used in this second four-bar phrase?

    (ii) Describe how the phrasing of the motif here differs from its phrasing in the first four bars printed above.

    (iii) Describe the bass part in relation to this phrasing.

(c) After these first eight bars what happens in the remainder of section 1?

Section 2

(d) Which instruments have the melody in this section?

(e) What thematic connection is there between this melody and the melody of section 1?

(f) In which other ways does the thematic structure of this section resemble that of section 1?

(g) There is a short link between this section and the recapitulation. What rhythmic devices does Tchaikovsky employ in this link in order to generate excitement for the recapitulation?

Section 3

(h) How does the recapitulation differ from section 1 in:

    (i) orchestration?

    (ii) form?

    (iii) tempo?

Music in the 20th Century

The final century of the millennium began with a feeling in the minds of some composers that the current vocabulary of music was exhausted. The process of evolution in the arts has tended to produce similar crises at surprisingly regular intervals, providing the dates are not taken too literally: we have seen it around 1600 (Baroque), 1675 (late Baroque), 1750 (Classical) and 1825 (Romantic). After 1900, though, the crisis began to seem much more acute. Music of all kinds had a wider audience than ever before. The rapid increase of population in the industrial West during the 19th century had brought a huge increase in music-making, both for the amateur in the home, church, brass band and choral society, and for the professional in the music hall, concert hall and opera house. The rise of cheap music printing and the inventions of the mechanical 'player piano' and gramophone recording in the late 19th century (followed by radio broadcasting in the 1920s) disseminated music on an unprecedented scale.

Until the early 19th century, music had always meant contemporary music. With just a few exceptions, works that were not reasonably current were soon forgotten. However, 19th-century interest in historicism of all kinds soon led to rediscoveries of Bach, Palestrina and other forgotten composers—to be followed by a conscious effort to revive plainsong and to preserve rural folk-song. Also at this time a clearer division between popular and serious music emerged, with ragtime making its full impact in 1900, to be followed by the arrival of jazz.

In this wide and varied musical climate, it would never have been possible for a single style, or even a limited number of similar styles, to emerge as it eventually did after 1600 and 1750. What happened instead was a much greater emphasis on **individualism**. As always, some composers initially proved hugely popular—and some of these have already started to fade into obscurity—while others produced works which were ridiculed at their premières, only later to be recognized as amongst the masterpieces of 20th-century music.

Sometimes the search for a new musical language led composers to become isolated from their audiences. As in other art forms, some of the more extreme experiments led to 20th-century music gaining a reputation for ephemeral novelty and even for being unapproachable, unfathomable and occasionally downright unpleasant. Because audiences no longer depended on a constant supply of contemporary music, performances of the 'classics' and revivals of 'authentic' early music, as well as pop and jazz, could easily move in to the fill the gap, as they still do to this very day. Nevertheless, it should be remembered that the 20th century is also the age of such enduringly popular works as *The Rite of Spring*, *The Planets*, *Carmina Burana*, *Peter and the Wolf*, Ravel's *Bolero*, *Rhapsody in Blue*, Elgar's Cello Concerto, *Façade*, *Belshazzar's Feast*, the *War Requiem* and Penderecki's *St Luke Passion*. A century of contrasts, indeed.

For some composers—and for a surprisingly long period—a central problem was posed by the somewhat flawed notion of the 'breakdown of tonality'. Flawed because, in reality, tonality cannot break down any more than $\frac{4}{4}$ time can break down—it can just stop being used. Flawed, too, because there are many examples, in jazz and popular music as well as in large sections of most of the works listed above, that show the major–minor tonal system to be alive and well, and perfectly capable of being adapted to the needs of a new musical language. Indeed, in a way that can only be explained by the tendency of all things fashionable to run full circle, tonal music is once again at the heart of the avant garde, as you can hear in the works of composers such as Reich, Tavener and Górecki (the rise of whose Third Symphony to both the top of the classical charts and number six in the pop LP charts early in 1993 somewhat dumbfounded the pundits). For much of the 20th century, contemporary serious music suffered under the notion that it must be 'difficult', could only appeal to a small number of enthusiasts, and needed a network of grants and subsidies, and publicly funded broadcasting to exist at all. Such a system has, of course, proved as necessary as the aristocratic patronage of old for some composers. The alternative idea that modern art music can have popular appeal, and the ability to 'sell' itself, seems peculiar in the late 20th century, even though it would not have seemed strange in earlier periods. Inevitably a reactionary element struggles against this, in the belief that anything popular must lack intellectual rigour or seriousness of purpose. 'Cross-over' composers such as Martland reject such simplistic arguments, though, by refusing to accept the artificial division of music into popular and serious categories.

This is not to imply that some sort of subversive Romanticism sprawled on, unchallenged and unchanged through the 20th century. At least as important as the attempts to replace the tonal system were those composers that sought to develop it in new ways. Debussy was already exploring the novel use of modal, pentatonic and whole-tone scales and of a new, colouristic approach to harmony and texture in the 1890s. Later, composers such as Hindemith looked to the technique of harmony based on fourths (quartal harmony) rather than thirds, or of harmony based on seconds and similar 'tone clusters'. Others incorporated elements of modality or the blues scale into the tonal system. Still others were less interested in pushing out the boundaries of harmony and tonality than in exploring the potential of rhythm—that element of Western music which is, to many other cultures, the most naïve and underdeveloped.

Romanticism did, however, continue without too many rude interruptions for the first decade or so of the century: the calm before the storm of the First World War, during which the rich, chromatic style of Wagner was culminating in the works of Mahler, Richard Strauss, and Elgar; when Puccini was following in Verdi's footsteps and Rachmaninov and Rimsky-Korsakov were perpetuating the Russian Romanticism of Tchaikovsky. The world in 1918, though, was a different place. Schoenberg's *Pierrot Lunaire* (1912), Stravinsky's *The Rite of Spring* (1913) and Holst's *The Planets* (1916) had appeared as just three of many harbingers of a new music; the arrival of the Americans in Europe towards the end of the war (1917, the year of the first jazz recording by The Original Dixieland Jass Band) heralded the start of a whole new era in popular music and the economics of war had finally put an end to the vast orchestras required by more excessive elements in late Romantic music, signalling a new, leaner era in which the chamber orchestra and smaller ensemble would rise to prominence.

Serialism

The early music of Arnold Schoenberg (1874–1951) includes the lush string sextet, *Verklärte Nacht* (1899) and the colossal *Gurrelieder* (for narrator, five soloists, three male choruses, eight-part choir and an orchestra of 140). Both works are in a rich, post-Wagnerian style, with an accumulation of chromatic and contrapuntal detail that challenges, but never entirely removes, the sense of key. Tension is heightened by long appoggiaturas on complex chords, creating dissonances that often resolve onto further dissonances—a technique typical of all late Romantic music. In order to maximize their expressive impact, Schoenberg's discords were becoming longer and their resolutions shorter and less obvious, to the point where any expectation of resolution was forgotten. Alongside this, the tonal signposts of recognizable tonic and dominant chords were becoming rarer until, in 1908, Schoenberg saw that, by abandoning the concept of key, he could use dissonance as freely and expressively as he wanted. Schoenberg disliked the term **atonality** ('without key'), preferring pantonality ('all keys'). Whatever the name, though, the lack of a tonal centre in music brought new organizational problems. At first, the best way to balance the expressive power of continual dissonance seemed to be brevity—a solution also adopted by Schoenberg's disciples, Berg and particularly Webern. Later, the use of a text helped provide a structure in the theatre music pieces, *Erwartung, Die glückliche Hand* and *Pierrot Lunaire*. In the latter, the melodrama (narrative spoken over music) of *Gurrelieder* is intensified to *sprechgesang* ('speechsong') in which the voice keeps to exact rhythms and follows an outline of relative pitches. Music of this period is often described as **expressionist**—a term borrowed from the visual arts and meaning the outward expression of hidden emotions (particularly the inner world of dreams and nightmares) often by means of shocking and distorted images. Schoenberg spent a long time grappling with the problem of structuring music without the use of tonality. The use of forms such as passacaglia, fugue and canon in *Pierrot Lunaire* pointed towards the possibility of counterpoint, which was where Schoenberg eventually found his answer—in the strict equality of all 12 semitones, and in their essentially contrapuntal treatment, provided by serial technique. Serialism was not Schoenberg's own invention, but he and his pupils Berg and Webern developed the technique (the three together being known as the Second Viennese School) and its principles influenced many later composers, especially in the years after 1945.

One of the unique aspects of serialism, at least in the context of Western music since the Renaissance, is that its structural system is almost impossible to discern by listening alone. It can be marvelled at on paper, like Bach's 'crab' canon in *The Musical Offering*, whose melody provides its own accompaniment when played backwards, and proponents of serialism would say that the listener is somehow subconsciously aware of the unity provided by serial technique. However, since this book is about aural perception, and the processes of serial music are very difficult to detect by ear alone, we shall shortly turn our attention to other strands in 20th-century music.

It is important to realize that serialism is only one way of organizing atonal music. Many 20th-century composers wrote atonal music, or used atonality in their vocabulary, without encountering problems of structure. In *The Rite of Spring*, for example, Stravinsky contrasted the most dissonant of harmonies with simple diatonic passages, and relied on the rhythmic strength of dance music and traditional techniques of repetition and variation for structure. The American composer Charles Ives was using atonality even before Schoenberg, but in a colouristic rather than structural way—his twin pieces *The Unanswered Question* and *Central Park In The Dark* (1906) are for two orchestras, one playing atonal music and the other tonal. They proceed, oblivious of each other, with different conductors and in different rhythms that never synchronize. A vivid example of atonal music by Ives will be found in *Sound Matters* No. 38—compare this with the serialism of Webern's Variations for Piano in *Sound Matters* No. 39.

Many aspects of 20th-century music show strong links with the past—a point that Schoenberg stressed in connection with his own music. The influence of traditional music from non-Western cultures has grown apace since Debussy heard the Javanese gamelan at the *Exposition Universelle* in Paris more than a century ago. Other links with the past include the continuing development of music rooted in national styles, notably by Bartók, Sibelius, Vaughan Williams and Manuel de Falla, the dying embers of Romanticism in Elgar, Rachmaninov and Richard Strauss, the neo-classicism of Stravinsky and Hindemith, the perpetuation of major genres such as the symphony (albeit in sometimes greatly changed forms), and in the revival of medieval techniques by composers such as Maxwell Davies and Birtwistle. Despite the individualism of 20th-century composers, such groupings reveal that various composers shared common aims, giving rise to the strands so often labelled as '-isms' of one kind or another.

Nationalism

While 19th-century nationalist composers were content to incorporate passing references to folk idioms, Béla Bartók (1881–1945) took a scientific interest in the folk music of Hungary and, with his friend and colleague Kodály, collected and categorized thousands of folk melodies from all over Eastern Europe. A few of these feature in his harmonizations of Romanian Folk Dances of 1915 (for piano, orchestrated 1917). The extracts on Tracks 48–50 include authentic Romanian melodies with Bartók's own harmonies, but you will find similar melodic contours in his other works, even when they are the product of the composer's own fertile imagination. The melodies use some of the characteristic scales of this region: listen out for the 'flat seventh' of the Dorian mode and the characteristic sharpened fourth of the Lydian mode. Sometimes less familiar modes are used, such as the Dorian with a flattened second or a sharpened fourth, seeming to give the music a more chromatic tint. Melodies frequently finish on the second degree of the mode and another common feature is the transposition of a whole phrase by a fifth.

The seven dances of this suite all have melodies with four phrases in patterns such as AABB and ABBA, with or without some variation of the repeated phrases. Bartók's harmonies include drones (pedals) on the tonic and dominant, modal progressions (including non-functional dominant sevenths) and tonal as well as modal cadences. Sometimes he includes heterophony but never, in these settings, any contrapuntal textures. The scoring (for a small orchestra of strings, two horns and double woodwind without oboes) is characteristically vivid.

Track 48

=== Test 102 ===

(a) Upon which of these modes is the clarinet melody based?

Lydian   Dorian   Dorian with a sharp fourth   Dorian with a flat second

(b) Which of the patterns below best indicates the phrase structure?

AABB   ABB^{1}A^1 AAB^{1}A^1 AA^{1}BB^1

(c) Upon which degree of the mode do each of these four phrases end?

(d) With which sort of cadence does Bartók end the dance?

Track 49

=== Test 103 ===

(a) Upon which of these modes is the piccolo melody based?

Lydian   Dorian   Dorian with a sharp fourth   Dorian with a flat second

(b) Which of the patterns below best indicates the phrase structure?

AABB   AABB^1 AAB^{1}A   AA^{1}BB^1

(c) Describe Bartók's harmonization, indicating how the accompaniment for the last two phrases differs from the accompaniment for the first two phrases.

Track 50

=== Test 104 ===

(a) Upon which of these modes is the first phrase of the violin melody based?

Lydian   Dorian   Dorian with a sharp fourth   Dorian with a flat second

(b) How does the second phrase of the violin melody differ from the first?

(c) Which of the patterns below best indicates the phrase structure?

AABB   AABB^1 AA^{1}AA^1 AA^{1}BB^1

(d) What are the most important differences between Bartók's harmonization of the first two phrases and his harmonization of the last two phrases?

Impressionism

Although Debussy (1862–1918) disapproved of the term, 'Impressionism' does convey something of the style of his music from the time of his famous *Prélude à l'après-midi d'un faune* (1894) onwards. Like the evocations of the play of light in the paintings of such Impressionists as Monet, Debussy's music conjures up evanescent images of nature by techniques which were in many respects quite new to Western music (though traces of them may be found even in Wagner, with whose music Debussy had a life-long love–hate relationship). His style is based upon an exploration of delicate timbral combinations and contrasts rather than a developing musical argument. Forms are free, the shape sometimes being determined by the programme (as in *L'après-midi d'un faune* which is based on a poem with the same title). Harmonies are often static or change very slowly, with chords being chosen primarily for their colour—try playing a dominant ninth on the piano and then shifting all of the notes down in whole-tone steps for a simple example of Debussy's parallel harmony. Bare fifths, chromatic and modal progressions also form part of his rich harmonic vocabulary. Rhythms are complex and often designed to sound almost non-metrical. Melodies may be modal or based upon pentatonic or whole-tone scales. Tonality is often vague or implied by pedals. All of these techniques are used in order to create musical impressions of the pictorial or verbal images which inspired his compositions.

In his two sets of *Préludes* (1910 and 1913) Debussy continued the tradition of the 19th-century characteristic piece. Each of them ends with a verbal phrase which gives a clue to the impression the music is meant to evoke, and some have detailed performance directions which give further clues. In the Sixth Prelude of Book 1 the instructions at the start, *Ce rythme doit avoir la valeur sonore d'un fond de paysage triste et glacé*, immediately suggests both sad emptiness and a frozen wilderness. The 'title' at the end, ...*Des pas sur la neige* ('... Footsteps in the snow'), confirms the impression the music has already given.

(a) This is the first bar of Debussy's *Des pas sur la neige:*

Sad and Slow ♩=44

Which of the following best describes the tonality of the first four bars?

major   minor   modal   chromatic   atonal

(b) In the next two bars four chords appear in the bass. Describe this progression.

(c) After a short unaccompanied melody, the figures quoted in question (a) are heard in an upper part for four bars. Describe the bass part in these bars.

(d) In the closing bars the melodic line transfers to the bass, ending with the rhythms of bar 1. What interval is formed by the two notes of these final figures?

(e) Describe how the metre and tonality of the last few bars differ from the metre and tonality in the first 11 bars.

Impressionism was not the only movement in the visual arts to have an impact on French music in the early 20th century. **Dada** was a rejection of the entire gamut of artistic pretensions of the establishment—its musical counterpart is to be found in some of the highly individual works of Erik Satie, such as the collage of ragtime, revolver, typewriter and siren in his ballet score *Parade* (1917), written for Diaghilev and the Russian ballet in Paris (with set and costume designs by Picasso). In the same tradition comes the bitonal ragtime of Milhaud's ballet *Le Bœuf sur le toit* (1919) and his setting of descriptions selected from a farm machinery catalogue in the song cycle, *Machines agricoles* (1919). More significantly, perhaps, Milhaud (one of the group of French composers known as *Les Six*) went on to become one of the first composers to explore some of the techniques of jazz in works such as his ballet *La Création du monde* (1923). The use of popular dance styles, unusual performing resources and original presentation by such French composers was a major influence on *Façade*, written in 1921–22 by the young British composer, William Walton.

Messiaen (1908–1992) was one of the major composers of the century. Although not himself an Impressionist, he was influenced by Debussy's use of colouristic harmony and his non-metrical rhythms. Messiaen radically and systematically developed both of these. In his 'modes of limited transposition' he devised new scale patterns, in some of which it proved possible to use conventional triads, and sevenths built on these, in ways which are entirely free of the implications of tonal harmony and yet which have an inner logic of their own. The superimposition of these familiar patterns result in vivid, pungent harmonies which are instantly recognizable as one of Messiaen's distinctive fingerprints.

Messiaen's interest in Indian music led him to develop rhythms in which the relative durations of notes are of the essence, rather than the regular beats of metrical music. To the ear the most obvious technique is Messiaen's use of the *valeur ajoutée* or 'added value', in which the same (usually very short) duration is added to each note-length in a rhythm pattern, producing irregularities such as bars of four-and-a-quarter beats. If this device is used systematically it will result in music which has no regular metre—and this is precisely what he does. However, it can, as in Indian music, result in the perception a new, very fast pulse whose regularity gives a whole extra metrical dimension to the music.

Excerpts from the final piece, *Dieu parmi nous* ('God among us'), of Messiaen's cycle of meditations for organ, *La Nativité du Seigneur* ('The Birth of Our Lord', 1935) are recorded on Track 52. The track begins with two slow, keyless passages giving an impression of eternity (similar sections recur like refrains throughout the first part of the piece), while the joy of Christians today is represented by the final toccata. Its driving intensity comes from the use of *valeur ajoutée* and, while the chords are derived from the modes of limited transposition, the effect of rooting the tonality in E major produces a thrilling climax to the theme of the nativity bringing 'God among us' on earth.

 Track 52

Test 106

There are three separate extracts from *Dieu parmi nous* on this track, each separated by a short silence.

(a) In extract 1:

   (i) What compositional device does Messiaen use in the first moderately fast set of descending parallel chromatic dissonances?

   (ii) What sort of chord is held on the keyboard for the rest of the extract?

   (iii) Describe the bass melody played on the organ pedals under this chord.

(b) In extract 2:

   (i) How does this passage of descending parallel chromatic dissonances differ from the similar passage in extract 1?

   (ii) What is the relationship between the slower section of this passage and the slower section in extract 1?

(c) In extract 3:

   (i) How does the first phrase on the pedals in this toccata differ from the pedal part in the first extract?

   (ii) What use is made of this phrase on the pedals in the rest of this extract?

   (iii) Describe the rhythm of the part above the first phrase on the pedals.

   (iv) Upon what sort of chord does this extract end?

Neo-classicism

Stravinsky (1882–1971) was an enormously talented chameleon whose style evolved and changed many times throughout a long life in which he was to be uprooted to Paris at the outbreak of the Russian revolution and uprooted again to America at the start of the war in 1939. He was a pupil of Rimsky-Korsakov but wrote that 'the musicians of my generation and myself owe most to Debussy'. The influence of both composers is evident in *The Firebird* (1910), the first work he wrote for Diaghilev's famous ballet company on its Paris tours. His second ballet score, *Petrushka* (1911) revealed a more original style, and in 1913 he completed a third, *The Rite of Spring*—the work for which he was initially most notorious and is now most famous. It is scored for a very large orchestra, with

[147]

quadruple woodwind (plus alto flute), eight horns, five trumpets (including a piccolo trumpet), three trombones, two tubas and six percussionists. The scoring stretches the dynamic and frequency ranges of the orchestra to its limits. But what outraged the first audience most was his use of atonal dissonances, such as the famous **bitonal** 'Rite chord' (E flat[7] superimposed on a chord of E major) and his pounding, non-metrical rhythms to express the subject of pagan ritual sacrifice. Where Schoenberg (whose *Pierrot Lunaire* Stravinsky had heard while completing *The Rite*) was expanding the tonal bounds of music, Stravinsky was opening up an untapped world of new rhythmic possibilities. Messaien later made a study of the rhythms in *The Rite*, the asymmetrical augmentation and diminution of rhythm patterns influencing his own work.

Soon after the end of the war, Diaghilev asked Stravinsky to arrange a ballet score from works by Pergolesi (1710–1736) and other 18th-century composers. The result was the ballet *Pulcinella* (Paris, 1920), the first of Stravinsky's neo-classical works. The term 'neo-classical' does not, surprisingly, refer to a revival of the Classical style but to the use, in a new context, of a variety of techniques and styles from the past. Stravinsky, in his neo-classical works, draws on ideas ranging from the 17th to the 19th centuries. When you listen to the extract from *Pulcinella* below, notice that it goes beyond the idea of mere arrangement, and becomes a total reworking of the original in modern terms. However, most neo-classical music, like Prokofiev's 'Classical' Symphony, tends to combine the harmonic vocabulary and angular lines of the composer's own invention with the textures and techniques, but not the actual content, of earlier music.

Like much music of the time, *Pulcinella* was written for comparatively small resources—an orchestra of only 33 players, used in soloistic textures of great clarity. The extract from the *Gavotta con due variazioni* on Track 53 is a re-working of the movement by Martini studied on page 112 (recorded on Tracks 18–21). Stravinsky wrote of *Pulcinella* that it was 'my discovery of the past, the epiphany through which the whole of my later work became possible'. This is certainly true, for *Pulcinella* heralds a series of original neo-classical masterpieces including the Handelian opera-cum-oratorio *Oedipus Rex* (1927), and the Bachian concerto *Dumbarton Oaks* (1938). An extract from Stravinsky's neo-classical ballet score, *Agon* (1956–57), can be found in *Sound Matters*, No. 42. Here is the score of bars 1–14 of Martini's original harpsichord gavotte on which Stravinsky's music is based:

Martini: Gavotta from Sonata in D (1742)

You are to compare Stravinsky's arrangement of this gavotte, recorded on Track 53, with the music of Martini's original version, printed on page 148. The extract continues for a further 18 bars beyond the end of the printed music.

(a) What two instruments play the printed parts in bars 1–10?

(b) What other change does Stravinsky make in these first ten bars?

(c) Describe Stravinsky's alteration of Martini's bass part in bars 11–13.

(d) What device is employed in the horn part in bars 11–13?

(e) Comment on the texture of the final four bars of the gavotte (not printed).

(f) What, apart from instrumentation, reveals that this excerpt from *Pulcinella* is not in a purely 18th-century style?

Post-Romanticism

Three elements of Romanticism are apparent in the early works of Jean Sibelius (1865–1957). Most obvious is the lavish orchestral colouring, owing much to Tchaikovsky. Second is his use of the programmatic tone poem, in the tradition extending from Liszt to Richard Strauss, and third is the Finnish nationalism which he himself created (though he had a Scandinavian precedent in Grieg). All of these find expression in symphonic poems such as *En Saga* (1892), inspired by the *Kalevala*, the great Finnish national epic. Sibelius, unlike Bartók, showed little interest in folk-song, but he tried to capture the heroic spirit of a country struggling to establish an identity free of the domination of Sweden and Russia.

As a boy, Sibelius played the violin at home in chamber music by the Viennese Classical composers and developed a deep understanding of the sonata principle, especially in the works of Haydn and Beethoven. It was probably this experience which fired Sibelius (like Brahms before him) to seek to develop the structural elements of his musical thinking in his seven symphonies. Each inhabits quite a different sound world and tackles structural problems in quite different ways, but all share the composer's aim of 'severity of form and profound logic'—a sharp contrast to the expansive, 'all-embracing' symphonic thought of Mahler.

This is not the place for analysis of those structures, but a couple of Sibelius's most characteristic traits can be heard in the extract from the finale of his Fifth Symphony (1919) on Track 54. First comes a scurrying scale figure on strings with chattering woodwind. Then the horns and timpani enter—notice how the fast scurrying figure gives way to a slower horn figure swinging backwards and forwards like a pendulum (Tovey aptly described it as 'Thor's hammer'). This ability to move from one prevailing speed to another in the most natural, yet telling, way is one of Sibelius's great achievements. At subsequent hearings you may become aware that, once 'Thor's hammer' is underway, the music appears to be moving at three different speeds simultaneously, like clouds at different altitudes, some apparently stationary, others lumbering past them and yet others racing by. This is another fingerprint of Sibelius's symphonic technique which, like all great music, satisfies both the intellect (in that it relates to the overall 'profound logic' of the work) and the emotions (in that these different speeds create tensions which crave for, and eventually achieve, release).

The second characteristic trait is the composer's handling of tonality. The scurrying figure contains chromatic notes which undermine the sense of tonality (especially the sharpened fourth and flattened seventh) and contribute to the stormy mood. By contrast, 'Thor's hammer' glistens in the sun of pure diatonicism. What is more characteristic is the huge tonal shift that occurs towards the end of the extract. Again, we experience the combination of the emotional thrill of this earth-shattering move, without departing from the 'profound logic' in which this climax represents the slowest of the simultaneously moving speeds, an underlying march of tonal centres heading with inevitable steps for the final deeply satisfying cadence. But that, of course, is an aspect of the symphony which we can hardly expect to address in this book!

Listen to the recording and identify the bass part given in the music below (it starts about 30 seconds into the track). Most of the questions relate to this music.

(a) The double basses enter 17 seconds into the track. How does their entry underline the tonality of E flat?

(b) How does the prominent horn ostinato ('Thor's hammer') relate to the double bass part quoted in the music below?

(c) How does the speed of the shortest notes in the woodwind counter-melody relate to the speed of the horn ostinato?

(d) Immediately after the end of the bass part below, the music changes key.

　(i) To which of the following keys does the music move?

　　B flat major　　C minor　　A flat major　　C major　　E major

　(ii) How does the bass part underline this new tonal centre?

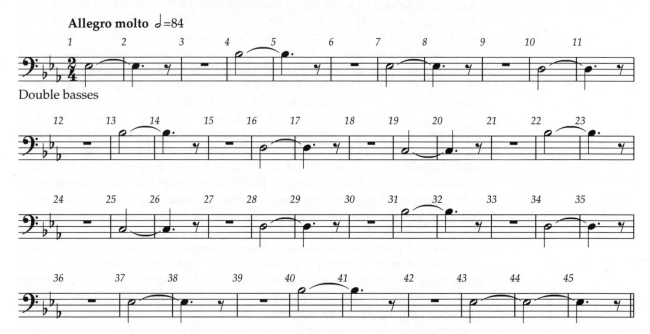

Sibelius: Symphony No. 5 (from the last movement)

The varied style of some composers defies attempts at labelling. In the music of Benjamin Britten (1913–1976), the English pastoral style of Vaughan Williams is evident in the modality of such early works as the *Hymn to the Virgin* (1930), yet, whilst still in his teens, Britten wrote the *Sinfonietta*, a chamber symphony with textures owing much to Schoenberg but including a distinctive pentatonic horn call in the first movement! European influences appear again in his homage to his teacher, the *Variations on a Theme of Frank Bridge* (1937), in which he affectionately parodies various European styles: early 19th-century Italian opera in the *Aria Italiana*, the early 18th-century French clavecinistes in the *Bourreé Classique*, 20th-century neo-classicism in the *Romance* and Mahler in *Wiener Walzer* (a parody of a parody!), *Funeral March* and *Chant*. Mahler's influence is again apparent in the wide-ranging melodies, chromaticism, insistent pedals and clear textures of the *Sinfonia da Requiem* (1940). Like Purcell before him, Britten's greatest achievement lies in his uncanny ability to reflect the rhythms and imagery of English verse in his song cycles. In the first two of these with opus numbers he set the poetry of his friend Auden, yet his next two cycles, *Les Illuminations* (1939) and *Seven Sonnets of Michelangelo* (1940) set French (Rimbaud) and Italian poetry in its original language with equal assurance. Such a diversity of influences sometimes leads to Britten's style being described as eclectic, yet Bach's compendium of German, Italian and French styles, genres and forms might be thought just as derivative. What matters is how such influences are used, and whether something new is created from them. In Britten's song cycle, *Serenade for Tenor, Horn and Strings* (1943), it would be hard to discern specific influences—they have been fused and transformed into a unique idiom. The style that was to ensure his success as perhaps the greatest 20th-century operatic composer is already evident in this work: a Mozartian clarity of texture and economy of means, an inspired use of tonal idioms ranging from the innocently diatonic to the tormentedly chromatic, an assured contrapuntal technique and satisfying formal structures which are motivically linked. But above all Britten gets to the core of his texts, and often throws completely new light upon them.

Track 55

Test 109

Here are the first six verses of an anonymous 15th-century dirge, which Britten uses as the text for one of the sections of his *Serenade for Tenor, Horn and Strings*. It tells of the soul's journey through purgatory and warns of the terrible consequences of a lack of charity in this life. All the questions relate to this text.

1   This ae nighte, this ae nighte,
      Every nighte and alle,
   Fire and <u>fleet</u> and <u>can</u>dle-lighte,
      And Christe receive thy saule.

2   When thou from hence away art past,
      Every nighte and alle,
   To Whinnymuir thou com'st at last;
      And Christe receive thy saule.

3   If ever thou gav'st hos'n and shoon,
      Every nighte and alle,
   Sit thee down and put them on;
      And Christe receive thy saule.

4   If hos'n and shoon thou ne'er gav'st nane,
      Every nighte and alle,
   The whinnies shall prick thee to the bare bane;
      And Christe receive thy saule.

5   From Whinnymuir when thou may'st pass,
      Every nighte and alle,
   To Brig o' Dread thou com'st at last;
      And Christe receive thy saule.

6   From Brig o' Dread when thou may'st pass,
      Every nighte and alle,
   To Purgatory fire thou com'st at last;
      And Christe receive thy saule.

(a) The first verse is unaccompanied and is based upon a descending minor triad. How do the notes on the underlined syllables relate to this triadic pattern? Describe each one individually.

(b) How does the melody of the last line of the verse relate to the melody of the second line?

(c) What use is made of the melody of verse 1 in the remainder of this extract?

(d) When the orchestra first enters how does Britten ensure musical continuity between the melody of verse 1 and this new theme on the orchestra?

(e) Comment on the tonality of the cello/bass melody in relation to the vocal melody of verse 2.

(f) At the word 'Whinnymuir' in verse 2 the violas enter. How does the tonality of the viola tune relate to both the cello/bass melody and the vocal melody in these first few bars?

(g) At the words 'hos'n and schoon' in verse 3 the second violins enter, and at the same words in verse 4 the first violins enter. What type of composition have you heard in the orchestra by the time the first violins have completed their melody?

(h) How does the string portamento at the end of the third line of verse 5 relate to the vocal melody?

(i) (i)   How does the string texture change when the horn enters?

   (ii)   Describe two other ways in which Britten achieves a musical climax at this point.

[151]

Another composer whose work resists the temptation to be pigeon-holed is Britten's friend, Shostakovich (1906–1975). He was just 11 when the October Revolution decisively changed the face of Russia, and he lived his life in the shadow of the Soviet state. Revolutionary zeal affected composers as much as it did any other citizen. His attempt to come to terms with the style of the Western avant garde was stymied when his opera *Lady Macbeth of Mtsensk* (1934) was described in the Communist press as 'chaos instead of music' shortly after Stalin heard it. Realizing that his modernism was unacceptable and could lead to the Gulag Archipelago, Shostakovich wrote his justly famous Fifth Symphony (1937) as 'a Soviet artist's reply to just criticism'. Decadent capitalist experiments had to be abandoned in favour of wholesome socialist realism expressed in clearly formulated structures (though the harmonies, textures and orchestration might often seem Mahlerian). In practice this meant that any form of atonal music was out of the question, and his new compositions had to conform to Soviet norms by being based on some sort of programme which glorified the struggle of the proletariat, whilst at the same time being constructed according to what amounted to a revenant sonata principle. At first it may seem surprising that Shostakovich was able to produce some of his greatest works under such a repressive regime, yet composers have always responded well to discipline, whether self-imposed or required by their conditions of employment.

Shostakovich's Seventh Symphony (1941) manifests both these elements. On the one hand it clearly depicts the suffering and heroism of the people of Leningrad (now St Petersburg) in a steadfast defence of their city in the face of Fascist aggressors. On the other, it is based upon the tonal system and motivic integration of Beethoven (with, of course, brilliant 20th-century orchestration and dissonant harmony). Far from being atonal, the symphony contains tunes of such diatonic clarity that the proletariat could whistle them after one hearing of the work (such a tune, representing the march of the Nazis upon Leningrad, is the subject of Bartók's bitter satire in his Concerto for Orchestra).

In later years Shostakovich's music became more introspective and doom-laden, sometimes including the motif D–E flat–C–B, the German letter names for which transliterate to D. Sch(ostakovich). The extract on Track 56 comes from his First Cello Concerto, Op. 107 (1959), which was written for Rostropovich (for whom Britten wrote his Cello Symphony). In this you will hear the following similarly obsessive motif, played at the start by the cello and developed throughout the first subject:

Allegretto

Solo cello

 Track 56

===== *Test 110* =====

You will hear an extract from the beginning of the Cello Concerto. This extract can be divided into four sections, as follows:

Section 1	Section 2	Section 3	Section 4
Based on the motif printed above	Begins with rising chromatic scales on woodwind	Begins and ends with sustained woodwind chords	Strings enter for the first time

(a) In **section 1**:

   (i)   What sort of chord does the orchestra play when it first enters?

   (ii) How does this chord cause tonal tension between the soloist and the orchestra?

(iii) Describe the texture and the orchestration of the orchestral accompaniment in the first 20 seconds.

(iv) In this same passage, how does Shostakovich treat the initial motif?

(v) What, in this same passage, does the cello borrow from the orchestral accompaniment?

(b) In **section 2**:

(i) how does Shostakovich develop the orchestral part of the first 20 seconds?

(ii) what special string techniques does the cellist employ?

(c) In **section 3**, what new type of rhythm appears in the cello part in the two passages of sustained woodwind chords?

(d) In **section 4**:

(i) what happens at the beginning of this section, in terms of the form of the extract?

(ii) the orchestra begins to play thematic material not heard in the accompaniment before: describe it.

Post-Modernism

Those observers who believe that the 150-year cycles and 75-year sub-cycles of renewal in the arts are something more than just coincidence were doubtless expecting to witness a change of direction in musical style after 1975, despite the fact that the individualism of 20th-century music warns against making too many assumptions about universal trends. With the benefit of a little hindsight, though, the death of Shostakovich in 1975 may perhaps have marked the passing of an era, since a new course in modern music is discernible in recent decades. The term 'post-modernism' has been hijacked from the visual arts (particularly architecture) as an umbrella word to describe this new direction. It is, however, one of the silliest labels of all, for it implies that music written 30, 50 or more years ago is still 'modern' and it ignores the irrefutable fact that what seems the mode of today will seem very old-fashioned to future generations.

Post-modernism is certainly part of the cycle of reaction and renewal that has been the ongoing process of Western art. Just as post-modernist architecture has rejected the functional severity of the buildings of the previous generation and turned to an aesthetic that makes obvious references to past historical styles, so music has turned again to tonal and modal styles that some once thought were exhausted. Just as the new architecture can sometimes appear pretentious—the supermarket sporting false porticos and gables, and graced with an atrium—so the new music can appear static and naïve. This, though, is perhaps to misunderstand its rationale, which centres around a rejection of the intellectualism of the earlier avant garde. Instead, it claims an identity for itself that does not require the understanding of a hierarchy of theories or the analysis of complex interrelationships, but which borrows an aesthetic from popular music and asks simply to be taken for what it is. In essence, it is the same feeling that the agenda of previous musical style has been fulfilled, and that a fresh start must be made with the basics, as has occurred at the start of every previous new stylistic period in music.

As early as 1969 the Polish composer Górecki (b. 1933) forsook Webernian pointillism to write *Three Little Pieces in Olden Style* which include references to 16th-century Polish song. Since then his style has become ever more simple and more modal. In his Third Symphony, the recent popularity of which was mentioned at the start of this chapter, Górecki makes reference to Polish folk-song and church music as well as Beethoven and Chopin. The style can be static and meditative (like that of the music of his teacher, Messiaen) but never overtly intellectual (like that of Boulez).

The music of the English composer John Tavener (b. 1944) has an inner stillness derived from the ancient Byzantine chant of his adopted Orthodox faith. *The Protecting Veil* for cello and orchestra was first performed at the Proms in 1989 and, like Górecki's Third Symphony, its recording achieved unprecedented sales for a piece of new music. Drones are used throughout long sections of the work, and microtones sometimes appear in its long repetitious incantatory melodies. The harmonic backdrop to these largely diatonic melodies is simple and slow moving with wide-spaced textures. There are occasional programmatic references (like the string chords which are meant to represent monastery bells), but the overall effect is of meditative stasis.

Tavener uses the serial techniques of inverted and reversed note-rows in his work, but when applied to essentially tonal material the results could not be more different to 12-tone serialism. He described his five-act stage work, *Mary of Egypt* (Aldeburgh, 1992), as a 'moving icon': that concisely indicates the huge gulf which separates this music from both the sonata-drama of the 18th and 19th centuries and the tortured Expressionism and cerebral serialism of some of the music of the earlier 20th century.

Track 57

Test 111

You will hear the second verse of Tavener's setting (1976) of a poem entitled *The Lamb* by William Blake (1757–1827). The words make little sense without the first verse, so, although only verse 2 is recorded here, both verses are printed. The questions relate only to verse 2.

Verse 1	**Verse 2**	*Line Number*
Little Lamb, who made thee?	Little Lamb, I'll tell thee	1
Dost thou know who made thee?	Little Lamb, I'll tell thee:	2
Gave thee life, and bid thee feed	He is called by thy name,	3
By the stream and o'er the mead;	For he calls himself a Lamb.	4
Gave thee clothing of delight,	He is meek and he is mild;	5
Softest clothing, wooly, bright;	He became a little child.	6
Gave thee such a tender voice,	I, a child, and thou a lamb	7
Making all the vales rejoice?	We are called by his name.	8
Little Lamb, who made thee?	Little Lamb, God bless thee!	9
Dost thou know who made thee?	Little Lamb, God bless thee!	10

(a) Describe the choir in terms of the number of voice parts and types of voice.

(b) Compare the choral textures of the settings of lines 1 and 2.

(c) Which of the following words best describes the melody of line 1?

    chromatic   atonal   modal   diatonic   pentatonic

(d) Listen carefully to the uppermost part of line 2, then to the bass part. How do these two parts relate to each other?

(e) Which of the following words best describes the melody of lines 3 and 4?

    chromatic   atonal   modal   diatonic   pentatonic

(f) What do the settings of lines 5 and 6 have in common with (i) line 2, and (ii) lines 3 and 4?

(g) (i) Which of the following words best describes the texture of the setting of lines 7 and 8?

        monodic   unison   homophonic   contrapuntal

    (ii) Which of the following words best describes the tonality of these same lines 7 and 8?

        chromatic   atonal   modal   diatonic   pentatonic

(h) How does the very last phrase of music relate to the three previous phrases?

(i) Comment on the metre of the whole setting.

Minimalism

Further examples of work that looks afresh at the building-blocks of music can be found in the style of the minimalist composers. Typical is the use of the most basic of tonal melodic motifs, deployed in the simplest of forms generated by interaction and repetition, often with no modulation or changes of tempo at all.

In C (1964) by Terry Riley (b. 1935) was one of the first such works. The composition consists of 53 melodic motifs of the utmost simplicity. For example, motif 1 consists of three crotchets on the same note E, all three with the same grace-note; motif 2 consists of two quavers and a crotchet in the pattern E–F–E, the first E having the same grace-note as motif 1; motif 3 consists of the same three pitches as motif 2, but it begins off the beat with a quaver. Each of these motifs is repeated as often as desired as each instrumentalist plays through all 53. Although some motifs introduce F sharp or B flat, these simply colour the slowly shifting chordal patterns which emerge from the phasing between the various instruments.

There are no contrasts, no drama, no development of ideas, simply organic mutations like the same object viewed in differing lights. Although the use of repetitious patterns has precedents in the music of Satie and the ostinato-based style of Orff, this hypnotic music has more in common with gamelan and other oriental music than with earlier Western styles. Indeed, in Riley's later works repetition is used in rhythmic cycles similar to the *tala* of Indian music. Like his contemporaries, Steve Reich and Philip Glass, Riley has gone on to explore the concept of **phase music**, in which the use of motifs that shift out of phase with one another at an almost imperceptibly slow rate gradually bring into focus a spectrum of new textures and patterns.

A particular phenomenon of late 20th-century music has been the interaction of previously separate types of music. Sometimes this may appear to be no more than the fashion of the moment—Vivaldi played on amplified strings, a little Classical music to enhance the classiness of a product in a commercial, or a world-famous opera singer appearing in the pop charts. In such matters, it is easy to fall prey to the promotional power of the music industry, itself a force that makes an enormous impact on the success (or otherwise) of new music in any sphere. Nevertheless, the merging of styles, already noted in jazz fusion and popular folk music, has made an impact on art music, too.

Steve Martland (b. 1959) is one of several young composers who refuse to recognize traditional distinctions between the various '-isms' of serious music on the one hand and jazz and pop on the other. In an interview reported in the monthly *Classic CD* (August 1990), he affirmed that he was a part of the radical British tradition of dissent and went on 'I reject the classical music establishment ... Music is about communication but you can only engage the imagination of an audience if you've got something to say about the world in which we all live'. This social relevance is reflected in the rock-style presentation of Martland's concerts, but he equally rejects the label of pop star: 'pop is all about production rather than the quality of the material ...The act of performing, that's where my music gets closest to rock ...There are pop people who enjoy my music on a surface level but who don't understand the technicalities and the intellectual things'. His philosophy centres on the idea that the patron of modern music is not the aristocrat of old, nor even corporate bodies such as the BBC or Arts Council, but quite simply the public and it is to them that composers must direct their work. To this end, the performance and promotion of his music is of paramount importance: 'It's my work I want people to know. The only way to do that is to get out there and sell yourself.' While Martland's promotional techniques are borrowed from the world of pop, in his music he admits to the influences of Bach and Stravinsky as well as 'downtown New York rap and earthy Dutch music'. He is, in short, a **cross-over** composer who, like Bach and Stravinsky, is prepared to utilize whatever resources and styles come to hand so long as they serve his purpose. Those resources include some of the techniques evolved by minimalist composers, as is evident in this extract from *Principia* (first performed at the City of Leeds College of Music in 1990).

You will hear part of an episodic composition which falls into well-defined sections. Three of these are recorded on this track. The first section (A) is repeated in modified form (A^1) after a shorter middle section (B).

(a) Describe the instrumentation.

(b) In **section A**:

    (i) How many different pitches are used in the melodic line?

    (ii) How is variety achieved with these melodic pitches?

    (iii) Suggest a suitable time signature.

    (iv) Describe the texture of the whole passage.

(c) In **section B**:

    (i) How do the rhythms of this section differ from those in section A?

    (ii) How do the chords here differ from those in section A?

    (iii) How does the tonality here differ from that of section A?

(d) How does the harmony at the start of section A^1 differ from the harmony at the start of section A?

Postlude

It is important to realize that we have not, in this chapter as in any other, had the space to provide a comprehensive survey of the music of the age. Rather, we hope to have introduced you to the aural recognition of some of the many styles of the music of the 20th century and to some of the techniques used. There are many others. You will find examples of music that includes aleatoric elements, graphic scores, modern 'music theatre' and electronic music in *Sound Matters* (Nos. 44–48) as well as other examples of the styles mentioned in this chapter. Beyond this, take every opportunity not only to broaden your listening, but to deepen it. Aim to take in more detail, recognize the procedures being used and become aware of the comparisons and contrasts, similarities and differences. Notice how the greatest music will reveal more and more of its detail with repeated listening. These things will, in turn, inform your historical and analytical studies in music, help you to evaluate and refine your performances, and assist in the the judgements you make in composition, for, in all of these things, it is the experience of musicians everywhere that **aural matters**.

Answers to the Tests

Melody Tests 1–6

Two-Part Tests 7–10

Track 22

Track 23

Track 24

Track 25

Track 26

Test 12 **Page 19** (a) (i) Interrupted (ii) Plagal (iii) Imperfect (iv) Perfect.
    (b) A descending scale, E down to A.
    (c) Minor: chord II (A minor).
    (d) Perfect.

Test 13 **Page 21** (a) Ib (F/A).
    (b) It is the same.
    (c) A triple suspension (i.e., the notes D, F and B natural are repeated from the previous bar) followed by a tonic chord of C.
    (d) V^7 (C^7).
    (e) Imperfect.
    (f) II^7b (Gm^7/B flat).
    (g) (i) Tonic, dominant and lower tonic (i.e., root, fifth and root again).
        (ii) A suspension on E, resolving upwards to F.

Test 14 **Page 23** (a) V^7d–Ib (D^7/C–G/B).
    (b) Suspension, passing-note, seventh.
    (c) F natural. It is chromatic, being cancelled by an F sharp in the same bar.
    (d) Plagal.
    (e) Preparation, suspension and resolution.
    (f) (i) D major (ii) B minor (iii) A minor.
    (g) The same chord, but the bass is an octave higher and has a passing-note.
    (h) Ic (G/D)—in other words, a cadential second inversion.

Test 15 **Page 24** (a) D major (the dominant).
    (b) Ib (G/B), VI (Em), V^{4-3} in D (A sus D).
    (c) Imperfect, perfect.
    (d) A minor, C major.

Test 16 **Page 25** (a) IV (Gm), V (A), flat VII (C).
    (b) A perfect cadence, decorated with a passing seventh on its first chord and a *tierce de Picardie* on its second chord.

Test 17 **Page 26** (a) V^7 (D^7).
    (b) It is the same but in sequence, a third lower (in the key of E minor).
    (c) (i) A false relation is caused by the singer's A natural.
        (ii) The singer has an appoggiatura (not a suspension) on the note C.
    (d) (i) Diminished seventh, (ii) Neapolitan sixth.
    (e) E minor

Test 18 **Page 28** (a) The chords change once per bar. They consist of the pattern I, IVc and a diminished seventh (E, A/E and dim. 7).
    (b) G natural, F sharp and E.
    (c) (i) G major (the flattened mediant).
        (ii) A tonic pedal (on G).
    (d) A diminished seventh followed by a dominant seventh of E (B^7).

Test 19 **Page 30** (a) A secondary dominant (E/G sharp) and V^7b (D^7/F sharp).
    (b) Bar 5 uses the progression I–IIIb (G–Bm/D) under-pinned by a tonic pedal: bar 9 uses the same progression but without the pedal.
    (c) B major and G major.
    (d) They are chromatic lower auxiliaries in thirds.
    (e) Perfect cadence in C major.
    (f) C sharp.
    (g) Dominant major ninth or dominant seventh with an appoggiatura.
    (h) A double appoggiatura, effectively creating the progression IVc–I (C/G–G).

Test 20 **Page 31** (a) It follows a similar scale pattern in tenths below the melody.
    (b) B flat major (the dominant).
    (c) Chord I of B flat minor.
    (d) An inverted pedal on the dominant (B flat).
    (e) Diminished seventh.
    (f) IIb (Fm/A flat).

Test 21 **Page 32** (a) An augmented sixth on the note C and V^7 in A minor (E^7).
    (b) An inverted pedal on E.
    (c) Neapolitan sixth (the violin plays F natural above the printed notes).
    (d) With a triple suspension.
    (e) (i) F major (the 'Neapolitan key') (ii) C major (iii) A minor.

Test 22	**Page 34**	Bar 2	Beat 3	Flat.
		Bar 4	Beat 1	Sharp.
		Bar 6	Beat 2	Sharp.
		Bar 7	Beat 2	Flat.
Test 23	**Page 35**			
	Track 39	Bar 1	Beat 3	Flat.
		Bar 3	Beat 2	Flat.
		Bar 4	Beat 1	Sharp.
	Track 40	Bar 2	Beat 2	Flat.
		Bar 3	Beat 4	Sharp.
		Bar 5	Beat 4	Sharp.
	Track 41	Bar 1	Beat 3	Sharp.
		Bar 2	Beat 3	Flat.
		Bar 4	Beat 1	Sharp.
	Track 42	Bar 1	Beat 2	Sharp.
		Bar 2	Beat 3	Flat.
		Bar 3	Beat 1	Flat.
Test 24	**Page 36**			
	Track 43	Bar 1	Beat 3	The A flat is sharp.
		Bar 2	Beat 3	The C is flat.
		Bar 3	Beat 1	Flat.
		Bar 4	Beat 1	Flat.
	Track 44	Bar 2	Beat 1	Flat.
		Bar 4	Beat 1	Flat.
		Bar 5	Beat 2	The F is sharp.
		Bar 8	Beat 1	Sharp.
	Track 45	Bar 1	Beat 1	The E is flat.
		Bar 2	Beat 2	The F is sharp.
		Bar 4	Beat 2	The first C is flat.
		Bar 6	Beat 2	The A is flat.
Test 25	**Page 37**			
	Track 46	Bar 2	Beat 1	The C is sharp.
		Bar 3	Beat 1	The F is flat.
		Bar 4	Beat 3	Sharp
		Bar 5	Beat 3	The top E is flat.
		Bar 7	Beat 2	The A is flat.
	Track 47	Bar 1	Beat 2	Sharp.
		Bar 2	Beat 4	Flat.
		Bar 3	Beat 4	Flat.
		Bar 5	Beat 2	Sharp.
		Bar 6	Beat 3	Sharp.
Test 26	**Page 39**	Bar 3	Beat 2	Oboe: D not F.
		Bar 5	Beat 4	Clarinet: B flat not B natural.
		Bar 7	Beat 1	Oboe: dotted quaver, semiquaver.
		Bar 8	Beats 1–2	Clarinet: dotted crotchet, quaver.
		Bar 11	Beats 1–2	Bassoon: dotted crotchet, quaver.
		Bar 12	Beat 1	Bassoon: F sharp not F natural.
Test 27	**Page 40**	Bar 1	Beat 2	Horn: B flat (changing the tonic triad into a dissonance).
		Bar 4	Beats 1–3	Trumpet: minim and two quavers (compare with bar 12).
		Bar 6	Beat 1	Trombone: D not F (creating an interrupted cadence).
		Bar 8	Beat 2	Horn: the quaver was B natural, not B flat.
		Bar 10	Beats 2–3	Trumpet: two quavers, crotchet (removing the syncopation).
		Bar 13	Beats 1–3	Trombone: minim, crotchet (spoiling the hemiola).
Test 28	**Page 41**	Bar 1	Beat 1	Bassoon: third semiquaver was F sharp not A sharp (making the imitation of the oboe part less exact).
		Bar 2	Beat 3	Bassoon: dotted quaver, semiquaver.
		Bar 4	Beat 1	Oboe: the top (tied) note was F sharp, not A.
		Bar 6	Beats 1–2	Bassoon: crotchet (untied) on D, quaver on B.
		Bar 7	Beat 1	Oboe: the second semiquaver was B, not D.
		Bar 8	Beat 2	Oboe: two quavers.
Test 29	**Page 42**	Bar 4	Beat 2	Top stave: last semiquaver was C natural, not C sharp.
		Bar 6	Beat 2	Bass stave: last quaver was B, not G.

		Bar 9	Beat 2	Bass stave: rest omitted, making the D a crotchet.
		Bar 14	Beat 1	Bass stave: F natural, not F sharp.
		Bar 19	Beat 2	Middle stave: quaver, two semiquavers.
		Bar 22	Beat 2	Top stave: last three semiquavers were played as a triplet of semiquavers, making the preceding tied note a quaver.
		Bar 25	Beat 1	Bass stave: D above the printed G.
Test 30	**Page 44**	Bar 1	Beat 2	Oboe: quaver (tied), four demisemiquavers.
		Bar 2	Beats 3–4	Oboe: three quavers (E–D–C).
		Bar 3	Beat 4	Flute: semiquaver, quaver, semiquaver (F–G–F).
		Bar 5	Beat 1	Oboe: semiquaver (tied), semiquaver, quaver.
		Bar 6	Beat 1	Bassoon: two semiquavers, quaver (G–E–D).
		Bar 6	Beat 2	Flute: triplet of quavers (E–A–G).
Test 31	**Page 45**	Bar 2	Beat 3	Clarinet: C natural, not C sharp.
		Bar 4	Beat 4	Oboe: dotted quaver rest, semiquaver on A.
		Bar 6	Beat 4	Oboe: D, not C.
		Bar 8	Beat 2	Bassoon: A, not G.
		Bar 10	Beats 1–2	Oboe: two crotchets (E–D).
		Bar 11	Beat 2	Clarinet: dotted quaver, semiquaver (B flat–C).
		Bar 13	Beat 3	Oboe: semiquaver, quaver ('Scotch snap').
Test 32	**Page 46**	Bar 1	Beat 3	Cello: D below the printed G.
		Bar 3	Beats 1–2	Viola: two crotchets (D–E flat).
		Bar 5	Beat 3	Cello: last quaver was E natural, not E flat.
		Bar 8	Beat 1	Viola: D, not C.
		Bar 10	Beat 3	Violin: dotted quaver, semiquaver (C–A).
		Bar 13	Beats 1–2	Violin: crotchet, quaver.
Test 33	**Page 47**	Bar 2	Beat 3	Horn: F, not E (changing the triad from minor to major).
		Bar 4	Beat 2	Trombone: D an octave lower than printed.
		Bar 5	Beats 3–4	Horn: two quavers, crotchet.
		Bar 8	Beat 2	Trumpet: dotted quaver, semiquaver.
		Bar 11	Beats 1–4	Trombone: A, not C (creating a minor triad).
		Bar 14	Beat 2	Horn: the second quaver was B natural, not B flat.
Test 34	**Page 48**	Bar 6	Beat 4	Oboe: a triplet of quavers (A–F–G).
		Bar 10	Beats 3–4	Oboe: the entry was on C, not A.
		Bar 12	Beats 2–3	Flute: quaver, dotted crotchet (D–E flat).
		Bar 18	Beat 1	Flute: E flat on second quaver (i.e., same as bar 17, beat 1).
		Bar 21	Beat 1	Flute: quaver, two semiquavers (B flat–C–D).
		Bar 25	Beat 1	Bassoon: second quaver was C, not A.
		Bar 29	Beat 3	Flute: first quaver was A flat, not A natural.
Test 35	**Page 50**	Bar 1	Beat 4	Bassoon: G, not F.
		Bar 2	Beat 4	Oboe: two semiquavers (F–E).
		Bar 3	Beat 3	Flute: triplet of semiquavers (B flat–A–G).
		Bar 4	Beat 2	Flute: the semiquaver was on E (removing the 'Corelli clash' in which the flute's anticipatory D should have coincided with the oboe's delayed resolution onto C sharp).
		Bar 5	Beat 4	Oboe: F, not G.
Test 36	**Page 51**	Bar 2	Beats 1–2	Violin: quaver, two semiquavers (F–G–F).
		Bar 3	Beat 3	Cello: the middle F of the three was played as D.
		Bar 4	Beat 4	Cello: tenor C, an octave lower than printed.
		Bar 6	Beat 1	Viola: G, not A.
		Bar 6	Beat 6	Violin: G flat, not G natural.
		Bar 7	Beat 6	Viola: the rhythm of the last two notes was played as an unequal triplet, as shown left, to align with the triplet of semiquavers in the violin. Schubert wrote this trio in 1817: in music up to about this time, such rhythmic adaptation would not be an 'error' but part of normal performing practice.
Test 37	**Page 52**	Bar 1	Beats 1–3	Cello: crotchet, quaver (F sharp–B).
		Bar 4	Beats 3–4	Violin: double-dotted quaver, demisemiquaver.
		Bar 6	Beats 2–3	Viola: F natural, not E.
		Bar 9	Beat 3	Cello: A, not F sharp.
		Bar 11	Beat 4	Viola: G sharp, not G natural.
Test 38	**Page 55**	(a) The melody sounds an octave higher than printed.		

(b) It is the same except for the last two notes, which have been altered to allow the phrase to end on the tonic.

(c) The rhythm is the same except in bar 2 (changed to crotchet, minim, crotchet). The melody begins and ends in the same way, but is different in the middle. The tessitura is higher—bar 1 is an octave higher than in phrase A.

(d) The second phrase.

(e) AA^{1}BA^1, or (if you feel the third phrase is not that different) AA^{1}A^{2}A^1.

(f) (i) Pattern iii   (ii) The last bar of the third phrase.

Test 39	**Page 56**	

(a) Phrase C.

(b) It is a fourth higher (i.e., the subdominant).

(c) The first repeated phrase (AA) is accompanied by a pedal (often called a drone in folk music) on the tonic. The repetition of these phrases at the end (A^{1}A^1) is harmonized with a variety of chords (I, Ib, IV, II and V) as you can hear if you listen to the bass notes played on the piano.

(d) Compound duple metre ($\frac{6}{8}$).

(e) Continuous identical note lengths (they are quavers) until a longer note (a crotchet) on the last note of each phrase.

Test 40   **Page 57**

(a) Dorian.

(b) Mixolydian.

(c) Major.

(d) Dorian.

Test 41   **Page 57**

(a) Triplet quavers.

(b) D.

(c) Dotted quaver, semiquaver, followed by a 'Scotch snap' (as in bar 6).

(d) They play in octaves.

(e) By playing the first degree and then the characteristic flat seventh of the mode.

Test 42   **Page 58**

(a) Line 1.

(b) The syllable 'gen-' of 'gentry'.

(c) The word 'of'.

(d) Monophonic.

Test 43   **Page 59**

(a) E.

(b) An octave.

(c) The word 'rally'.

(d) 'Word' (line 2) and 'quelled' (line 4). They mark the end of sections.

(e) AA^{1}BB^{1}AA^1. This is a verse (BB^1) and chorus (AA^1) structure (not Classical ternary form because the middle section is not in a different key).

(f) Pentatonic.

Test 44   **Page 60**

(a) The cadence in bar 4 is imperfect, while the cadence at the end of line 2 is perfect.

(b) It is a three-bar phrase.

(c) It stays on one note (the dominant).

(d) Bare fifths and octaves above a repeated dominant.

(e) The first two lines of music are repeated to different words.

(f) A three-part homophonic texture for male voices (two tenor parts and bass). The printed passage is the first tenor: this forms a simple harmony part above the main melody, which is in the middle (second tenor) part.

Test 45   **Page 61**

(a) (i) Verse 2, lines 1 and 2.
    (ii) Verse 1, line 2.
    (iii) Verse 1, line 1.

(b) (i) Lines 2 and 3.
    (ii) Line 4.
    (iii) Line 3.
    (iv) Line 1.
    (v) Line 2.

(c) The metre is not constant: it changes to match the stresses of the words.

Test 46   **Page 62**

(a) With a mordent.

(b) The melody is essentially the same, but has been slightly modified to accommodate some differences in the rhythm of the words of verse 2.

(c) ABAB ABCD

(d) A chorus of male voices sings mainly in thirds and sixths with the soloist.

(e) Lines 3 and 4 of the verses (CD).

(f) A flat seventh is added in the second half of bar 2 (leading to a chord of B flat).

(g) It is composed of primary triads (i.e., the major chords, I, IV and V). They sometimes have (flat) sevenths added.

Test 47   Page 63

(a) It is decorated with a pair of grace-notes either side of the main note (i.e., on F and D flat).

(b) The fourth degree (the note A flat).

(c) Phrase A.

(d) 1. The melody is freely augmented (longer note values).
2. Vibrato and/or portamento (a slide in pitch) on the word 'eart' (heart).

Test 48   Page 64

(a) ABBA or ABB^{1}A^1 (there are slight variations in both phrases A^1 and B^1).

(b) Pattern (ii).

(c) The chords in these three bars have sevenths: the others are plain triads.

(d) A plagal cadence.

Test 49   Page 66

(a) Heterophonic.

(b) Pentatonic.

(c) Drum rolls are used for colour and effect, possibly representing the parting clouds, while the finger cymbals are used rhythmically to mark strong beats.

Test 50   Page 66

(a) (i) *yo* (ii) *in*.

(b) Quasi-heterophonic. *Shamisen* and *shakuhachi* shadow each other, more or less in unison, and the voice follows.

Test 51   Page 67

(a) It is passed to and fro between *sitar* and *sarod* with improvised variations.

(b) 1, 5 and 8 or *sa*, *pa* and *sa^1*.

(c) It is used in both natural and flattened form (like a major and minor third).

Test 52   Page 67

(a) The second degree (*re*) is omitted.

(b) The fourth degree (*ma*) is sharpened and the sixth degree (*dha*) is flattened.

Test 53   Page 68

(a) The first includes plucked and bowed string instruments, flutes, voice and xylophone. The second consists only of tuned metal percussion and drums.

(b) The first is multi-layered, resonant and quite gentle. The second is more unified, damped and much harder.

(c) The first has a more or less constant quiet dynamic level. The second changes abruptly between loud and soft.

(d) The first is slow and continuous, the second is fast and disjunct.

(e) The first is in *slendro*, the second is in *pelog* (omitting notes 4 and 7).

Test 54   Page 69

(a) A fourth.

(b) Pattern (iv).

(c) A ten-beat cycle with accents on 1, 4, 7 and 8:   **1** 2 3 **4** 5 6 **7** **8** 9 10.

Test 55   Page 69

(a) It uses the last phrase of the verse, with a part in contrary motion above.

(b) Verse 1: unison and octaves. Verse 2: men sing the melody, women sing a counterpoint. Verses 3 and 4: women sing the melody, men sing a different counterpoint (with some use of imitation).

(c) It gradually speeds up, but slows down dramatically for the final phrase.

Test 56   Page 70

(a) Sung in parallel tenths, using call-and-response technique.

(b) It moves from duple to triple metre, but it retains the same basic pulse.

Test 57   Page 70

(a) No regular metre. The rhythms follow the 'mood' of the singer.

(b) A semitone higher (B flat major) then a tone above that (C major)—the guitarist is simply shifting up the fingerboard to produce parallel chords.

(c) Pattern (iii).

Test 58   Page 71

(a) The fifth.

(b) Pattern (iv).

(c) Pattern (i).

(d) AABB^{1}CC^1.

Test 59   Page 72

(a) A pedal point.

(b) Imitation.

(c) (i)   It is the same melody but 'jazzed up' with a syncopated rhythm.
(ii)   This syncopated version of the tune reappears at the end, but this time sung by men and women in unison.

(d) 1: guitar or ukelele (*cavaquinho*).   2: high-pitched drum (*tamborim*).
3: low-pitched drum (*surdo*).   4: tambourine (*pandeiro*).
5: medium-pitched drum (*contra-surdo*).

Test 60	**Page 72**	(a) A chord of B minor.

Test 60   **Page 72**   (a) A chord of B minor.
(b) They play the same simple melody in parallel fourths
(c) The tonic and the minor (i.e., flat seventh).

Test 61   **Page 75**   (a) In (free) inversion.
(b) It modulates to the dominant.
(c) It is almost the same except that the bass figure is replaced by a flat seventh (in order to pass through subdominant harmony at the start of bar 13).
(d) Cycle of fifths (i.e., V^7 of V^7 of V^7 of I).
(e) (i) Bar 6^4 (ii) Bars 13^1 to 14^2 (iii) Bar 7^3 or Bar 15^1.

Test 62   **Page 77**   (a) The quavers are played in a rhythm which approximates to the pattern shown right. These are called 'swung quavers' or 'jazz quavers' and are one of the key features of early jazz in particular.
(b) C minor (the mediant minor, or relative minor of the dominant).
(c) (i) It has an independent counter-melody, with triplets and chromaticism, instead of plain, single notes. It is also higher in tessitura.
   (ii) The ending is modified to remain in the tonic (major) key.
(d) A descending scale articulated (tongued) in even notes, not swung quavers.
(e) Lines 2 and 3 are the same, but line 4 is not.
(f) The notes on the third beats are anticipated by a quaver (i.e., it is syncopated).
(g) Piano and banjo (the rhythm section).
(h) Glissando (since the pitches are continuous, you might say portamento).
(i) The cornet enters in the last bar of the previous of the strain.
(j) It is a long anticipation (almost a semibreve) of the note in the next bar, effectively creating a 'blue' seventh.
(k) Strain 2 and (with slight differences) strain 3. It is not related to strain 1.

Test 63   **Page 79**   (a) Swung rhythm, or jazz quavers. Notice that they are printed as dotted quaver–semiquaver pairs, unlike the even quavers of the previous extract. However, triplet groups give a closer approximation than either method.
(b) Electric guitar (still a new instrument in 1945), using rhythm (iii).
(c) Muted trumpet (using a bucket mute).
(d) A long descent to an indeterminate pitch at the end of the note. Variously known as a 'fall', a 'fall-off' or a 'spill'.
(e) It uses essentially the same chords, featuring the rising semitone, but in a different rhythm.
(f) By shortening the semibreve to a minim the pattern enters at one-bar intervals instead of two-bar intervals.
(g) It requires a flat symbol. It is one of many 'blue notes' in the piece.
(h) A slide from the semitone below. Known as a 'smear', it is a tiny microtonal glissando (not a pitch bend, which takes the shape of a mordent, sliding up or down from the true note and back again).
(i) 12-bar blues, as in the first two sections.
(j) It is riff, or ostinato, in which the same rhythm pattern is repeated throughout, changing pitch levels to match the chord progressions.

Test 64   **Page 80**   (a) With a mordent.
(b) Bars 3–4 are a repetition of bars 1–2, bars 5–6 form a free sequence.
(c) A descending chromatic scale, followed by two dominants an octave apart.
(d) Immediately after the introduction it is played in double time (i.e., starting in quavers), giving an effect of diminution. Notice that thereafter the motif is not used—it is the harmony that forms the basis for the improvisation.
(e) Pizzicato string bass and rhythm guitar.
(f) (i) Chord subsitutions instead of two bars of D. You might equally well say the harmonic pace is increased as the pattern becomes $D–Bm–Em–A^7$.
   (ii) The E^7 and A^7 chords are each extended to occupy two bars. Thus, tonic harmony is not reached until the start of the next section.
(g) The key drops a tone to C major (i.e., the key of the flattened leading note).
(h) Mordents at *(x)*; smear, slide or (in string players' terms) portamento at *(y)*.
(i) Triplet quavers, each with a lower chromatic auxiliary.
(j) Grappelli goes through the chord sequence only three times and produces a more continuous improvisation, without the breaks that Reinhardt had.

Test 65   **Page 83**   (a) Muted trumpet and vibraphone.
(b) A pizzicato walking bass in crotchets (it outlines the chord patterns but is independent of the piano left hand).

(c) The underlying chord pattern is essentially the same in both bars.

(d) Mostly the same, but the ending is modified to finish in the tonic.

(e) Cycle of fifths.

(f) Section 2, making the overall structure AA^{1}BA^1.

(g) The cymbal maintains a steady beat, but the drums have many off-beat accents, some matching the soloists and some cutting across their rhythm.

Test 66   Page 85

(a) Homophonic three-part texture, with harmony in parallel major sevenths and tritones.

(b) Semitone. A fall, or downward portamento.

(c) A military pattern on the snare drum, then fills on the toms alternating with snare, followed by a rapid pattern on cymbal.

(d) Minor third.

(e) (i) The same minor third.

    (ii) The opening minor third is extended into a motif that begins and ends with the third and that features triplets. This is repeated and then developed into a rising figure.

(f) It mainly plays chords in the rests of the wind parts.

(g) The same chord pattern is retained, but there is a new melody for high, muted trumpet. The other instruments play only fragments of the motif featured in the first chorus.

(h) The bridge is in triple time—you might just have been able to detect some fragments of fast waltz rhythm. However, it is highly obscured by cross-rhythms and duplets, and might best be simply described as polyrhythmic.

Test 67   Page 88

(a) The tonic (A).

(b) It is the flat seventh (G natural): a 'blue note'.

(c) Triplet of crotchets.

(d) Bar 5.

(e) Bar 6.

(f) It is based largely on triadic patterns.

(g) Tonic harmony.

Test 68   Page 89

(a) In sequence, one step lower.

(b) The relative minor (B flat minor).

(c) Each phrase starts one note lower than the previous phrase.

(d) (i) Tambourine.

    (ii) It plays mostly single notes on the second and fourth beats of each bar.

(e) In verse 1, bowed strings play sustained notes in unison, at first shadowing the voice and later providing a counter-melody in a higher register. In the first half of verse 2, sustained harmonies are supplied by the bvox and cellos, while pizzicato violins doubled by xylophone play a new motif over the long notes at the end of each vocal phrase. Lower strings again shadow the vocal line at first and the high violin counter-melody returns.

(f) (i) Verse 1 ends with an imperfect cadence; verse 2 with a perfect cadence.

    (ii) They are approached by secondary dominants, forming a cycle of fifths (B flat major–E flat major–A flat major–D flat major).

Test 69   Page 91

(a) (i) An acciaccatura (ii) A mordent.

(b) A descending scale, from C to C an octave lower. There was a chromatic passing-note at the end of bar 2.

(c) (i) Quavers (ii) A fill on the toms (using a sextuplet of semiquavers).

(d) The dominant (G).

(e) (i) A triplet of crotchets.

    (ii) Downward and upward glissandi.

    (iii) An appoggiatura or added sixth (the note A above C major harmony).

(f) Plagal.

(g) The harmonic scheme of the introduction is used throughout the extract (and throughout the entire song): twice in the verse and once in the chorus.

Test 70   Page 92

(a) (i) A similar part but (mostly) a third higher.

    (ii) It continues sequentially down the notes of an A major triad: bar 2 starting on A and bar 3 on E. Bar 4 consists of a single note (D).

    (iii) Descending crotchets, in the pattern A–E, in each bar.

    (iv) In bar 4 the chord changes to B minor.

    (v) The second half of each verse repeats the music of the first half.

(b) The words 'did before' are sung to a 'blue third' (effectively C natural) while the word 'now' is sung to the normal major third (C sharp).

(c) The word 'and'.

(d) It is an improvisation over the same chord pattern as verses 1 and 2.

(e) Augmentation on the words 'I know you love me'.

Test 71   Page 94

(a) (i)   Rhythmic anticipation (the chord on 'green' sounds a semiquaver earlier than the notation suggests).

    (ii)   G sharp (to create a modulation to the dominant).

    (iii) Portamento to the next note.

    (iv) Dotted rhythm: the rhythm on these three beats was changed to dotted quaver, semiquaver, crotchet (followed by a crotchet rest).

    (v)   Passing-note added (on the note B).

(b) They move in consecutive fifths.

(c) On 'wearing it' (bar 12).

(d) Almost all of the cadences are inverted, ending on a first inversion or even a second inversion triad.

(e) The third (F sharp).

(f) Three-part (A.T.B.) homophony.

(g) (i)   It is faster.

    (ii)   The melody is essentially the same although there are small changes, largely to accommodate differences in the scansion of the words.

    (iii) The chords are the same, but are now in root position apart from the dominant triad (A major) which is sometimes used in first inversion.

Test 72   Page 97

(a) Septuple metre (i.e., $\frac{7}{4}$).

(b) A harpsichord sound, used to embellish the same riff as the marimba.

(c) The same syncopated pattern, based on tonic and dominant notes, is used throughout this section. The repeated tonic at the start of every bar gives the effect of a pedal.

(d) It is based on the same tonic–dominant pattern, but with passing-notes and generally moving in contrary motion to the bass.

(e) It is a descending chromatic part below the main melody.

(f) A major.

(g) Minor third.

(h) Tonic (of B minor).

(i) The main drum part stays the same, but isolated notes are added from bar 17, using first the sound of a *cuíca* (a Brazilian drum that makes the swooping pitches heard) and then a whip.

Test 73   Page 99

(a) Phrase 2.

(b) Four voices: boy treble, male alto, tenor and bass. All four are solo voices.

(c) He retains all but one of the pitches, alters the rhythm and adds his own melismatic ending.

(d) They all use the same plainsong phrase in imitative counterpoint.

(e) A suspension: the treble sustains a note which becomes dissonant as the lower voices move to the penultimate chord (see the example on page 99).

Test 74   Page 100

(a) Phrase 2 is non-imitative counterpoint; phrase 3 is imitative.

(b) Fast rising scales in close imitation.

(c) Phrase 6 is homophonic; phrase 7 is polyphonic.

(d) By varied vocal scoring: first the lowest three voices, then the highest three voices, finally all four voices.

(e) Slowly descending scales follow each other imitatively, perhaps suggesting a procession of saints following Christ.

(f) (i)   The trebles sustain one note (the tonic) against the shifting harmonies and counterpoints of the lower voices (an inverted pedal).

    (ii)   A decorated suspension in the tenor part.

Test 75   Page 101

(a) Phrase 7.

(b) By contrapuntal overlapping of the music for the two phrases.

(c) The setting of the words *miserere nobis* ends with a perfect cadence and a chord of a bare fifth, but phrase 7 overlaps phrase 8 in the motet.

Test 76   Page 102

(a) By using a single unaccompanied voice.

(b) Phrase 2 is homophonic while phrase 3 is polyphonic.

(c) By very close imitation.

(d) Long sustained notes (almost like a dominant pedal towards the end).

(e) Alternating duple and triple metre with syncopation (accents on the second beat of triple time bars).

(f) The same major key throughout, with brief modulations to the dominant.

Test 77	Page 103	(a) By adding a running quaver counterpoint above the melody and by simplifying the supporting harmonies.

Test 77   **Page 103**

(a) By adding a running quaver counterpoint above the melody and by simplifying the supporting harmonies.

(b) By adding a running quaver counterpoint in the bass with a simple inner part filling in the harmonies.

(c) The harmonic progression. (Writing new material to fit the existing chord pattern is a very common variation technique—always listen out for this possibility if a variation seems to have no other connection with its theme).

(d) Imitation (on a point derived from the second eight-bar phrase on Track 7.

Test 78   **Page 105**

(a) (i)   The second cornetto plays the melody in canon with the first cornetto.

(ii)   They are lively, dance-like and dotted.

(iii)   It is in triple time, with a syncopated cadence, and is mainly homophonic.

(iv)   All four sections end with a perfect cadence.

(b) (i)   Organ, theorbo (a large lute) and cello.

(ii)   It is a sequence of the first. Both phrases end with imperfect cadences.

(iii)   A three-note rising chromatic figure, heard three times in rising sequence.

(c) (i)   Two cornetti.

(ii)   The second phrase is a melodic and harmonic sequence of the first (the entire passage is transposed up a tone). In the second phrase the cornetto parts are embellished with improvised ornamentation.

(iii)   Both phrases end on a tonic chord with a major third, in passages which were in the minor (i.e., a *tierce de Picardie*).

(iv)   A false relation.

(v)   Polychoral antiphony between the choirs in the triple-time passage, and 14-part homophony with some independent part movement in the duple-time passage.

(vi)   I and V (an indication of emergent major–minor tonality).

(vii)   False relations and suspensions.

Test 79   **Page 108**

(a) The subject is inverted. You may also notice that the original subject and its inversion are treated in stretto (full marks if you heard this!).

(b) The subject is heard in augmentation then repeated in sequence.

(c) (i)   The augmented subject is now inverted then repeated in sequence.

(ii)   The chords are all dissonant and chromatic—more precisely, they are all versions of that distinctive discord known as a diminished seventh.

(iii)   A perfect cadence (it leads to a coda over a tonic pedal, not recorded).

Test 80   **Page 110**

(a) 'Hemiola' is the most concise answer. You could explain that two bars of the $\frac{3}{4}$ metre are articulated as three minims, effectively creating a bar of $\frac{3}{2}$ time.

(b) An imperfect cadence in the tonic key (of A minor). It is a special kind of imperfect known as a 'Phrygian cadence' (the chords IVb–V in a minor key).

(c) Melodic sequence.

(d) The relative major (C major).

(e) Apart from a couple of bass notes the second four bars are a repeat of the first four bars but, at *piano*, they sound like an echo.

(f) Any one of bars 15, 27 or 31.

Test 81   **Page 112**

(a) The consequent modulates to a perfect cadence in the dominant (A major).

(b) (i)   The three notes in bar 12 are replaced by a semibreve on B in bar 14.

(ii)   It is transposed up a tone (sequence).   (iii) An appoggiatura or suspension.

(c) It is chordal (homophonic) instead of being in a two-part texture.

(d) Ic–V–I (Ic in this context is a 'cadential six-four' and the three chords together form a typical cadence pattern in *galant* and Classical music). The ornament is a turn.

(e) The original melody is surrounded by almost continuous triplet figuration.

(f) The bass is surrounded by quaver figuration, including broken chords.

(g) Both the original phrase structure and harmonies have been retained, but the melody has been omitted.

Test 82   **Page 113**

(a) In bars 4–6 the rising chromatic violin part of bars 7–9 is played in the bass: in bars 7–9 the syncopated violin part of bars 4–6 is played in the bass. This interchange of the two parts is known as contrapuntal inversion.

(b) (i)   Two unaccompanied solo violins.   (ii) They are in parallel thirds.

(iii)   Sequence.

(c) The first three bars.

(d) (i)   Two unaccompanied solo violins playing sequences in parallel thirds.

(ii)   It is in canon ('In imitation' is only half the story!).

(iii)   First a cycle of fifths, then alternating tonic and dominant chords.

(e) It is transposed (to the dominant minor), otherwise it is exactly the same.

Test 83	**Page 114**	(a) Counter-tenor (or male alto).

Test 83 **Page 114**
(a) Counter-tenor (or male alto).
(b) (i) 'let me' (ii) 'me weep'.
(c) By introducing the melody for the obbligato violin before the cadence so that the phrasing of bass and melody do not synchronize.
(d) (i) The ground is extended, by inserting three extra bars in the middle.
(ii) More anguished appoggiaturas and chromaticism above this extension.
(e) The obbligato violin echoes the singer's short phrases a fifth higher.
(f) Prominent dotted rhythms are used for the first time.

Test 84 **Page 115**
(a) Phrase 4.
(b) Phrase 2 is a repeat of phrase 1.
(c) (i) Appoggiaturas. (ii) They resolve up in phrases 1 and 2 and down in phrase 3.
(d) The order in which phrases occur is altered and the four-bar phrase is omitted (the order is now 1–2–4–3 and phrase 5 is omitted).

Test 85 **Page 117**
(a) The first extract is *secco* recitative sung by a tenor, the second is accompanied recitative and is sung by a bass.
(b) (i) By placing this word on the highest note.
(ii) An appoggiatura. (iii) A perfect cadence.
(c) (i) An appoggiatura.
(ii) By starting to modulate and by using a very dissonant appoggiatura.
(iii) By chromatic melodies and harmonies.

Test 86 **Page 118**
(a) They both begin with the same tune.
(b) (i) Melody-dominated homophony, in a major key.
(ii) By using warlike mock fanfares (the twice-repeated rising triadic figure).
(c) Both are set to long, virtuosic melismas.
(d) The music begins and ends in minor keys.
(e) They are ornamented, notably with an initial rising scale figure.
(f) They are partial repeats of the orchestral introduction, i.e., ritornellos.
(g) Ternary/ritornello form: this is a *da capo* aria (although only the first few bars of the repeat are recorded in this extract).

Test 87 **Page 118**
(a) The bass on the word *Gloria*.
(b) The alto on the word *Zungen*.
(c) The bass on the words *mit Harfen*.

Test 88 **Page 118**
(a) (i) Strings and oboes alternating antiphonally.
(ii) Syncopated. (iii) Long notes tied over to form suspensions.
(b) It uses motifs from the orchestral ritornello in reduced scoring.
(c) (i) Fugal three-part imitiation.
(ii) Three-voice imitation upon a rising scale figure (*hoch* = high).
(iii) Detached chords (*wach auf* = wake up!).
(d) Ternary, or part of a ritornello structure (ritornello–chorus–ritornello).

Test 89 **Page 120**
(a) (i) G minor.
(ii) The minor key reflects the meaning of *pianti* ('tears') and *pene* ('pains') and it could also reflect the 'change' mentioned in the next line of text.
(b) (i) The opening of the melody is for instruments only, the chromatic passing-notes (on *sen* and the last syllable of *trapassò*) are omitted and the end of the phrase is remodelled and lengthened.
(ii) Perfect, Ic–V^7–I.
(c) Line 2 (*Nel languire amando ognor*). It changes to the tonic minor to illustrate the words ('in everlasting longing...').

Test 90 **Page 121**
(a) Homophonic.
(b) A major.
(c) Bars 3–4. They are repeated in a freely modulating sequence.
(d) (i) The motif in bar 4 of the printed music.
(ii) The rhythm is syncopated (caused by repetitions of the motif's two-beat rhythm pattern in triple time). The texture consists of detached chords under the motif.
(e) From the two quavers.
(f) At the beginning of section B. It is played by the cello with detached chords in the upper strings. The three-note motif is repeated in rising sequence.
(g) From the *da capo* of the minuet (because the sections are not repeated).

Test 91 **Page 125**
(a) (i) All three instruments in bare octaves. Bars 14 and 15.
(ii) Rising chromatic scale (chromatic passing-notes are typical of Mozart).
(iii) Bars 5–6 (on the oboe). (iv) Imitation.

(v)   Melody with homophonic accompaniment: repeated block chords and broken chords briefly on the clarinet.

vi)   A tonic pedal. Although F is the dominant of B flat, this oft-repeated F does not form a dominant pedal: F is the *tonic* of the key at this point.

(b) (i)   The first three notes of bars 1–2. They have been freely inverted to give a descending diminished triad instead of an ascending major triad.

(ii)   Bars 29–32 are in the minor while bars 33–38 are in the relative major (C minor and E flat major respectively).

(iii)   Bars 12–15.

(c) (i)   The tonic (B flat).

(ii)   Some phrases have been transposed down a fifth and others up a fourth. There are thus some shifts of octave in the recapitulation version.

(d) (i)   Bars 1–4.

(ii)   They imitate the oboe part.

(iii)   Bars 26–28 (the codetta) are repeated almost exactly in the last three bars of the movement.

Test 92   Page 126

(a) (i)   Like bars 1–4, the melody is constructed from the three-note motif of the first beat of bar 1, but now modulating to the dominant (D major).

(ii)   The first eight bars are repeated.

(iii)   After a harmonized repeat of bars 17–18, transposed up an octave, there is a modification to allow a modulation back to the tonic (G major).

(iv)   Binary form.

(b) (i)   It is in the relative minor (E minor).

(ii)   There are no repeats; the tune is now played over triplet broken chords.

(iii)   The first four-bar phrase is repeated in sequence.

(iv)   All eight bars are repeated with slight variations (the triadic figures are now in semiquaver rhythm).

(v)   The accompaniment is now in semiquaver broken chords and the tune disappears at the repeat, to be replaced by broken octaves.

Test 93   Page 128

(a) The transition.

(b) It is in the tonic (i.e., transposed down a fifth) in the recapitulation.

(c) It imitates the first bar of the second subject.

(d) Violins play descending arpeggios (major, minor, diminished seventh) followed by a rising sequence. All this over a pedal.

(e) The second phrase is a free sequence of the first.

(f) It begins with a very fast and syncopated version of the Adagio.

(g) (i)   From bars 40–41 (the opening of the first subject: *x*).

(ii)   From bar 82 (*y* in the second subject).

Test 94   Page 130

(a) (i)   (Bowed) tremolo.

(ii)   The first is minor; the second is major.

(iii)   It echoes the last three notes of the *idée fixe*.

(b) (i)   Double stopping.

(ii)   They are in canon.

(iii)   Triangle (you might just be able to hear timpani as well).

(c) (i)   Violins, cellos, then violins again.

(ii)   They are all shorter than either of the two phrases of the *idée fixe*.

(iii)   Overlapped phrasing.

(d) (i)   The wind and lower violas sustain a tonic/dominant drone. The upper violas have chords in the same rhythms as the oboe and piccolo melody.

(ii)   Flute and harp. The harp is using harmonics.

(iii)   The viola melody is based on the following motifs from the *idée fixe*: the rising arpeggio of bar 3, the falling third and sixth of bars 1–2, and the final three-note figure of both phrases (bars 4 and 8 respectively).

Test 95   Page 132

(a) Voice and piano in bare octaves.

(b) Double dotted.

(c) A harmonized echo of the last phrase of the vocal part (the melody is in the bass, two octaves below the pitch used by the vocal part).

(d) They are in the (tonic) major with chordal accompaniment as opposed to the minor tonality and bare octaves of lines 1–2. This helps illustrate the portrait of lines 1–2 coming to life in the poet's imagination in lines 3–4.

(e) The first dissonance is a suspension onto a complete dominant seventh which carries the music to the key of the flat submediant (a typically sensuous Schubertian tertiary modulation), but the second dissonance is a bare tritone resolving on to an equally bare minor sixth (both intervals doubled in octaves).

(f) The piano epilogue is a tonic minor version of the major key interlude at the end of verse 1, thus negating the effect of the warm major tonality of the last two lines of the text.

Test 96   Page 133

(a) The semiquaver turn with acciaccatura at the end of the introduction.
(b) It modulates to the dominant.
(c) Clarinet.
(d) Cello.
(e) Chromaticism and the use of the (tonic) minor.
(f) A perfect cadence in the tonic key.
(g) Faster harmonic rhythm and modulation to the (mediant) minor.
(h) A feminine imperfect cadence (Ic–V, more typical of Classical than of Romantic music: here is suggests Othello's forced courtesy).
(i) Violins doubled by an oboe. They play a rising sequence.
(j) It is set to an expressive appoggiatura on the highest notes of the phrase.

Test 97   Page 134

(a) Three trombones.
(b) (i) A falling perfect fourth.
　　(ii) It is the inversion of the rising perfect fourth in the instrumental melody of bars 1, 3, 5, 6 and 7.
(c) (i) Clarinet (notice the subtle difference in timbre between this and the bass clarinet used in the first two bars).
　　(ii) Horn. (iii) Cellos.
(d) Harp.
(e) Violins.

Test 98   Page 136

(a) Root position chords (IV and I) with suspensions.
(b) The piano part imitates the descending scales.
(c) x
(d) (i) The pulse is arranged in three groups of minims instead of two groups of dotted minims (it is effectively in $\frac{3}{2}$ time because the first two beats of x are repeated three times in each bar).
　　(ii) The quavers are phrased in groups of three so as to set up a cross rhythm both with the prevailing $\frac{6}{4}$ time and with the $\frac{3}{2}$ metre of the violin: the piano part is, in effect, in $\frac{12}{8}$ time.
(e) z, inverted and freely augmented.
(f) The piano plays the same melody as the violin, but an octave higher and a bar later (imitation).
(g) (i) z
　　(ii) Sequence and fragmentation (i.e., the first two notes are detached and repeated) producing the effect of a stretto.
　　(iii) It imitates the violin and, when fragmentation occurs, it plays in cross-rhythm with it (the left hand has a simple broken chord accompaniment).
(h) Bars 3–4.
(i) y, x, then y again. x is treated in sequential imitation between right and left hands.
(j) The second subject of the exposition (a new tune in the dominant begins at bar 36: the tonality is too stable for this to be from the development, and the second subject in the recapitulation would usually be in the same key as the first subject).

Test 99   Page 139

(a) Bar 1.
(b) (i) The melody is higher (by about a fourth).
　　(ii) It ends with a chromatic sequence of secondary dominant chords which replace the original diatonic cadence.
(c) (i) Chromatic harmony which briefly refers to minor keys replaces the more diatonic harmonization of the first phrase.
　　(ii) The third beat.
(d) It is effectively in $\frac{2}{4}$ time (the lowest bass notes coming on alternate crotchet beats).
(e) A chromatic appoggiatura.
(f) (i) The original end of phrase C is replaced by a falling chromatic sequence.
　　(ii) The original end of phrase C is replaced by a clear perfect cadence.
(g) A tonic pedal suggesting bagpipes.

Test 100   Page 140

(a) Bars 1–2 are repeated.
(b) Repetition; sequence; the last three notes only are then treated in the same ways.
(c) (i) The descending melodic minor scale.   (ii) Root position triads.

(d) They are in canon at the octave.
(e) Bar 19 is repeated in sequence.
(f) The relative major (E flat).
(g) There an exact repeat of the first phrase, a variant, and then a louder version.
(h) It is scored for full orchestra. Upper strings and woodwind play the original oboe melody, and middle strings, horn and a trombone play the canonic bassoon part. Cymbals, bass drum and triangle emphasize the heavy beat.

Test 101   Page 141

(a) Bar 2, beat 2.
(b) (i)   The second, third and fourth notes (two semiquavers and a quaver).
    (ii) It is cross-phrased (i.e., phrased over the bar-line).
    (iii) The bass part plays off the beat, emphasizing the cross-phrasing.
(c) The first eight-bar phrase is repeated, but ending with a plagal cadence. The first eight-bar phrase is then repeated exactly but louder and in fuller scoring. Finally the second eight-bar phrase (with its plagal cadence) is also repeated very loudly and in tutti scoring.
(d) Lower strings and lower woodwind (bass clarinet and bassoons).
(e) It uses the motif of two semiquavers and a quaver first heard in bar 1.
(f) It has a similar two-bar sequence and the whole eight-bar phrase is repeated.
(g) Cross-phrasing and syncopation.
(h) (i)   More prominent, and continuous parts for heavy brass, timpani and tambourine.
    (ii) There is only one repetition of the eight-bar phrase, but the section with cross-phrasing is greatly extended.
    (iii) There is a gradual accelerando towards the end.

Test 102   Page 145

(a) Dorian.
(b) ABB¹A¹.
(c) Phrase 1 ends on the fifth, phrase 2 on the fourth, the last two on the first.
(d) Perfect (the seventh degree is sharpened to form a dominant in the accompaniment).

Test 103   Page 145

(a) Dorian with a sharpened fourth (producing the noticeable augmented seconds).
(b) AABB.
(c) A double pedal on the first and fifth degrees of the mode (the latter twice moving up a semitone in the last two phrases). These two notes are sustained like a drone by the clarinets and are articulated as an ostinato figure by the upper strings.

Test 104   Page 145

(a) Lydian.
(b) It is transposed down a fifth.
(c) AA¹AA¹.
(d) The first two phrases are harmonized over a pedal, the second two begin with a minor chord, followed by two chords moving up in step to the final major chord.

Test 105   Page 146

(a) Modal.
(b) Root position triads moving down by step (producing consecutive fifths).
(c) A chromatic melody in crotchets.
(d) A tritone.
(e) The metre and tonality are both vague whereas the ostinato figure in the first 11 bars helped establish a tonal centre of D and a sense of pulse.

Test 106   Page 147

(a) (i)   Sequence.   (ii) A seventh chord (like a dominant seventh).
    (iii) A part in which both intervals and note-lengths become progressively closer as it descends (the intervals start with a fourth and end with a semitone).
(b) (i)   It is slower, the melody contains no semitones and there is a pedal point.
    (ii) The descending pedal phrase is inverted and much higher, supported by chords which are more dissonant than before.
(c) (i)   It begins and ends on the same note, thus firmly establishing the major tonality suggested by the parts above it.
    (ii) It is repeated twice, the second time with the final note delayed by repetitions of the final four-note figure. This figure is then detached and repeated several times.
    (iii) An irregular group of fast notes is repeated twice (they are articulated as 4+4+4+6 and might be heard as a group of three crotchets plus a dotted crotchet, a simple example of *valeur ajoutée*).
    (iv) A tonic chord with an added 6th.

Test 107   Page 149

(a) Oboe and bassoon, then horn for the last four bass notes. There are a few small differences of pitch in the bassoon part.
(b) Sustained inner parts have been added, played by a horn and another bassoon,